Negotiating Identity in Modern Foreign Language Teaching

Matilde Gallardo
Editor

Negotiating Identity in Modern Foreign Language Teaching

palgrave
macmillan

Editor
Matilde Gallardo
Faculty of Arts and Humanities
King's College London
London, UK

ISBN 978-3-030-27708-6   ISBN 978-3-030-27709-3 (eBook)
https://doi.org/10.1007/978-3-030-27709-3

© The Editor(s) (if applicable) and The Author(s) 2019

This work is subject to copyright. All rights are solely and exclusively licensed by the Publisher, whether the whole or part of the material is concerned, specifically the rights of translation, reprinting, reuse of illustrations, recitation, broadcasting, reproduction on microfilms or in any other physical way, and transmission or information storage and retrieval, electronic adaptation, computer software, or by similar or dissimilar methodology now known or hereafter developed.

The use of general descriptive names, registered names, trademarks, service marks, etc. in this publication does not imply, even in the absence of a specific statement, that such names are exempt from the relevant protective laws and regulations and therefore free for general use.

The publisher, the authors and the editors are safe to assume that the advice and information in this book are believed to be true and accurate at the date of publication. Neither the publisher nor the authors or the editors give a warranty, expressed or implied, with respect to the material contained herein or for any errors or omissions that may have been made. The publisher remains neutral with regard to jurisdictional claims in published maps and institutional affiliations.

Cover credit: Mykola Velychko/Alamy Stock Photo

This Palgrave Macmillan imprint is published by the registered company Springer Nature Switzerland AG
The registered company address is: Gewerbestrasse 11, 6330 Cham, Switzerland

To Dave and Sofía

Foreword

At the heart of *Language Acts and Worldmaking*, one of the four major projects that together constitute the AHRC-funded initiative Open World Research Initiative, is the exploration of 'language as a material and historical force which acts as the means by which individuals construct their personal, local, transnational and spiritual identities' (https://www.languageacts.org/about-us/our-vision/), a process which is referred to as 'worldmaking'. This project, and more specifically one of the strands of that project entitled *Diasporic Identities and the Politics of Language* strand, has inspired this timely and revealing volume edited by Matilde Gallardo, which has compiled a collection of inspirational narratives and reflections from teachers of modern languages in the UK.

It is important to acknowledge the particularly challenging context in which these women are working hard to encourage language learning. The long-acknowledged lack of motivation for learning other languages in the UK has for many decades stimulated innovation amongst language teachers, who have pushed the boundaries of pedagogy in an attempt to share their own enthusiasm for and joy in the learning of languages. Recently, however, it has felt as if more and more obstacles are being put in their way, as political changes have disrupted the curricular and pedagogical reforms instigated during the years of the National Languages Strategy (2002–2010), which were designed to enhance motivation, provide a more appropriate and inclusive curriculum as well as a diversity of accreditation systems, and to build on the vast multilingual resources that are present in our schools, communities and cities. This has been even more recently compounded by the political, economic and social insecurities triggered by the Brexit referendum and its on-going repercussions, and by the ensuing sense of increasing insularity, which sits at odds with the vision of language teachers to open minds and encourage communication between people from different backgrounds. Language teachers themselves are by definition plurilingual and pluricultural, either because they have migrated to the UK themselves for a range of reasons or, even if born in the UK, because they have spent years learning other languages, spending time with people from different backgrounds, and living in and moving between other countries. The risks associated with potential loss of the right to live and work in the UK and loss of secure opportunities to work across borders and boundaries means that language teachers are therefore particularly affected by the current political developments.

This volume focuses on explorations of language teacheridentity, which is intimately bound up with other dimensions of identity and indeed the multiple plurilingual, pluricultural and transnational identities that characterise most language teachers. Exploring identities is always methodologically challenging as they are so slippery. Nevertheless, this book has succeeded in pulling together a rich and insightful range of perspectives, constructions and beliefs, by developing a community of practice that has led to the application of various forms of narrative research, including autobiographical narratives, as well as practitioner enquiry and reflection, all underpinned by a commitment to the idea of teaching and researching being two sides of the same coin.

My own trajectory, both as a researcher and as a teacher, has been characterised by a commitment to finding ways of motivating language learners and valuing multilingualism and plurilingualism. I have always been concerned by the disaffection that develops when the environment is not conducive to facilitating learning in an inclusive way and I soon recognised that such disaffection could affect teachers as much as learners. In 2000, I reconceptualised disaffection as 'a search for a voice in a context of disenfranchisement' (Lamb 2000a), arguing that, if such 'voice' is nurtured, welcomed and listened to, both learners and teachers can find ways of negotiating their space within the constraints of the systems and structures in which they are operating. If not, disaffection can turn into more negative forms of resistance, such as withdrawal or other behaviours that in turn can lead to failure and despair. I mention this here because I believe that Matilde Gallardo's volume not only offers the space for voices to be heard but also illustrates the different ways in which teachers themselves make their voices heard. In so doing, the teachers are able to draw on their inner reserves, to remind themselves of their values, ideals, personal theories and motivations, to reflect critically on these in order to challenge any of their own assumptions, and to develop resilience. For me, this is characteristic of a critical form of teacher autonomy, in which teachers 'empower themselves by finding the spaces and opportunities for manoeuvre' (Lamb 2000b: 127) in order to find ways of moving ever closer to their ideals *despite* the constraints. As such, these narratives offer 'spaces of hope', a construct developed by the radical geographer David Harvey (2000), which, though referring to urban communities disenfranchised by capitalist development in cities around the world, is nevertheless enlightening for and relevant to our communities of teachers in its argument for the 'construction of collective identities, of communities of action, of rules of belonging' (p. 241) in order to achieve for themselves a greater inclusion of their own identities and a greater sense of hope.

The strength of narrative and identity research is that it enables us to reflect on our own situations and to find new ways of thinking that can stimulate creativity and optimism. I am honoured to have had the opportunity to read this volume and to indulge in my own responses to its focus and contents. I hope the readers of these wonderful contributions will feel equally inspired to think, question, relate, remember why they became language teachers and how they developed, and find new ways of inspiring others to love languages as much as they do.

Professor Terry Lamb, B.Sc. (Hons), P.G.C.E.,
M.A., Ph.D., F.R.S.A., Chevalier dans
l'Ordre des Palmes Académiques
Department of Humanities
University of Westminster
London, UK

References

Harvey, D. 2000. *Spaces of Hope*. Edinburgh: Edinburgh University Press.

Lamb, T.E. 2000a. Reconceptualising Disaffection—Issues of Power, Voice and Learner Autonomy. In *Combating Social Exclusion Through Education*, ed. G. Walraven, C. Parsons, D. Van Veen, and C. Day, 99–115. Louvain, Belgium and Apeldoorn, The Netherlands: Garant.

Lamb, T.E. 2000b. Finding a Voice—Learner Autonomy and Teacher Education in an Urban Context. In *Learner Autonomy, Teacher Autonomy: Future Directions*, ed. B. Sinclair, I. McGrath, and T.E. Lamb, 118–127. Harlow: Addison Wesley Longman.

Professor Terry Lamb A former secondary school languages teacher for 16 years, Terry previously also had numerous roles in the Universities of Nottingham and Sheffield, such as Professor of Languages and Pedagogy, Director of Initial Teacher Education, Director of Learning and Teaching, and Director of a range of Masters programmes. He is now Professor of Languages and Interdisciplinary Pedagogy and Director of the Centre for Teaching Innovation at the University of Westminster. He has published extensively in the areas of multilingualism and learner and teacher autonomy and is founder editor of the academic journal *Innovation in Language Learning and Teaching*. He has carried out consultancies and presented keynote papers in many countries and his numerous research projects have included several at the European Centre for Modern Languages of the Council of Europe in Graz. Terry has worked closely on languages strategy and curriculum with the UK and other Governments in countries such as Australia, the Czech Republic, France and Malaysia, and in 2010 was awarded the honour of Chevalier des Palmes Académiques by the French Prime Minister.

Terry is Vice President (and former President and Secretary General) of FIPLV (Fédération Internationale des Professeurs de Langues Vivantes), an NGO of both UNESCO and the Council of Europe.

Website: https://www.westminster.ac.uk/about-us/our-people/directory/lamb-terry#publications.

Acknowledgements

I wish to express my gratitude to the following colleagues for kindly reading and giving their valuable feedback on the different chapters of this book:

Dr. Inma Álvarez (The Open University), Dr. Alan Bainbridge (Canterbury Christ Church University), Dr. Richard Kiely (University of Southampton), Dr. Jai McKenzie (University of Nottingham), Dr. Cristina Ros i Solé (Goldsmiths College London), Dr. Cathy Watts (University of Brighton) and Professor Dorota Werbińska (Pomeranian University, Poland).

To Professor Terry Lamb from the University of Westminster, to Dr. Inma Álvarez and the Diasporic Identities team at the Open University and to Dr. Ana de Medeiros at King's College London for their support and encouragement.

I would also like to take this opportunity to thank Professor Catherine Boyle, Chair of the *Language Acts and Worldmaking* project at King's College London, for giving me the opportunity to be part of such an exciting research enterprise.

Finally, I would like to thank the language teachers who directly or indirectly have been involved in this project for sharing their stories with us. Without them, this book would not have become a reality.

Contents

1 Introduction to Negotiating Identity in Modern Foreign
  Language Teaching 1
  Matilde Gallardo

2 Transcultural Voices: Exploring Notions of Identity
  in Transnational Language Teachers' Personal Narratives 17
  Matilde Gallardo

3 Language Teacher/Translator Gendered Identity
  Construction: From Dilemmatic to Agentive—Big Lives
  Through Small Stories 45
  Tanya Linaker

4 "When I Am Teaching German, I Put on a Persona":
  Exploring Lived Experiences of Teaching a Foreign
  Language 69
  Maria Luisa Pérez Cavana

5 Becoming a Language Professional in Higher Education:
   A Psychosocial Case Study 91
   Donata Puntil

6 Modern Language Teacher Identity Formation Through
   Engagement with Exploratory Practice: The Future
   Will Tell 117
   Assia Slimani-Rolls

7 How a Community of Practice Shapes a Modern Foreign
   Language Teacher's Views of Herself as a Teacher
   over Time and Space: A Biographical Case Study 143
   Christina Richardson

8 Constructing Hybrid Identities in the Language
   Classroom 167
   Lorenza Boscaini and Debora Quattrocchi

9 The Journey to Becoming a Language Teacher:
   Motivation and Engagement with the Process
   of Professional Development and Lifelong Learning 185
   Laura Puente Martín and Susanne Winchester

Conclusion 203

Index 207

Notes on Contributors

Lorenza Boscaini holds a B.A. (Hons) in Modern Foreign Languages and Literature from Ca' Foscari, Venice University in Italy. She gained an M.A. in Bilingual Translation at the University of Westminster, London, and later on became an Associate Fellow of the Higher Education Academy (AFHEA) in the UK. She is currently an Associate Lecturer in Italian at the Open University where she also teaches Intercultural Communication. Lorenza's interests range from translation and interpreting, linguistics, language learning through process drama, to identity formation, bilingualism, multiculturalism and minority languages.

Maria Luisa Pérez Cavana, Ph.D., SFHEA studied Philosophy, History and Education in Spain and Germany. She is a lecturer in Languages at the Open University. Her main research interests are in the field of promoting learner autonomy and a learner-centred pedagogy through the use of ePortfolios in relation to language learning. She is part of the expert team for the European Language Portfolio (ELP) at the European Centre for Modern Languages (ECML) in Graz. She has also developed a model of Personal Development Planning (PDP) adapted to distance education. She is currently using phenomenology as a research method to study the lived experience of learning a language.

Matilde Gallardo, M.A., Ph.D. is currently a Visiting Research Fellow at King's College London where she also teaches Applied Linguistics. She contributes to language teacher training in M.A. and Doctorate programmes in the UK and in Spain. As well as being a language teacher educator, Matilde has taught Spanish and applied linguistics in a number of universities in the UK where she developed cross-institutional collaborative projects for MFL teachers and led two successful Aimhigher projects for secondary schools. She has published on the history of Spanish language teaching in the UK, language teaching in blended contexts and dyslexia and language teaching. Her current research is on narratives and transnationalism in language teaching.

Tanya Linaker has an M.A. in Russian Studies from SSEES, UCL and an M.A. in Applied Linguistics from Birkbeck College, London. After teaching at Northumbria University, Tanya moved to King's College London where she has taught Russian since 2002. As Team Leader in the Modern Language Centre at King's, she is responsible for the delivering of Slavic and Middle Eastern language courses. She is also Centre Education Lead. Tanya shares her expertise in teaching and assessment with colleagues from Cambridge, Manchester, Warwick and Reading Universities where she is an External Examiner. She has been a recipient of research and development grants. Her areas of research include gendered professional identity and innovative language teaching pedagogy.

Laura Puente Martín has worked as an Associate Lecturer, author and consultant in Spanish at the Open University since 2002. She has an Honours Degree and a Ph.D. in English Philology from the University of Salamanca (Spain). She is the co-author of Cambridge IGCSE Spanish as a First Language (Cambridge University Press). In the field of secondary education, she has worked as a Foreign Language Assistant, and as examiner for a leading Examination Board in the United Kingdom. Laura Puente Martín is a Fellow of the Higher Education Academy (FHEA) in the UK.

Donata Puntil is a Programme Director at the Modern Language Centre, King's College, London, where she is responsible for internal and external staff development and intercultural training activities. Donata has an extensive teaching and research experience in teaching Italian as a FL, in Second Language Acquisition and Intercultural Studies. She has presented at national and international conferences on the above subjects with a particular focus on the role that culture plays in language teaching. Donata is also an accredited Psychoanalytic Psychotherapist and practices this profession on a part-time basis. She is a member of the BPC (British Psychoanalytic Association).

Debora Quattrocchi graduated in Modern Languages and Literature in Italy, completed a B.A. Hons in English at Birkbeck College, London and an MRes in English Literature at Middlesex University, London. She currently works as an Associate Lecturer in Italian at the Open University where she also teaches an introduction to Applied Linguistics module. She is a Fellow of the Higher Education Academy (FHEA) in the UK and is interested in pedagogy, sociolinguistics, multilingualism and language and identity.

Christina Richardson is currently a Visiting Lecturer in Language Education at King's College London, where she works on the Modern Language Post Graduate Certificate in Education and on the B.A. in English Language and Linguistics, and the M.A.s in ELT and Applied Linguistics and TESOL. She also contributes to the M.Ed. in Bilingualism in Education at the University of Birmingham. Prior to becoming a teacher educator, Christina taught French, German and Spanish in secondary schools in the UK. Christina's Ph.D. research looked at inclusive practices in mainstream schools with a particular focus on supporting students with dyslexia in learning a modern language.

Assia Slimani-Rolls is a Reader of Applied Linguistics and Education. She is Head of Research and Professional Development in the Institute of Languages and Culture at Regent's University London. Her research interests include Exploratory Practice (a form of practitioner research), language learning, language teacher education and continuing professional development. Her belief in the collaborative work by teachers and learners to understand better their classroom practice has been heightened further since working with language teachers and learners on several projects to implement Exploratory Practice in their classroom which led to her latest co-authored publication *Exploratory Practice For Continuing Professional Development—An Innovative Approach For Language Teachers* (2018).

Susanne Winchester has worked as an Associate Lecturer, author and consultant in German at the Open University since 1996. She has over 28 years of experience as a teacher, examiner, curriculum coordinator and teacher trainer in secondary, further and higher education. She is an experienced examiner and is the author of *Talk German* 2 in the BBC Active Series. She completed her Doctorate in Education (E.d.D) at the Open University in 2015. Her research focused on the use of digital vocabulary trainers. Susanne Winchester is a Fellow of the Higher Education Academy (FHEA) in the UK.

List of Tables

Chapter 2

Table 1   Participants' characteristics   22

Chapter 4

Table 1   Participants' details   74

Chapter 5

Table 1   Participants' demographic data   101
Table 2   Stages of the data collection   103
Table 3   Main themes in the narrative accounts   104
Table 4   Narrative categories   105

1

Introduction to Negotiating Identity in Modern Foreign Language Teaching

Matilde Gallardo

1 Identity in Language Teaching

The field of teacher identity is a complex area that has been a subject of study in Second Language Acquisition (SLA) since the 1980s. Language teacher identity research originated in a variety of areas in applied linguistics and general educational research, such as teacher knowledge/teacher cognition, teacher beliefs, professional development and reflective practice. It is a concept that has been addressed predominantly from the perspective of English as a foreign/second language (EFL/ESL) (e.g. Taylor et al. 2013; Park 2017; Werbińska 2017); the language learner's perspective (e.g. Murray et al. 2011; Taylor 2013) and secondary teacher education (e.g. Grenfell et al. 2003; Pachler et al. 2014).

Within the area of second language teacher education (SLTE) teacher identity has attracted increasing interest in the last two decades (e.g. Varghese 2005; Richards 2006; Beauchamp and Thomas 2009; Kanno and Stuart 2011; Kramsch 2014; Block 2014; Barkhuizen 2017; Pavlenko and

M. Gallardo (✉)
Faculty of Arts and Humanities, King's College London, London, UK
e-mail: Matilde.gallardo@kcl.ac.uk

Norton 2018) with researchers paying particular attention to teachers as object of study—their beliefs and attitudes about teaching, as well as on how they construct their professional identity in relation to the subject knowledge and their teacher training experience. Research on language teacher identity also focuses on teachers reflecting on their experience of teaching with the aim of improving practice (e.g. Farrell 2007). Other studies have emphasized the role of the teacher in developing learners' intercultural competence (e.g. Byram and Kramsch 2008) and the importance of knowledge in constructing teachers' professional identity because it is informed by practice and developed in the classroom (e.g. Jiménez Raya and Lamb 2008; Murray et al. 2011). This line of research stresses the importance of teacher professional identity development for good language teaching while recognizing that it "[...] promotes social equality" (De Costa and Norton 2017, p. 4).

The idea of *good language teaching* has also been explored from the perspective of teacher emotions. The notion of *the good language teacher* as an "emotional, passionate being" (Hargreaves 1998, p. 835) has been advanced by researchers (e.g. Sutton and Wheatley 2003; Zembylas 2005; Dewaele 2010; King 2015) for whom good teaching, "[...] an inherently emotional endeavour" (King 2015, p. 98), is not solely considered in terms of achieving good subject knowledge and being familiar with pedagogical techniques. Language teachers' emotions such as the belief of caring for their learners and the feelings of responsibility for learners' motivation and progress have also guided teachers' pedagogical choices and professional development (Isenbarger and Zembylas 2006; O'Connor 2008) with the aim of enhancing their practice and meeting the expectations of learners, educational institutions and society. The latter aspect resonates within research on teacher professionalism that places language teacher professional identity within the materiality of the broader educational and institutional context where it is constructed. This includes the inherent inconsistencies between educational policies and practices which may require language teachers to demonstrate autonomy and accountability at the same time (Sachs 2001, p. 150); the complexities of more diverse than ever classrooms; and the demands of changing scenarios in a globalized world.

Research on language teacher identity has developed from a sociocultural perception of a collective identity which is negotiated and developed through communities of practice (professional teachers' identity, national-based groups of individuals with a common culture and language) to include teachers' complex and flexible individual identities (Canrinus et al. 2011) which integrate "[…] the individual and the social, making individuality a social and socially regulated affair" (Van Leeuwen 2009, p. 21), as well as their multidimensional identities (e.g. Duff and Uchida 1997; Tsui 2011; Kanno and Stuart 2011; Morgan and Clarke 2011; Cheung et al. 2015; Varghese et al. 2005, 2016; Barkhuizen 2017). As an example, Block (2015) referred to language teacher identity as how individuals self-position and are positioned by others as teachers, how they affiliate to different aspects of their work and how they build attachments to communities of practice. On the other hand, social psychologists have advocated the role of personal agency in shaping teachers' lives (Vähäsantanen 2015) and in making decisions about their own professional learning. The role of agency is also present in recent research which focuses on the importance of teachers' motivation as an aspect of their professional identity construction (Mercer and Kostoulas 2018). Theoretical frameworks from the perspective of self-efficacy (Bandura 2015), self-determination or achievement goal theory (Deci and Ryan 2012) have shed light on the reasons why individuals become teachers and the part that motivation plays in their professional development and classroom practices.

In this book we follow the epistemological exploration of teacher knowledge, beliefs and attitudes, as well as post-structuralist approaches to sociocultural aspects including gender, diaspora, educational and social affiliations and status, all of which are significant in the development of language teacher identity (Wilkins et al. 2012; Tabouret-Keller 1997). We adopt the socio-constructivist position of viewing language teacher identity as socially constructed, as a learning trajectory which is defined by the relation between the local and the global (Wenger 1998; Block 2017); as a continuous process of negotiation, potential change and constant dialogue (Akkermann et al. 2011), where the personal and the professional selves converge into oneself that results in the *becoming* of a language teacher, represented by teachers' personal stories (Beijaard et al. 2004). In so doing, we endorse the notion of language teachers as agents in the formation of their own identity within the social and educational contexts which they inhabit and to which they make a contribution.

2 Aims of This Book

This book is about modern foreign language (MFL) teachers researching their own and other teachers' experiences of identity construction and negotiation in the context of teaching and living in the UK. The idea of the book originates from the Language Acts and Worldmaking project,[1] led by King's College London and, more specifically, from a collaboration with the *Diasporic Identities and the Politics of Language* strand of that project led by the Open University, which investigates the role of MFL teachers in the UK with a view to challenging perceived attitudes and preconceptions about modern language education.

In broad terms, this volume aims to shed light on MFL teachers as agents in the construction of their own professional identities. Particularly, it intends to explore how their identity is shaped by contextual factors as well as cultural and linguistic influences; how they convey the interconnectivity between their professional and personal lives; how they voice their reasons for becoming language teachers; and what motivates them to engage in professional development and research.

Nevertheless, since MFL teacher professional identity is often related to national-based groups of people with a common cultural denomination and language, we have approached the topic mainly, although not exclusively, from the perspective of migration and transnationalism that characterizes the teaching of modern languages in the UK tertiary sector, as studied by Block (2017) in his research of transnational MFL teachers in London. The term *transnational*, derived from narrative, transcultural, and media theory approaches to memory studies (Erll 2011; Rothberg 2014; Assmann 2014) is used in this context to refer to migrant language teachers who have settled in the UK. However, in the MFL teaching milieu, the idea of the transnational may go beyond the physicality of the different spaces teachers may inhabit to reach the more abstract diverse linguistic and cultural identities which make them who they are.

The focus of the book is therefore upon pluricultural and plurilingual MFL practitioners and the role that their socio-educational, cultural and linguistic characteristics play in the making of their professional identity. The cultural dimension of MFL teacher identity is an under-researched area. This book aims to make a contribution to the field addressing not only that aspect of MFL teachers' identities, but also teachers' thoughts on the relevance of their cultural identities to their practices (e.g. how they position themselves with the language they teach; their emotions and beliefs about cultural representation in the classroom; their cultural and subject affiliations; their engagement with professional development and research). It also explores the intersection between their exposure to different pedagogical methods, educational policies and institutional dynamics and the expectations they face from learners, fellow practitioners and policy makers.

The contributors in this book have approached the task from the perspective of Practitioner Inquiry (e.g. Murray 1992; Cochran-Smith and Lytle 2004; Lytle 2008) and Autobiographical Narrative (e.g. Gee 2000; Nunan and Choi 2010; Barkhuizen et al. 2014; De Fina and Georgakopoulou 2015; Clandinin 2016). Essential to both of these perspectives is the idea of *reflection* on critical situations and events where teachers exercise their agency concerning their own professional practice and experiences. Equally essential is the narrative process that enables teachers to make sense of the world and to understand their own and other people's lives. As experienced language teachers and teacher educators with a transnational background in most cases, we belong to the community of practitioners which is the object of study in this book. Theirs and our voices are present through their autobiographical stories and our personal accounts. As teacher-researchers we have engaged with the process of research as a method to generate knowledge about MFL teachers' identity that can enhance how they are perceived in the social and educational establishments and raise awareness of key issues affecting the profession. It is often said that teachers and researchers are disconnected from the same community (Block 2017). As a collective endeavour, the making of this book generates a community of teacher-researchers whose voices encapsulate those of other practitioners with whom we share similar scenarios and interest in developing ourselves professionally.

This collection represents a fresh insight into understanding a key element in the educational and sociopolitical debate surrounding the discipline of modern foreign languages in the UK—the teachers' voices and their sense of agency in shaping their professional lives. This represents an original contribution to the field of MFL teacher identity research in the current climate of the national decline of the subject and the fractured environment in which these teachers often operate in Higher Education—this being in research-focused Language Departments and Language Centres, frequently depicted as non-research active and as service providers of supplementary foreign language skills.

3 Overview

This introduction started by examining the main theoretical approaches underpinning language teacher identity research within SLA and applied linguistics. The ensuing chapters offer, using diverse methodological approaches, unique insights into the role of experience, emotions and social factors in shaping teachers' identities; their personal orientations to their journeys to becoming language practitioners; their beliefs and ideas about the profession and their self-perceptions as members of communities of practice and citizens of a complex and diverse world. Following a social-constructivist qualitative auto-narrative-oriented approach, the chapters in this book include methods of investigation such as narrative inquiry (Nunan and Choi 2010; Johnson and Golombek 2002), psychosocial case study (Riessman 2003), positioning analysis (Bamberg and Georgakopoulou 2008), phenomenology (Finlay 2009) and engagement with exploratory practice (Allwright and Hanks 2009), among others.

The contributions that constitute this volume have been arranged in two parts. Part 1 (chapters 2–7) consists of a collection of chapters based on empirical research from the perspective of the practitioners themselves—teachers researching teachers' professional identity and their lived experiences of teaching. The authors' reflectivity on their own histories as language educators and/or as transnational language teachers is present in their investigation. Part 2 (chapters 8 and 9), consists of the personal accounts of four teachers who, using an auto-ethnographic approach, narrate their experiences of becoming MFL teachers. They exemplify many of the claims made in part one chapters and highlight the teachers' conscious examination of their trajectories, memories, experiences and, ultimately, their negotiation of identities in their professional and lived contexts. This situated reflection enables them to conceptualize, to go deeper and evaluate their own experiences as migrants, but also as learners and teachers. All four teachers acknowledge the liberating, although initially challenging, effect of writing their autobiographical narratives, which they recognize as a valuable opportunity to reflect on their personal and professional journeys to become the practitioners they are today.

Chapter 2, by Matilde Gallardo, unveils transnational language teachers' perceptions of identity in the context of their transcultural lives by engaging a small group of practitioners with the process of reflection through autobiographical narratives. Following a post-structuralist, post-modern conceptual orientation, the chapter discusses how teachers' complex and diverse linguistic and cultural identities generate a constant process of rethinking their identity which challenges assumed notions of national identity and memory. The author reflects on the dialogic nature of identity as well as on the practitioners' sense of agency in managing conflicting attitudes and values across diverse sociocultural and linguistic worlds. The chapter shows that, notwithstanding the educational changes, societal uncertainties and difficulties faced by transnational language teachers in the UK, their sense of identity remains strongly connected to their practice and their relationship with their learners and other practitioners.

In Chapter 3, Tanya Linaker's case study offers an insight into the gendered professional identity construction of Russian female teachers and translators in the UK, based on the narrated interaction between a practitioner and the researcher. Through the chapter the author gives voice to the under-represented Russian female community of language professionals in the UK of which the author is part, revealing their positioning not only within their professional discourse but also within the discourses of motherhood, immigration, and gender ideology. The chapter considers the so-called *Soviet gender paradox*—equality of labour without domestic equality (Ashwin 2006) and demonstrates how the boundaries between the personal and the professional are blurred among these migrant women due to sociocultural and historic state of affairs. Linaker approaches her research through small storytelling discursive interactions and the discourse of immigration and professional success.

Chapter 4 by María Luisa Pérez Cavana investigates the lived experience of two language teachers through in-depth interviews using a phenomenological approach. Phenomenology is an under-researched methodology in relation to language teachers' lived experiences. The author draws from the work of philosophers such as Husserl, Heidegger and Merleau-Ponty to investigate questions such as *What is it like to teach a language that is not your mother tongue? How is the sense of self when teaching a foreign language? How does the language-teacher-self relate to their "normal" self?* The chapter argues that to be a language teacher is grounded in being able to "personify", enact and embody a language that may not necessarily be one's mother tongue, resulting therefore, in contradictory identities which are not always in conflict. Her research positions itself within sociocultural and post-structuralist theory which establishes the complexity and multiplicity of language teachers' identities, as well as within the debate around Native Speaker (NS) versus Non-Native Speaker (NNS), a prevailing discussion in Second Language Acquisition (SLA) research.

Donata Puntil's Chapter 5 takes the investigation of the correlation between the personal and the professional in the trajectory of language professionals to an innovative dimension by positioning her study within a psychosocial framework. By questioning conscious and unconscious factors she brings the focus of her analysis of MFL teachers' autobiographical narratives not only to the told story, but to the untold, to what is implied, but not explicitly narrated. Her aim is to represent the interrelation between the personal and the professional in the unfolding of language teachers' nomadic stories of professionalization. This is mediated by the author's reflection on her own nomadic journey and her own professional background as a language educator and a qualified psychoanalytic psychotherapist. The professional settings of language centres in UK universities in which many language teachers operate are central to Puntil's investigation because of their impact on teachers' motivation and interest in further professional development.

In Chapter 6, Assia Slimani-Rolls further explores the formation of the professional identity of a group of modern language teachers as practitioner researchers through the analysis of their narratives following their participation in a longitudinal Exploratory Practice (EP) project co-directed by the author. Through her chapter, Slimani-Rolls provides a pertinent account of the theoretical framework of EP and discusses what teachers tell us about their experiences of engaging with classroom and practice research under the EP project. The current decline of modern languages in England and its effect on teachers' working conditions are discussed realistically by the author, who clearly articulates the difficulties encountered by MFL teachers to engage with research opportunities. She also identifies the precarious environment in which MFL teachers in higher education in the UK exercise their profession and the obvious impact of these factors on teachers' professional identity.

Drawing on her professional background as a language teacher educator, Christina Richardson considers in Chapter 7 how language teacher identity develops over time and how affiliation to communities of practice shapes that development. Taking a biographical case study approach and building on the author's previous doctoral research, this chapter explores the development of Maria's identity, a teacher of French, in relation to the environmental and social influences of her subject department within a secondary school setting. Building on Bourdieu and Wacquant's (1992) notions of *habitus* and *dispositions* and Wenger's (1998) *communities of practice*, the chapter discusses the situated nature of learning as a useful framework for exploring *identities in practice* and *identity (trans)formation in practice*. Richardson's study adds to the body of research that highlights the important relationship between subject affiliation, identity and agency, suggesting that a strong identity as an educator, a strong sense of agency and ongoing engagement with formal education and research may be key factors in sustaining a satisfying and ever-developing teaching career.

In Chapter 8, Lorenza Boscaini and Debora Quattrocchi reflect on their identities, both on a personal and professional level, and how they have developed across space and time through their own experiences of language learning and classroom interaction with their learners. Both narratives highlight the challenges as well as the cultural and pedagogical adjustments that the narrators have experienced as transnational language teachers in the context of the MFL classroom. They also emphasize the difficulties in reconciling cultural and linguistic differences in their teacher/mediator role at a time of fast-paced social and educational changes and greater awareness of multiculturalism.

In Chapter 9, Susanne Winchester and Laura Puente Martin tell their stories of becoming language teachers which converge in a vivid passion for both learning and helping others to learn. They acknowledge that early childhood learning experiences, as well as critical incidents early in a teaching career can have a significant influence on later professional choices, while empowering individuals to be active agents in developing their own professional identity. Their reflective accounts illustrate how the authors' identity as language teachers is intertwined with their experiences and identity as language learners, in addition to being shaped by their active engagement with specialized professional training and shared practice within their academic communities.

The conclusions of this volume include final remarks and reflections on the distinctive insights into the multiple and complex factors shaping MFL teachers construction of their professional identity offered in this volume.

We hope the stories and studies in this book will allow readers to gain a better understanding of who the people behind the profession of MFL teacher are, what moves them to succeed in sometimes complex and difficult circumstances and what are their thoughts about their profession. This volume offers an accurate understanding of the community of MFL practitioners and by doing so, it makes a contribution to the discipline of MFL studies in the UK.

Note

1. For more information about the Languages Acts and Worldmaking project (funded by the Arts and Humanities Research Council's Open World Research Initiative) see the following website, https://languageacts.org/.

References

Akkerman, Sanne F., and Paulien C. Meijer. 2011. A Dialogical Approach to Conceptualizing Teacher Identity. *Teaching and Teacher Education* 27: 308–319.

Allwright, Dick, and Judith Hanks. 2009. *The Developing Language Learner: An Introduction to Exploratory Practice*. Basingstoke: Palgrave Macmillan.

Ashwin, Sarah. 2006. Dealing with Devastation in Russia: Men and Women Compared. In *Adapting to Russia's New Labour Market: Gender and Employment Behaviour*, ed. Sarah Ashwin, 1–30. London: Routledge.

Assmann, Aleida. 2014. Transnational Memories. *European Review* 22 (4): 546–556.

Bamberg, Michael, and Alexandra Georgakopoulou. 2008. Small Stories as a New Perspective in Narrative and Identity Analysis. *Text and Talk* 23: 377–396.

Bandura, Albert. 2015. Self-Regulation of Motivation and Action Through Internal Standards and Goal Systems. *Goal Concepts in Personality and Social Psychology* 23: 19–85. https://doi.org/10.4324/9781315717517.

Barkhuizen, Gary (ed.). 2017. *Reflections on Language Teacher Identity Research*. New York: Routledge.

Barkhuizen, Gary, Phil Benson, and Alice Chik. 2014. *Narrative Inquiry in Language Teaching and Learning Research*. New York and London: Routledge.

Beauchamp, Catherine, and Lynn Thomas. 2009. Understanding Teacher Identity: An Overview of Issues in the Literature and Implications for Teacher Education. *Cambridge Journal of Education* 39 (2): 175–189.

Beijaard, Douwe, Paulien C. Meijer, and Verloop Nico. 2004. Reconsidering Research on Teachers' Professional Identity. *Teaching and Teacher Education* 20 (2): 107–128.

Block, David. 2014. *Second Language Identities*, 2nd ed. London: Bloomsbury.

Block, David. 2015. Becoming a Language Teacher: Constrains and Negotiations in the Emergence of New Identities. *Bellaterra Journal of Teaching and Learning Language and Literature* 8 (3): 9–26.

Block, David. 2017. Journey to the Centre of Language Teacher Identity. In *Reflections on Language Teacher Identity Research*, ed. Gary Barkhuizen, 31–36. New York: Routledge.

Bourdieu, Pierre, and Loïc Wacquant. 1992. *An Invitation to Reflexive Sociology*. Chicago and London: The University of Chicago Press.

Byram, Katra, and Claire Kramsch. 2008. Why Is It So Difficult to Teach Language as Culture? *The German Quarterly* 81 (1): 20–34.

Canrinus, Esther T., Michelle Helms-Lorenz, Douwe Beijaard, Jaap Buitink, and Adriaan Hofman. 2011. Profiling Teachers' Sense of Professional Identity. *Educational Studies* 37 (5): 593–608.
Cheung, Yin Ling, Selim Ben Said, and Kwanghyun Park (eds.). 2015. *Advances and Current Trends in Language Teacher Identity Research*. London: Routledge.
Clandinin, Jean. 2016. *Engaging in Narrative Inquiry*. Abingdon and New York: Routledge.
Cochran-Smith, Marilyn, and Susan L. Lytle. 2004. Practitioner Inquiry, Knowledge, and University Culture. In *International Handbook of Self-Study of Teaching and Teacher Education Practices*, ed. John J. Loughran, Mary L. Hamilton, and Vicki K. LaBoskey, 12. Dordrecht: Springer. https://doi.org/10.1007/978-1-4020-6545-3_16.
Deci, Edward L., and Richard M. Ryan. 2012. Motivation, Personality, and Development Within Embedded Social Contexts: An Overview of Self-Determination Theory. In *The Oxford Handbook of Human Motivation*, ed. Richard M. Ryan, 85–107. New York: Oxford University Press. https://doi.org/10.1093/oxfordhb/9780195399820.013.0006.
De Costa, Peter I., and Bonny Norton. 2017. Introduction: Identity, Transdisciplinarity and the Good Language Teacher. *The Modern Language Journal* 101. https://doi.org/10.1111/modl.123680026-7902/17/3-14.
De Fina, Anna, and Alexandra Georgakopoulou (eds.). 2015. *The Handbook of Narrative Analysis*. Chichester and Malden: Wiley Blackwell.
Dewaele, Jean-Marc. 2010. *Emotions in Multiple Languages*. London: Palgrave Macmillan.
Duff, Patricia, and Yuko Uchida. 1997. The Negotiation of Teachers' Sociocultural Identities and Practices in Postsecondary EFL Classrooms. *TESOL Quarterly* 31 (3): 451–461.
Erll, Astrid. 2011. *Memory in Culture*. London: Macmillan.
Farrell, Thomas S. C. 2007. *Reflective Language Teaching: From Research to Practice*. London: Continuum.
Finlay, Linda. 2009. Debating Phenomenological Research Methods. *Phenomenology and Practice* 3 (1): 6–25.
Gee, James Paul. 2000. Identity as an Analytic Lens for Research in Education. *Review of Research in Education* 25: 99–125.
Grenfell, Michael, Kelly Michael, and Diana Jones. 2003. *The European Language Teacher: Recent Trends and Future Developments in Teacher Education*. Oxford: Peter Lang.
Hargreaves, Andy. 1998. The Emotional Practice of Teaching. *Teaching and Teacher Education* 14 (8): 835–854.

Isenbarger, Lynn, and Michalinos Zembylas. 2006. The Emotional Labour of Caring in Teaching. *Teaching and Teacher Education* 22: 120–134. https://doi.org/10.1016/j.tate.2005.07.002.
Jiménez Raya, Manuel, and Terry Lamb (eds.). 2008. *Pedagogy for Autonomy in Modern Languages Education in Europe: Theory, Practice and Teacher Education.* Dublin: Authentik.
Johnson, Karen E., and Paula R. Golombek. 2002. *Teachers' Narrative Inquiry as Professional Development.* Cambridge: Cambridge University Press.
Kanno, Yasuko, and Christian Stuart. 2011. Learning to Become a Second Language Teacher: Identities-in-Practice. *Modern Language Journal* 95 (2): 236–252.
King, Jim. 2015. "It's Time, Put on the Smile, It's Time!": The Emotional Labour of Second Language Teaching Within a Japanese University. In *New Directions in Language Learning Psychology, Second Language Learning and Teaching*, ed. Christina Gkonou, et al., 97–112. Springer. ProQuest Ebook Central. http://ebookcentral.proquest.com/lib/kcl/detail.action?docID=4179464. Accessed 15 January 2019.
Kramsch, Claire. 1998. *Language and Culture.* Oxford: Oxford University Press.
Kramsch, Claire. 2014. Teaching Foreign Languages in an Era of Globalization: An Introduction. *Modern Language Journal* 98: 296–311.
Lytle, Susan L. 2008. At Last: Practitioner Inquiry and the Practice of Teaching: Some Thoughts on Better. *Journal for Research in the Teaching of English* 42 (3): 373–379. http://repository.upenn.edu/gse_pubs/153.
Mercer, Sarah, and Achilleas Kostoulas. 2018. *Language Teacher Psychology.* Bristol: Multilingual Matters.
Morgan, Brian, and Mathew Clarke. 2011. Identity in Second Language Teaching and Learning. In *Handbook of Research in Second Language Teaching and Learning*, ed. Eli Hinkel, 817–836. New York: Routledge.
Murray, Garold, Xuesong Gao, and Terry Lamb (eds.). 2011. *Identity, Motivation and Autonomy in Language Learning.* Bristol: Multilingual Matters.
Murray, Louis. 1992. What Is Practitioner Based Enquiry? *Journal of In-Service Education* 18 (3): 191–196. https://doi.org/10.1080/0305763920180309.
Nunan, David, and Julie Choi (eds.). 2010. *Language and Culture. Reflective Narratives and the Emergence of Identity.* New York and London: Routledge.
O'Connor, Kate E. 2008. "You Choose to Care": Teachers, Emotions and Professional Identities. *Teaching and Teacher Education: An International Journal of Research and Studies* 2 (1): 117–126.
Pachler, Norbert, Michael Evans, Ana Redondo, and Linda Fisher. 2014. *Learning to Teach Foreign Languages in the Secondary School.* London: Routledge.

Park, Gloria. 2017. *Narratives of East Asian Women Teachers of English: Where Privilege Meets Marginalization*. Bristol: Multilingual Matters.

Pavlenko, Aneta and Norton Bonny. 2018. Imagined Communities, Identity, and English Language Learning. In *International Handbook of English Language Teaching*, ed. Jim Cummins and Chris Davidson, 669–680. New York: Springer.

Richards, Keith. 2006. Being the Teacher: Identity and Classroom Conversation. *Applied Linguistics* 27 (1): 51–77.

Riessman, Catherine. K. 2003. *Narrative Analysis*. London and Newbury Park, CA: Sage.

Rothberg, Michael. 2014. Locating Transnational Memory. *European Review* 22: 652–656.

Sachs, Judyth. 2001. Teacher Professional Identity: Competing Discourses, Competing Outcomes. *Journal of Education Policy* 16 (2): 149–161. https://doi.org/10.1080/02680930116819.

Sutton, Rosemary E., and Karl F. Wheatley. 2003. Teachers' Emotions and Teaching: A Review of the Literature and Directions for Future Research. *Educational Psychology Review* 15 (4): 327–358. https://doi.org/10.1023/A:1026131715856.

Tabouret-Keller, Andrée. 1997. Language and Identity. In *The Handbook of Sociolinguistics*, ed. Florian Coulmas, 315–326. Oxford: Blackwell.

Taylor, Florentina. 2013. Relational Views of the Self in SLA. In *Multiple Perspectives on the Self in Second Language Acquisition*, ed. Sarah Mercer and Marion Williams, 92–103. Bristol: Multilingual Matters.

Taylor, Florentina, Vera Busse, Lubina Gagova, Emma Marsden, and Barabara Rooksen. 2013. Identity in Foreign Language Learning and Teaching: Why Listening to Our Students' and Teachers' Voices Really Matters. *ELT Research Papers 13–02*.

Tsui, Amy B.M. 2011. Teacher Education and Teacher Development. In *Handbook of Research in Second Language Teaching and Learning*, ed. Eli Hinkel, 21–40. New York: Routledge.

Vähäsantanen, Katja. 2015. Professional Agency in the Stream of Change: Understanding Educational Change and Teachers' Professional Identities. *Teaching and Teacher Education* 47. https://doi.org/10.1016/j.tate.2014.11.006.

Van Leeuwen, Theo. 2009. Discourses of Identity. *Language Teaching* 42 (2): 212–221. https://doi.org/10.1017/S0261444808005508.

Varghese, Manka, Brian Morgan, Bill Johnston, and Kimberly A. Johnson. 2005. Theorizing Language Teacher Identity: Three Perspectives and Beyond. *Journal of Language, Identity & Education* 4 (1): 21–44. https://doi.org/10.1207/s15327701jlie0401_2.

Varghese, Manka, Suhanthie Motha, Gloria Park, John Trent, and Jenelle Reeves. 2016. Language Teacher Identity in (Multi)lingual Educational Contexts. Special Issue, *TESOL Quarterly* 50 (3). https://doi.org/10.1002/tesq.333.

Wenger, Etienne. 1998. *Communities of Practice: Learning, Meaning, and Identity*. Cambridge: Cambridge University Press.

Werbińska, Dorota. 2017. *The Formation of Language Teacher Professional Identity. A Phenomenographic-Narrative Study.* Słupsk: Akademia Pomorska w Słupsk.

Wilkins, Chris, Hugh Busher, Michalis Kakos, Carmen Mohamed, and Joan Smith. 2012. Crossing Borders: New Teachers Co-constructing Professional Identity in Performative Times. *Professional Development in Education* 38 (1): 65–78.

Zembylas, Michalinos. 2005. Emotions and Teacher Identity: A Poststructural Perspective. *Teacher and Teaching: Theory and Practice* 9: 214–238. https://doi.org/10.1080/13540600309378.

2

Transcultural Voices: Exploring Notions of Identity in Transnational Language Teachers' Personal Narratives

Matilde Gallardo

1 Introduction

The internationalisation of Modern Foreign Language (MFL) teaching and related occupations in the UK can be traced back to the sixteenth century, to the movement of transnational collectives such as diplomats, merchants, reformers and political emigrés (Gallardo 2006). It is also linked to global economic migratory phenomena in the Western economy in contemporary times. Transnational language teachers, as cultural transmitters, have played a valuable role in shaping and influencing social, cultural and educational attitudes while belonging to *communities of memory* (Erll 2011) and establishing interconnectedness between distinct worlds. They may retain connections with their place of origin through national group membership, frequent visits to the home country and use of electronically mediated communication, but their multidimensional identity also needs to be understood from the perspective of the self and the process

---

M. Gallardo (✉)
Faculty of Arts and Humanities, King's College London, London, UK
e-mail: Matilde.gallardo@kcl.ac.uk

© The Author(s) 2019
M. Gallardo (ed.), *Negotiating Identity in Modern Foreign Language Teaching*, https://doi.org/10.1007/978-3-030-27709-3_2

of assimilation and integration into the host society they experience. As pluri-cultural and pluri-lingual individuals with multiple memberships—linguistic, cultural, national, professional—teachers embody the idea of the transnational, understood as movement in space across national borders (Rothberg 2014). They also represent the concept of transculturality (Welsch 1995), as they move in cross-cultural spaces and operate in a world of translations and reconfigurations of established cultural national themes, references, representations, images and concepts (Assmann 2014).

Following a post-structuralist, post-modern conceptual orientation (Giddens 1991; Akkerman and Meijer 2011) in which identity is understood as "[…] a dynamic personal life project that is nevertheless conditioned by the social context" (Werbińska 2017, p. 21), in this chapter I investigate the experiences and perceptions of identity of six transnational MFL teachers living and working in the UK, manifested in their personal narratives in the form of meaningful reflective accounts. My aim is to reveal how transnational language teachers approach the process of identity construction by looking at the situated nature of their narrated experiences and beliefs and the contextual factors influencing their personal and professional choices and how these may correspond with the values and attitudes they transmit to their learners. In particular, I want to explore the following questions: How do transnational language teachers identify themselves with being language teachers in the context of their transcultural experiences? What is their interpretation of key concepts which are intrinsic to the idea of identity, such as *homeland, otherness, change, belonging*? What are their feelings and beliefs about the activity of teaching and the profession?

Through this investigation I aim to make a contribution to the field of MFL teacher identity and more specifically to the under-researched topic of transnational language teacher identity construction.

2 Theoretical Framework Underpinning the Study

The field of language teacher identity which originated in applied linguistics and general educational research has attracted increasing interest in the last decade or so. In sociocultural theory (Wenger 2006; Kramsch 1998; Varghese 2018) the notion of identity, understood to mean the aggregate of a person's self beliefs which may be private or public and may differ from one relational context to another (Taylor 2013), relates to *desire*, "the desire for recognition, the desire for affiliation, and the desire for security and safety" (Norton 1997, p. 140). In post-structuralist theory (Akkerman and Meijer 2011; Norton 2013), identity is interpreted as the reflexive construction of the self, as a process which connects knowledge, personal and social change and which involves constant adaptation and adjustment (Giddens 1991). This idea is based on the assumption that individuals are flexible and adaptive and also that they exercise agency making decisions about shaping their professional lives and values (Pavlenko and Lantolf 2000; Kalaja et al. 2016; White 2018). Under post-modern views, identity emerges as a multiple, hybrid and heterogeneous mindset made up of several selves, which is subject to change and interwoven with social, political and global factors, rendering the nature of the identity construct dynamic (Nunan and Choi 2010). It is also subject to the associations and attachments individuals may forge with the communities which they encounter and with whose ideals, norms and values they may identify.

Transnational language teachers, as members of the diverse multicultural urban landscape resulting from the movement of peoples (Simpson and Hepworth 2010; Modood 2013), are a representative case of the hybrid, multiple and dynamic identities already considered. Their personal experiences conditioned by the geographical and cross-cultural spaces they inhabit are affected by the processes of assimilation, integration and citizenship which define the societal culture in which they negotiate a sense of individual social self and group identity as members of communities of practice (Wenger 2006). However, the internal life history of the person must also be considered in this process. Ricoeur (1981) referred to this both in terms of *idem* (sameness, permanence in time) and *ipse* (self, individuality) and to the mediating role that *narrative identity* plays in the dialectic relationship existing between those two aspects. Likewise, narrative identity, as stated by Werbińska (2017), has to be understood not as an enumeration of events in somebody's life, but as "[…] finding "the key" through which a person can reach the meanings of his or her existence" (2017, p. 24).

In this chapter the idea of a collective language teacher identity, whereby there are national-based groups of people with a common cultural denomination and language, is rejected in favour of considering the individual teachers' voices making meaning of their personal experiences and perspectives and taking into account *the social world* as well as *the self* as intrinsically related elements (Canrinus et al. 2011; Varghese 2018; Van Leeuwen 2009).

Among the identity frameworks examined for the purpose of this chapter (Barkhuizen 2017; Barkhuizen et al. 2014; Varghese et al. 2016; Cheung et al. 2015; Norton 2013; Tsui 2011), I focus attention on the "Three As Language Teacher Identity Framework" (3ALTIF) by Werbińska (2016, 2017). This reviews the impact that institutional and personal environments have on teachers' professional identities by showing how language teacher professional identity is constructed around the three domains of *affiliation, attachment* and *autonomy*. It provides a holistic approach to discussing key questions in relation to language teachers' professional identity, which include "Who am I as a language teacher?" (affiliation), "How do I teach?" (attachment) and "What am I allowed to do?" (autonomy) (Werbińska 2016, p. 137). These concepts and questions are highly relevant to my study on transnational language teachers' construction of identity which is the basis of this chapter.

3 The Study

This chapter investigates the perceptions and beliefs of identity in a group of six transnational MFL teachers in the UK. The idea originated from meetings with fellow language teachers in which questions around our own identity as transnational individuals and as members of the MFL teaching profession emerged as a frequent topic of debate. The need to share experiences and views, as well as to reflect on the processes that shaped our lives and those of fellow practitioners, became critical in the present climate of the decline of modern languages as an academic subject and the socio-economic and political scenarios that affect many transnational individuals in the UK.

3.1 Methodology

The investigation was conducted using a Narrative Inquiry methodological approach (Clandinin and Connelly 2000; Clandinin 2016), which places teachers' voices at the core of the inquiry in the form of reflective stories.

From the perspective of sociocultural theory, narrative appears to be naturally connected to teacher biographies and autobiographies (Moen 2006; Nunan and Choi 2010; Barkhuizen et al. 2014; De Fina and Georgakopoulou 2015). Similarly, teachers appear to value engaging with the reflective autobiographical process because it allows them to explore their narrated identity as they re-construct and re-connect their personal and professional selves (Bukor 2011), which becomes part of the act of inquiry (Nunan and Choi 2010; Belcher and Connor 2001). In the case of transnational language teachers, retroactive first-person narratives are especially relevant because they offer insights into their experiences of cross-cultural struggles (Pavlenko and Lantolf 2000) and allow them to analyse "spatial and temporal scenarios that go beyond the here and now", as explained by De Costa and Norton (2017, p. 6).

The personal narratives allowed teachers participating in this study to create descriptions about their experiences and also allowed me as a researcher to develop my own narrative to make sense of the experiences of others. As all human action is dialogic in nature (Bakhtin 1986), it is the interaction between these teachers' voices and my own voice and my personal reflection as a transnational language teacher, that creates meaning of their perceptions of identity in relation to the social contexts which they inhabit. This is what Moen (2006) following Ricoeur (1981) calls an *open work*, as the meaning in the researcher's final narrative report "opens for a wide range of interpretations by others who read and hear about the report" (Moen 2006, p. 62).

As a researcher, I encouraged participating teachers to look back and to reflect both on past and present actions that shaped their lives as transnational and transcultural language teachers, while I also reflected on the connections between their experiences and my own story as a member of the profession. I subsequently interpreted their stories within the theoretical framework of identity already presented in this chapter. Through this process, the participants and I became auto-ethnographers when constructing

Table 1 Participants' characteristics

Participants' characteristics
• The six participants (P1, P2, P3, P4, P5, P6) are female • Four are Spanish (P1, P2, P3, P4 and teach Spanish language and culture, with one teacher also teaching Intercultural Communication (P1). Two teachers were Italian and teach Italian language and culture (P5, P6) • They have an average of between fifteen and eighteen years teaching experience (more in some cases) and currently work in tertiary education, although some also have experience of secondary and further education • All of them have been educated to degree level in relevant subjects (language studies, translation, English language) and have additional post-graduate qualifications (three MAs, two PhDs and one PGCE/TEFL) • They have lived in at least two countries, including the UK and other European countries • They are fluent in at least two languages, English being one of them. Three teachers also spoke other European languages

our own stories (De Fina and Georgakopoulou 2015) and reflecting on our identities.

3.2 Participants

Language teachers participating in this study did so in the context of the Diasporic Identities and the Politics of Language (DIPL) research project under which this study was carried out. The DIPL is a research strand of the Language Acts and Worldmaking project, already mentioned in the introductory chapter of this book. It investigates the role of modern language teachers in the UK with a view to challenging perceived attitudes about language education.

From an initial workshop in January 2017 organised by the DIPL team at King's College London for MFL teachers interested in joining the project, six language teachers voluntarily agreed to participate in this study and contribute their autobiographical narratives. They generally share the characteristics of the larger cohort of language teachers involved in the overall project, which can be seen in Table 1.

The ethical aspects of this investigation were considered and the British Educational Research Association (BERA 2018) guidelines were adhered to.

3.3 Data Collection and Analysis

The investigation benefited from a previous initial survey with twenty-nine MFL teachers carried out under the umbrella DIPL project in 2017 in which I was also involved. The initial survey encouraged teachers to talk about their personal stories as language teachers in the UK, to discuss their feelings about the profession and the challenges in doing the job. This provided the context which led to the investigation into teachers' personal narratives, the focus of this chapter. Six teachers responded favourably to the expression of interest sent to all participants in the DIPL project. The process for obtaining the data, based on Long et al. (2012) consisted of the following stages:

Stage 1: A short personal details questionnaire to establish participants' profile (languages spoken, mother tongue(s), years of teaching experience).

Stage 2: A personal reflection on the concept of identity prompted by open questions such as: what does identity mean to you?; what do you consider markers of identity?; what factors may influence identity?. This information helped to establish participants' understanding of the concept in the first instance and also prepared them for the in-depth narratives.

Stage 3: A personal narrative (between 500–600 words) in which participants reflected upon and expressed their beliefs about their identity as transnational and transcultural individuals and language teachers. For the purpose of this task, participants were prompted with a list of meaningful keywords related to the discourse of identity (e.g. transculturality, adaptation, sameness/otherness, interconnectedness, citizenship) which they could choose to use or not in their narratives. The selection of keywords originated in the concepts that were more prominently used by respondents in the DIPL initial survey.

Teachers sent their narratives in written form, except for one who preferred to send a recorded narrative, which was later transcribed. English was used as a common language in all narratives to facilitate the analysis.

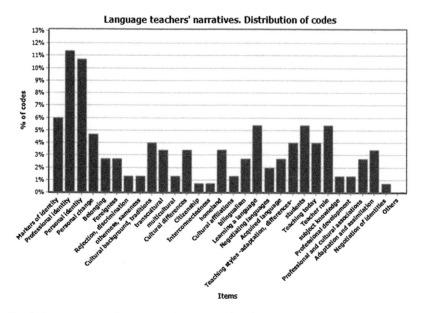

Fig. 1 Language teachers' narrative categories chart

The narratives were collected over an extended period of time (October 2017–April 2018) to give participants flexibility of opportunity to engage with the task in a reflective way.

The scrutiny of the six narratives was approached using thematic analysis (Braun and Clarke 2013; Guest et al. 2012) followed by a narrative analysis (Werbińska 2016) informed by the researcher's personal reflection. The thematic analysis looked for commonalities emerging from teachers' accounts, but it also highlighted contrasting views and experiences. Firstly, I scrutinised the data using QDA Milne qualitative research software to identify general themes and categories, as well as the frequency of their use, as shown in Fig. 1.

Secondly, I considered the common themes and interpreted them in the light of the theoretical framework underpinning the study to fully understand the beliefs underlying the stories and to provide answers to the research questions. The analysis was followed by my personal reflection in the form of an "open work" narrative report (Moen 2006, p. 62), as previously explained.

3.4 Analysis of Findings

The following six themes emerged from stages 2 and 3 of the data collection: perceptions of identity, language and identity, emotions and identity, culture and identity, teacher agency and visions of teaching, as explained below:

3.4.1 Perceptions of Identity

As the general theme of the narratives, the notion of identity underpins all themes and categories in the personal accounts, but examining teachers' interpretation of the concept, it emerges as the aggregate of the many aspects which make up who teachers are. As some respondents commented:

> There is no fixed notion of identity and we all adopt many identities according to the role we have in certain life scenarios (e.g. mother; daughter; teacher; commuter; customer; etc.). (P5)
>
> Identity is a deeply personal part of someone that can be composed of many different aspects, such as language(s), culture(s), profession, interests [...] religion, beliefs. (P6)
>
> Identity is more about how I view myself, rather than how others view me [...]. Cultural background I was brought up in, but also the one I created for myself in my formation years and in my academic life. (P1)

These statements suggest identity is about how individuals perceive themselves in the two spheres of the *personal* or private and the *professional* or public (Miller 2009; Taylor 2013), which are closely intertwined. This coexistence of identities, as justified by post-structuralist Second Language Acquisition (SLA) research (Norton 2013), is taken a step further when teachers define themselves in terms of their multifaceted *professional* identity as language teachers and as researchers:

> I see myself mainly as a Spanish language teacher. (P3)
> My professional identity is also an important part of my life. I am proud to be a language teacher, a linguist, a researcher, a teacher of Spanish

linguistics (and I'm proud to be so, despite being considered second-class teaching, unfortunately), and to be part of associations and groups of language teachers in the UK. (P4)

These extracts suggest that teachers' beliefs about identity can be contextual and spatial and some clearly highlight the disassociation between the individual's positive sense of professional identity and the negative perception of the profession externally, as seen in the above comment. The extracts also highlight the importance of language as a marker of identity (Ushioda 2009; Lightbown and Spada 2013) and reinforce the ambivalence between "achieved" or "inhabited" identity—the identity people themselves articulate or claim—and "ascribed" or "attributed" identity—the identity given to someone by someone else, in Miller's words (2009, p. 173).

Among the markers of identity, defined by Norton (2013) as subjective sub-identities, teachers mentioned cultural background, place of birth, nationality and change. *Change* and the process of transformation it conveys are intrinsic to the idea of identity as a dynamic, ever-evolving aspect of life: "Identity is not something fixed at some early point in life: it is in constant change" (P1). It also defines how teachers create their professional identity through a process of constant negotiation of their relationship to the outside world (Varghese 2018; Norton 1997). In addition, change is also inherent in the notion of diaspora, understood as hybrid, fluid and non-static communities, "[…] always creolizing the languages and values they encounter in diverse lands" (Canagarajah and Silberstein 2012, p. 82). As observed in the following comments, the diasporic identity of transnational language teachers appears to be shaped by their encounters as migrants with new cultural contexts as much as by the changes they adopt and embrace:

> Cultural background, personal cross-cultural life experiences, and sociocultural factors […] because I am an immigrant, I feel that part of my identity is quite shaped by them. (P2)
> How much I have changed as an individual having left one set of defined cultural and linguistic parameters in my country of origin and having embraced a new one in a new country […]. How does working and

functioning as a social being in a new country, adopting a new culture and language, transform an individual? (P5)

3.4.2 Language and Identity

In post-structuralist theory, identity is defined as "self-conscious and ongoing narratives that individuals perform, interpret and project in actions and language" (Block 2007, p. 27). Learning a language, a key aspect of identity formation in sociocultural theory (Kramsch 1998; Ricento 2005; Lantolf 2011), was considered by teachers to be a positive and logical consequence of a transnational life: "Living abroad has also offered me the great opportunity of learning other languages" (P4). Furthermore, in the case of competent multilanguage users, language, as carrier of cultural attitudes, behaviours and ideas, is an open door to building new identities and navigating across cultures; a process of personal growth:

> Being bilingual, since an early age the strong relationship between language and culture was to play a key role to turn me into a keen linguist. (P6)
> English has opened me the doors to a new world and culture, and allows me to communicate with many different people. (P4)
> Learning and using a new language means learning and adopting not only a new vocabulary but a new understanding of behaviours and attitudes, an entire new culture. (P5)

Simpson and Hepworth (2010) explain how language is intrinsic to the construction of identity and this also applies to migration contexts where the encounter with a new culture and a new language takes place. It can be added that identification with the new language is a key factor in negotiating relationships with other communities and establishing affiliation and proximity with the members of those communities (Werbińska 2017). Participants' narratives showed examples of teachers' agency in communicating across languages, in connecting with individuals and communities and their established cultural models. They also show a sense of personal satisfaction in achieving this goal, as suggested in the following comments:

I consider myself, rather, an Anglophile. I am deeply interested in the culture of the Anglophone world. This interest does not necessarily stem from experience, but from knowledge of history, literature and art. (P1)

While being in England I used to speak Spanish frequently as this is the language I teach and most of my colleagues are from Spanish-speaking countries. [...] Now that I am in Spain I consider that English is also part of my identity. Being able to understand and speak this language fluently makes me very pleased [...] I also enjoy the possibility of changing identity just by changing the language of communication or even the dialect used [...]. (P4)

These comments suggest that as teachers move between communities at home and abroad, they negotiate social and institutional relations with other groups. They also illustrate that switching personas reveals not a unitary, static identity but the dynamic sense of self, which, according to Belcher and Connor (2001), is a consequence of the experience of being multilingual and navigating across languages.

As explained by Ricento (2005), transnational language teachers operate in distinct but interrelated communities in which, "bilingualism [...] is the norm" (2005, p. 906). However, being *bilingual* can be an emotionally charged experience, not exempt from conflict and anxiety as language and discourse are always interwoven with power relationships and ideologies. This is highlighted in the following respondent's views:

It was not always easy having to bridge the gap between the Venetian culture embedded in the language spoken at home and the Italian language taught at school. This bilingual experience highlighted people's acceptance or rejection, even discrimination at times. (P6)

This example of *diglossia* not only refers to the physicality of the different linguistic contexts inhabited by the person, but also to the more complex, invisible, although perceptible, different linguistic and cultural selves which make individuals who they are.

3.4.3 Emotions and Identity

The positive emotions associated with the personal satisfaction of learning a new language are counterbalanced by the negative feelings experienced by some teachers when negotiating their sense of self in differing cultures. Teachers' stories often talk of feelings of *foreignness*, *otherness* and additionally of idealised nostalgic memories of the homeland. They show that on the surface they may consider themselves integrated into their adopted environment, but as transcultural individuals who move between cultures and nations they have a stake in maintaining strong memories of, and emotional connections with, their places of origin, as exemplified by the following comments:

> Basic aspects I was used to (the sunshine, the silence of the countryside, the beauty of the landscape, the delicious and fresh food, the happiness of the people…) are really appreciated after having missed them while being abroad in large busy and grey cities like London […]. As a consequence of living abroad for many years, I appreciate much more my place of origin and my life at home. (P4)
> Of course, the idea of homeland acquires a much profound (even idealised) meaning though, if one is forced to leave their country due to political and social unrest.[…]. (P5)

As identities are relational and constituted partly from the outside (Modood 2013), teachers' views of themselves are often influenced by outsiders' perceptions and social expectations, which can lead to emotions and feelings of inadequacy and eventually to negative feelings about belonging and identity, as illustrated by comments such as:

> In this city, I hardly ever felt like home. (P4)
> How fragile my own sense of identity has become […] Why am I perceived as a 'stranger' when I return to my hometown?. Yet why do I not, still after 25 years, feel as if I belonged to this country -where I have lived for so long- either?. Why am I still a 'foreigner' here? (P5)

The idea of *foreignness* understood as difference, often becomes a marker of identity for transnationals who do not recognise themselves in either the home society nor the adopted one. As migrants who have left behind their homeland encouraged by the perspective of a better future, work opportunities and social mobility, these teachers could be identified as members of diasporic communities with shared languages, cultural traits and professional identities who embody *difference*, not similarity. This can lead to homogeneous conceptions of national communities (Rothberg 2014) which become entangled with the idea of nation-state and national memory. However, memories are not fixed mechanisms but are affected by everyday interactions and exchanges across different social groups. As carriers of memories and stories, transnational language teachers move between the local (past, history, cultural experiences) and the global (the encounters, translations, adaptations and process of identity construction and redefinition) and this makes them question and challenge national stereotypes and ideologies. One of the teachers explained:

> People label me as Spanish because of where I was born and what my passport says, but my Spanish identity is my relationship with that part of myself: e.g. Am I typical Spanish person? How do I fit in Spanish society? Has this changed over time? It is interesting how people are taken aback by aspects of myself that are not "typically" Spanish for them […].Spanish culture is collectivistic and there are elements of this that I have always found difficult, even as a child […]. Maybe individuals who are perfectly happy and integrated within the societies where they were born do not experience a thirst for change and adventure, they do not feel dissatisfied to the point where they pack up their bags and leave. (P1)

Thus the negative connotations of *difference* and the feelings of inferiority and insecurity, not to mention prejudice, stereotyping and exclusion attached to it (Modood 2013) are contrasted with a positive view in which difference frees individuals from the constraints of *being a national*, and allows them to develop a critical approach to their own culture, as explained here:

> Curiously enough, within a foreign country you can be happily adjusted even if you never feel you are like the native population, because there is no external or internal pressure for you to be. Being perceived as a foreigner can be liberating. (P1)

It doesn't mean that I completely identify with my cultural background; on the contrary, there are some aspects with which I don't feel identified at all, including religion or giving too much details about people's private lives. (P4)

We live in a world fond of waving flags and boasting about their own countries. How does this make me feel about my national identity? I am a bit sceptical about this. I find it difficult to feel chauvinistic about the achievements of my country. Sometimes I come across students who seem to be very idealistic not only about Hispanic culture, but also about the personality of the population: e.g. "Spanish people are so nice"! (P1)

This critical approach is extended to the current unsettling sociopolitical discourse which affects migrant citizens in the UK, as experienced by many European language teachers. Some teachers actively challenge the discourses of nationalism ingrained in many sectors of society and defend their right to maintain their transnational and transcultural identities, as explained by two respondents:

Contrary to Theresa May's sadly narrow minded view that *citizen of the world* means citizen of nowhere, I believe we are all citizens of the world today, exactly because of its interconnectedness. (P5)

Connections are good both in the UK and in the motherland but the writer is reluctant to go through the naturalisation process, even after the governmental stance on immigration, subsequent to the Brexit 2016 referendum result. (P6)

3.4.4 Culture and Identity

Teachers' narratives show that their understanding of the world and themselves is not fixed by their birthplace, nationality or the culture they have been brought up in, but by the different cultures they have experienced, as the following comments suggest:

What has really influenced my appreciations of the world has been the great opportunity of living in different countries with people from many different cultural backgrounds. Only after getting to know better other cultures, I can really understand and appreciate my own background. (P4)

Nowadays, people are immersed in more than just one culture: we travel for work, for pleasure (although not always this interchange defines our identity), we migrate, we learn from different cultures in different ways (movies, friends, learning a language). (P2)

These statements highlight a sense of global citizenship which supports the notion of *transculturality* (Welsch 1995) and *multiculturalism*, understood not as a fixed process of assimilation but as a dynamic activity which is also the most successful form of integration (Modood 2013).

On the other hand, negotiating their identity and sense of belonging to *imagined communities* (Kanno and Norton 2003) and *figured worlds* (Varghese 2018) of professional networks marks the lives of many transnational language teachers in the UK, for whom the close relationship between territoriality, language and the associated cultural social settings raises the need for creating cultural and professional affiliations and attachments. Wenger's (2006) view of identity points to the sense of community membership, as well as to the multi-membership and the relation between the local and the global. As members of the educational establishment, a constructed community in itself with rules and modus operandi, language teachers' affiliation to cultural and professional associations plays a key role in developing a collective identity and maintaining a sense of attachment and belonging. It is also important for their professional development as much as for their emotional wellbeing, as one respondent explained:

Being a member of the Italian Cultural Institute means that I am informed and invited to events [...] relevant to the Italian culture happening in the UK, particularly in London. These events are mostly important and relevant to my role as a language teacher, help me to keep up-to-date with developments in my country. [...] They are also events that I truly enjoy and that give me pleasure. (P6)

Teachers are also aware of the benefits of collaboration with colleagues as a key aspect of their professional development, as explained by a participant:

I am influenced by my colleagues' views, as they are important in my life. Getting to know colleagues from many different cultures has made me realise of features of my own identity [...]. I still feel part of the UK language teaching culture and associations and I am very happy to be able to work and collaborate with colleagues who live thousands of miles away, thanks to the advances of technologies. (P4)

3.4.5 Teacher Agency

Teacher agency, as previously discussed and as stated by White (2018), refers to teachers' conscious choices within their professional contexts. This includes "relationships with learners and colleagues [...] participating in ongoing professional development opportunities [...] and adapting themselves to the diverse requirements of their working contexts" (White 2018, p. 196).

Participants' narratives show that agency, as influenced by situations outside the classroom, plays a role in the process of identity construction. The data suggests that membership of professional and cultural networks means opportunities for personal satisfaction and professional growth. It also means engagement and positioning in the debates affecting modern language subjects in the context of UK educational policies. Narratives offer an insight into the realities of the profession from the perspective of the practitioners themselves, such as the characterising uncertainty of "the unstable contracts as a language teacher and a lecturer in prestigious universities" (P4), or the multiplicity of occupations held in addition to teaching, including translator and interpreter, as stated in the following comment:

> As I work for different employers I also feel that different institutions' pedagogic policies, job contracts or expectations may affect the way one performs in the classroom having to vary one's identity. (P6)

Precariousness, insecurity and constant changes in the educational environment appear to affect many professionals' working conditions and trigger attitudes of action:

> There are many battles to be fought in teaching and HE in particular and I sometimes see myself as a rebel or an activist fighting against injustice and

bad senior management choices, as sadly the system has really let us down. (P5)

This aspect of identity, *activism*, vindicates the profession and the discipline against the perception of MFLs as "second-class teaching" (P4) and the many changes in educational policies that affect teachers' jobs and teacher training education (Kramsch 2014; De Costa and Norton 2017). In spite of these difficulties, teachers' narratives show, in Werbińska's words, "individual agentive powers […] when confronted with critical events and tensions or forced to make decisions" (2017, p. 45) related to their role as teachers, their teaching styles and the importance of pedagogical and subject knowledge, as explained in the next section.

3.4.6 Visions of Teaching

The multidimensionality of language teaching implies different personas within the teacher role, which teachers need to learn and absorb. Some teachers saw themselves as educators or facilitators, functions which go beyond the mere language and cultural instruction or knowledge transfer:

> I believe that the ethical aspect of my role as a teacher (and the one I value the most) is to absorb, digest and translate change into a language my students can understand, regardless of the subject I teach […]. This is what education should be about, not just getting good marks and passing a module. (P5)

Fulfilling this multiplicity of functions requires active agency in making adjustments to achieve the "transformable identity" (King 2015, p. 107) that helps teachers to become *performers* and to create emotional distance from their role, as suggested by one respondent:

> In the world of work […] we have a persona […]. I have always found it intriguing that so many teachers who appear to be very lively and extroverted in the classroom claim to be, really, shy and quiet people. Teachers have to be permanently on show, right in front of their pupils […]. It is interesting how so many of them claim to have this "double personality". (P1)

This transformable identity requires reflection about the language classroom as a community in which identities are forged and negotiated through interaction and language, as explained below:

[…] a place where students share a concern or a passion for something they do and learn how to do it better as they interact regularly, we can understand that every individual/student in the language classroom is shaping her/his own identity, and overall, negotiating it with the other participants in the community. (P2)

In this learning community, the interaction between teacher and learner is a key factor that requires teachers to have conceptual and pedagogical knowledge, as well as communicative knowledge of the language they teach (King 2015). However, as Varghese (2018) explains, pedagogical content knowledge is often an area of conflict for language teachers. While for some, subject knowledge is important to determine their professional identity, "Knowledge of my subject […] determines my professional identity, makes me proud of what I do and the way I do it" (P6); for others, competence in their subject is not enough:

I don't think 'knowledge of a specific subject' determines my professional identity. Being competent in my area and acting professionally in my sphere of work enriches my professional identity by making me feel adequately equipped to do my job well. But ultimately I don't recognise myself as a teacher of Italian only – I would find this extremely limiting. (P5)

Teachers found they have to adapt their practices and teaching styles to the needs and characteristics of their learners, and this includes awareness of different cultural backgrounds:

My teaching style had to change and adapt too. In Italy I would not need to teach language through 'examples' as I have to do here. There are also different levels of sensitivity between the two cultures (Italian and British) and how we talk in a class in the UK is very different (more cautious) from how we would talk in a class in Italy […]. (P5)

Teaching Italian to English speakers […] was quite different to teaching adults who had good command of English but were native-speakers of other languages [...]. It became apparent that it was necessary to adjust language teaching materials to the need to understand and reconcile the intercultural differences in attitudes and skills. (P6)

Narratives show that teachers' beliefs of what is and is not good teaching practice come from their experiences in the classroom, as well as from their reflective involvement with pedagogical curriculum design and planning.

4 Discussion and Personal Reflection

The aim of this chapter was to investigate the experiences and perceptions of identity in six transnational MFL teachers living and working in the UK, manifested in their personal narratives. The analysis of these narratives has revealed, among other aspects, that transnational language teachers embed the concept of dynamic, hybrid and non-static identities, which is also consistent with the notion of diaspora (Canagarajah and Silberstein 2012). Teachers approach the concepts of *difference* and *sameness* in different ways as they move across diverse contextual and spatial cultural and linguistic settings with ease. However, attachment to their subject and affiliation to communities related to their profession provide personal satisfaction and reassurance. These also bring them a connection and continuity with their past experiences and selves, relieving the feelings of anxiety brought about by the process of integration into host environments.

Reflecting upon and writing my interpretation of these six narratives has allowed me to be critically conscious about my own lived experiences as a transnational language teacher in the UK: a woman, a migrant, a teacher of Spanish, teacher of linguistics, researcher and teacher educator; but also a daughter, a mother, a spouse, a friend and a colleague.

Moen (2006) states that "a voice can never exist in isolation [...] Thus a voice is overpopulated with other voices, with the intentions, expectations, and attitudes of others" (2006, p. 58). In the act of finding my autobiographical voice, I find myself in the voices of these six women teachers, in the complexity of their feelings and beliefs about their place in the societies and communities they inhabit; reflecting about their attachments to teaching networks and learning communities; recognising their sense of belonging and displacement. I also find myself in their determination to succeed in their profession and their pride in being a language teacher in sometimes hostile environments; in their passion for learning and supporting their learners.

In my interpretation of these narratives I am aware of their situational subjectivity, subject to *here* and *now*, prone to change, as well as to the fact that my relationship with them may be equally affected and influenced by space and time as much as by the multiple voices and beliefs which inhabit deeply myself. The fact that these teachers are known to me might have also influenced my interpretation in that I know of their personal circumstances, their professional attitudes and roles, their feelings and emotions, which may take me beyond the narrative of their texts. But since "meaning and understanding are created when voices engage in dialogue with each other" (Moen 2006, p. 58), this reinforces the dialogic nature of the process of narrative and my own narrative as a transnational language teacher (whose professional identity is constructed by the interaction between lived individual experiences, the professional settings I have encountered and my personal history).

Reflecting on these accounts has made me understand the diasporic nature of the MFL teaching profession in the UK, represented by the sample in this study as much as by my own life history. Transnational language teachers are part of the migratory phenomenon that characterises the global economy. Immigration is perceived "as an act of adventure, a new beginning of one's life in a land of promise and prosperity" (Park 2017, p. 4). We are members of a community which is defined by strong interest in personal and professional growth as well as by economic factors. We move between communities, between opportunities for learning and learning is associated with improving job possibilities, but also with developing a sense of self that goes beyond affiliations to inherited cultures to embrace other cultures, a dimension which manifests itself in the classroom.

In our professional lives as transnational and transcultural language teachers who benefit from being part of academic and pedagogical discourses associated with the values of openness, tolerance and equality, we may consider ourselves to be privileged. However, we must not forget that inequity, prejudice and precariousness affect many of us, showing, therefore, that both privilege and otherness go hand-in-hand in our journeys as we negotiate their coexistence throughout our lives.

5 Conclusion

In this chapter I have attempted to unveil transnational language teachers' experiences and perceptions of identity in the context of their transcultural lives by engaging a small group of practitioners with the process of reflection through autobiographical narratives and by providing my own interpretation and meaning of their perceptions of identity in relation to the cross-cultural and social contexts which they inhabit. The analysis of the narratives has provided the following findings which respond to the initial questions I raised in this chapter:

1. Teachers' conceptualised identity appears as an aggregate of the private (the personal) and the public (the professional) spheres in which they exist. However, it is the multidimensional aspects of their identity as teachers that define them.
2. Language is a distinct a marker of identity and, as competent plurilanguage users, learning a new language is an achievement and a source of personal satisfaction. It is also an opening to developing new cultural identities, and confirms that teachers' sense of self is not fixed by a particular culture or language. In addition, it highlights their acceptance of *change* as intrinsic to the idea of identity, as a dynamic, ever-evolving aspect of life.
3. In contrast, narratives revealed feelings and experiences of *otherness*, *difference* and visions of the *homeland*, which affect teachers' integration into the host society as much as their sense of *belonging* to the home society to which they often return. This tension generates a constant process of rethinking their identity, as well as engendering a critical view of assumed notions of national identity and memory.
4. Teachers' beliefs about the multifaceted identity of the teaching profession evidences their role as agents in the process of adaptation, performing their role and developing awareness of their learners' needs. Teachers also highlight their active role in developing subject and

pedagogical knowledge through membership of professional communities and through collaboration with other teachers.

The findings of this study show that, in spite of the educational changes, uncertainties and difficult conditions of service that affect many professionals, transnational language teachers' sense of identity is strongly connected to their practice and the relationship with their learners and other practitioners. They also show their sense of agency in managing conflicting attitudes and values across diverse sociocultural and linguistic worlds. Narrative Inquiry has facilitated the process of reflection and enabled me as a researcher to develop a critical approach to experience the experiences of the participating teachers.

While this study presents many limitations due to the small number and range of languages and of participating teachers, it also reveals the value of this research and highlights the need for more research on transnational MFL teachers. Questions which need exploring include: what motivates them to become language teachers? What critical life experiences contribute to shape their professional identity? How do these experiences influence their attitudes and beliefs about themselves as members of social and cultural groups?

Similarly, more research is needed about transnational language teachers as agents of change in society and as transporters of ideas, histories and ideologies which are transferred, confronted and negotiated in the language classroom.

References

Akkerman, Sanne F., and Paulien C. Meijer. 2011. A Dialogical Approach to Conceptualizing Teacher Identity. *Teaching and Teacher Education* 27: 308–319.
Assmann, Aleida. 2014. Transnational Memories. *European Review* 22 (4): 546–556.
Bakhtin, Mikhail. 1986. Speech Genres and Other Late Essays. In *The Dialogic Imagination*, ed. and trans. Michael Holquist and Caryl Emerson, 259–422. Austin: University of Texas Press.

Barkhuizen, Gary (ed.). 2017. *Reflections on Language Teacher Identity Research*. New York: Routledge.

Barkhuizen, Gary, Phil Benson, and Alice Chik. 2014. *Narrative Inquiry in Language Teaching and Learning Research*. New York and London: Routledge.

Belcher, Diane, and Ulla Connor (eds.). 2001. *Reflections on Multilateral Lives*. Clevedon: Multilingual Matters.

Block, David. 2007. The Rise of Identity in SLA Research, Post Firth and Wagner (1997). *The Modern Language Journal* 91: 863–876. https://www.academia.edu/9242414/The_rise_of_identity_in_SLA_research_post_Firth_and_Wagner_2007_.

Braun, Virginia, and Victoria Clarke. 2013. *Successful Qualitative Research: A Practical Guide for Beginners*. London: Sage.

British Educational Research Association [BERA]. 2018. *Ethical Guidelines for Educational Research*, 4th ed. London. https://www.bera.ac.uk/researchers-resources/publications/ethicalguidelines-for-educational-research-2018. Accessed 20 March 2019.

Bukor, Emese. 2011. Exploring Teacher Identity: Teachers' Transformative Experiences of Re-constructing and Re-connecting Personal and Professional Selves. Working Papers in Language Pedagogy 7, 48–73. Accessed 15 April 2018.

Canagarajah, Suresh, and Sandra Silberstein. 2012. Diaspora Identities and Language. *Journal of Language, Identity & Education* 11 (2): 81–84. http://dx.doi.org/10.1080/15348458.2012.667296.

Canrinus, Esther T., Michelle Helms-Lorenz, Douwe Beijaard, Jaap Buitink, and Adriaan Hofman. 2011. Profiling Teachers' Sense of Professional Identity. *Educational Studies* 37-5: 593–608.

Cheung, Yin Ling, Selim Ben Said, and Kwanghyun Park (eds.). 2015. *Advances and Current Trends in Language Teacher Identity Research*. London: Routledge.

Clandinin, Jean. 2016. *Engaging in Narrative Inquiry*. Abingdon and New York: Routledge.

Clandinin, Jean, and F. Michael Connelly. 2000. *Narrative Inquiry: Experience and Story in Qualitative Research*. San Francisco: Jossey-Bass.

De Costa, Peter I., and Bonny Norton. 2017. Introduction: Identity, Transdisciplinarity and the Good Language Teacher. *The Modern Language Journal* 101: 3–14. https://doi.org/10.1111/modl.12368.

De Fina, Anna, and Alexandra Georgakopoulou (eds.). 2015. *The Handbook of Narrative Analysis*. Chichester and Malden: Wiley Blackwell.

Erll, Astrid. 2011. *Memory in Culture*. London: McMillan.

Gallardo, Matilde. 2006. Anglo-Spanish Grammar Books Published in England in the Nineteenth Century. *Bulletin of Spanish Studies. Hispanic Studies and Researches on Spain, Portugal and Latin America* 83 (1): 73–98.
Giddens, Anthony. 2004 [1991]. *Modernity and Self-Identity*. Oxford: Blackwell.
Guest, Greg, Kathleen M. MacQueen, and Emily E. Namey. 2012. *Applied Thematic Analysis*. Thousand Oaks, CA: Sage.
Kalaja, Paula, Ana Barcelos, Mari Aro, and Maria Ruohotie-Lyhty (eds.). 2016. *Beliefs, Agency and Identity in Foreign Language Learning and Teaching*. Basingstoke: Palgrave Macmillan.
Kanno, Yasuko, and Bonny Norton. 2003. Imagined Communities and Educational Possibilities: Introduction. *Journal of Language Identity & Education Identity* 4: 241–249. https://doi.org/10.1207/S15327701JLIE0204_1.
King, Jim. 2015. "It's Time, Put on the Smile, It's Time!": The Emotional Labour of Second Language Teaching Within a Japanese University. In *New Directions in Language Learning Psychology, Second Language Learning and Teaching*, ed. Christina Gkonou et al., 97–112. Springer. ProQuest Ebook Central. http://ebookcentral.proquest.com/lib/kcl/detail.action?docID=4179464. Accessed 15 January 2019.
Kramsch, Claire. 1998. *Language & Culture*. Oxford: Oxford University Press.
Kramsch, Claire. 2014. Teaching Foreign Languages in an Era of Globalization: An Introduction. *Modern Language Journal* 98: 296–311.
Lantolf, James P. 2011. Integrating Sociocultural Theory and Cognitive Linguistics in the SL Classroom. In *Handbook of Research in Second Language Teaching and Learning*, ed. Eli Hinkel, 303–319. New York: Routledge.
Lightbown, Patsy M., and Nina Spada. 2013. *How Languages Are Learned*. Oxford: Oxford University Press.
Long, Debra L., Clinton L. Johns, and Eunike Jonathan. 2012. A Memory Retrieval View of Discourse Representation: The Recollection and Familiarity of Text Ideas. *Language and Cognitive Processes* 27 (6): 821–843. http://dx.doi.org/10.1080/01690965.2011.587992.
Miller, Jennifer. 2009. Teacher Identity. In *The Cambridge Guide to Second Language Teacher Education*, ed. Anne Burns and Jack C. Richards, 172–182. Cambridge: Cambridge University Press.
Modood, Tariq. 2013. *Multiculturalism*. Cambridge: Polity Press.
Moen, Torill. 2006. Reflections on the Narrative Research Approach. *International Journal of Qualitative Methods* 5 (4): 56–69.
Norton, Bonny (ed.). 1997. Language, Identity and the Ownership of English. *TESOL Quarterly* 31 (3): 409–429.

Norton, Bonny. 2013. *Identity and Language Learning: Extending the Conversation*. Bristol: Multilingual Matters.
Nunan, David, and Julie Choi (eds.). 2010. *Language and Culture: Reflective Narratives and the Emergence of Identity*. New York and London: Routledge.
Park, Gloria. 2017. *Narratives of East Asian Women Teachers of English: Where Privilege Meets Marginalization*. Bristol: Multilingual Matters.
Pavlenko, Aneta, and James A. Lantolf. 2000. Second Language Learning as Participation in the Reconstruction of the Selves. In *Sociocultural Theory and Second Language Learning*, ed. James A. Lantolf, 155–177. Oxford and New York: Oxford University Press.
Ricento, Thomas. 2005. Considerations of Identity in L2 Learning. In *Handbook of Research in Second Language Teaching and Learning*, ed. Eli Hinkel, 895–910. New York: Routledge.
Ricoeur, Paul. 1981. *Hermeneutics and the Human Sciences*. Cambridge: Cambridge University Press.
Rothberg, Michael. 2014. Locating Transnational Memory. *European Review* 22: 652–656.
Simpson, James, and Michael Hepworth. 2010. *Identity Online: Multilingual English Language Learners' Textual Identities in and Out of Class*. Leeds: University of Leeds.
Taylor, Florentina. 2013. Relational Views of the Self in SLA. In *Multiple Perspectives on the Self in Second Language Acquisition*, ed. Sarah Mercer and Marion Williams, 92–103. Bristol: Multilingual Matters.
Tsui, Amy B.M. 2011. Teacher Education and Teacher Development. In *Handbook of Research in Second Language Teaching and Learning*, ed. Eli Hinkel, 21–40. New York: Routledge.
Ushioda, Ema. 2009. A Person-in-Context Relational View of Emergent Motivation, Self and Identity. In *Motivation, Language Identity and the L2 Self*, ed. Zoltán Dörnyei and Ema Ushioda, 215–228. Bristol: Multilingual Matters.
Van Leeuwen, Theo. 2009. Discourses of Identity. *Language Teaching* 42 (2): 212–221. https://doi.org/10.1017/S0261444808005508.
Varghese, Manka. 2018. Drawing on Cultural Models and Figured Worlds to Study Language Teacher Education and Teacher Identity. In *Language Teacher Psychology*, ed. Sarah Mercer and Achilleas Kostoulas, 71–85. Bristol: Multilingual Matters.
Varghese, Manka M., Suhanthie Motha, John Trent, Gloria Park, and Jenelle Reeves (eds.). 2016. Language Teacher Identity in (Multi)lingual Settings. *TESOL Quarterly* 50 (3): 545–571.

Welsch, Wolfgang. 1995. Transculturality—The Puzzling Form of Cultures Today. *California Sociologist* 17 (18): 19–39.
Wenger, Étienne. 2006 [1998]. *Communities of Practice: Learning, Meaning and Identity*. New York: Cambridge University Press.
Werbińska, Dorota. 2016. Language Teacher Professional Identity: Focus on Discontinuities from the Perspective of Teacher Affiliation, Attachment and Autonomy. In *New Directions in Language Learning Psychology, Second Language Learning and Teaching*, ed. Christina Gkonou et al., 135–157. Springer, ProQuest Ebook Central. http://ebookcentral.proquest.com/lib/kcl/detail.action?docID=4179464. Accessed 15 January 2019.
Werbińska, Dorota. 2017. *The Formation of Language Teacher Professional Identity: A Phenomenographic-Narrative Study*. Słupsk: Akademia Pomorska w Słupsk.
White, Cynthia. 2018. Language Teacher Agency. In *Language Teacher Psychology*, ed. Sarah Mercer and Achilleas Kostoulas, 196–210. Bristol: Multilingual Matters.

3

Language Teacher/Translator Gendered Identity Construction: From Dilemmatic to Agentive—Big Lives Through Small Stories

Tanya Linaker

1   Introduction

This chapter presents a case study of a bilingual Russian female teacher/translator in the UK. The aim of the chapter is twofold: to give voice to a female community of professional bilinguals in the UK of which I am part of and to gain a better understanding of the significance of gendered identity construction through small story analysis (Bamberg 2006). In doing so, I intend to make a contribution to the field of research on small stories (Bamberg 2006; Bamberg and Georgakopoulou 2008) as a site of gendered identity construction using a positioning analysis approach (Bamberg 1997). I use positioning analysis as a tool for interpreting and analysing the narrator's identity claims against interactive claims through interplay between three positioning levels—to the story characters, to the interlocutor and to the global discourse.

T. Linaker (✉)
King's College London, London, UK
e-mail: Tanya.linaker@kcl.ac.uk

My interest in this subject and more specifically in the identity of Russian female teachers/translators in the UK originates in my affiliation with this community and our common educational, cultural and ethnic background as well as our professional status and migration experiences. Therefore, my own experiences as a member of this group, as well as my perspective as an inside researcher will be included in the analysis of the narratives.

2 Theoretical Framework

The subject of Russian–English bilingual gendered professional identity construction in educational settings is still an under-researched area with only a few studies conducted in the USA and in Canada. They focus on themes which include women's immigration and professional development (Kouritzin 2000), gender ideology affecting language learning (Polanyi 1995), second language learning and identity interaction (Pavlenko and Norton 2018), agency in second language learning (Pavlenko and Piller 2001), gender, bilingualism and language maintenance (Pavlenko 2001) and bilingual autobiographic memory and discursive relativity (Pavlenko 2003). From these studies, I draw on the aspects of immigration, gender ideology and bilingual agency within the framework of female bilingual identity construction through the process of storytelling. I intend to further bridge the gap between research on gender and bilingualism by situating my study within a minority community of bilingual Russian teachers and translators in the UK.

This study is seated within a social constructionist framework and therefore views identity as a construct, existing as a series of actions, which changes according to particular social and communicative contexts (Gumperz 1982; Antaki and Widdicombe 1998; De Fina 2009; Blommaert 2005) emerging in social interaction, which is fluid and dynamic and implies the socially positioning of self and others (Bucholtz and Hall 2010). Individuals are agents shaping their reality in the frame of their social restrictions and communicative orientation (Archakis and Tsakona 2012). Therefore, culture, language and identity as experienced by individuals in their everyday lives (Nunan and Choi 2010) are part of the process of identity construction through social interaction. In connection with this, identity has also been studied from a dilemmatic perspective which reaches the following three main sociocultural aspects: staying the same in the face of change, being unique vis-à-vis being the same as others and being agentive yet subjected to the outside agents of the broader sociohistorical context (Bamberg 2011). Further studies on the dilemmatic nature of identity have considered areas of research which are relevant to my investigation, including: teachers' continuity/discontinuity, permanence/change dilemma (Werbińska 2016), positioning within and at the same time outside the community of practice (Eckert and McConnell-Ginet 1992; Archakis and Tzanne 2005) and acting agentively while conforming at the same time to the dominant gender ideologies (Baxter 2003).

With this chapter, I hope to make a contribution to the body of research on the dilemmatic nature of identity, which has determined my position in analysing the dilemmatic agency of a Russian female teacher/translator's identity construction. Therefore, this theoretical framework pays particular attention to gender, and more specifically gendered professional identity, as an aspect of identity in the context of professional immigrant Russian women in the UK.

Gender is considered in interaction with other dimensions of social identity, such as race, age, religion, nationality, class, culture and multilingualism. The relationship between these aspects of identity has been noted in immigrant narratives, where the boundaries between the personal and the professional are blurred due to sociocultural and historic circumstances: immigrant women's second language practices impeded by the gendered practices of their communities (Menard-Warwick 2009) and the empowerment of multilingualism (Mills 2004) in which code-switching is considered to be a site of identity construction through encoding different identities (Myers-Scotton 2005) and transgressing traditional constraints of gender discourse (Gardner-Chloros 2009).

The area of research on gendered professional identity in social contexts, a topic particularly relevant to my study, includes studies on the workplace as a site of social interaction and gender performance (Holmes 2005; Holmes and Schnurr 2006) as well as more recent scholarship focusing on gender identity performance and societal expectations (Litosseliti 2014), women in the workplace breaking through the *glass ceiling*

(Mullany 2010), gendered discourse (Coates 2015) and individual agency resisting stereotyped subject positioning (Baxter 2003). This body of research has revealed the fluidity and dynamics that characterise the interaction between gender and professional identities while also challenging ideological positions that prevent women from breaking through the glass ceiling in which the issues of flexibility, work–home balance and childcare are particularly salient. In this chapter I have referred to the *Soviet gender paradox*—equality of labour without domestic equality (Ashwin 2006) and have adopted a multilevel framework of gender ideology, which distinguishes between traditional, egalitarian and independent ideologies with the latter emerging as prevalent in contemporary Russia (Ashwin and Isupova 2018).

Relevant to this investigation is also the concept of *diaspora*, understood not as a static and stable aspect of identity connected to homeland, but as a shifting and changing concept in which individual identities are constructed and negotiated through multilingual strategies. This allows the members of given heritage groups to travel between languages and communities (Canagarajah and Silberstein 2012). This concept has been explored from cultural and political perspectives as a site of identity construction in relation to contemporary Russian speaking diasporic communities. For example, Isurin (2011) explores the Russian immigrants' perception as outsiders both in their home and host countries, while Byford (2012) identifies the Russian speaking diaspora abroad as a powerful instrument in international political relations across a global network of state-backed associations. My research echoes Nikolko and Carment's view (2017) of Russian speaking diaspora as a fragmented and unstable community with an element of alienation and detachment between its members. This deliberate disassociation from the traditional ideologies (i.e. gendered separate spheres in the employment and family domains) is explained later as an aspect of dilemmatic identity—acting as part of the community, yet performing uniqueness by challenging the community's traditional values (Bamberg 2011).

My study of female teacher/translator identity construction is contextualised by professional discourse, discourse of immigration, motherhood and childcare. It builds on existing research of teacher identity construction through small storytelling (Juzwik and Ives 2010; Soreide 2006; Watson

2007), teacher identity co-construction through discursive interactions (Johnson 2006) and discourse of immigration and professional success (Janssens et al. 2006). My analysis is mediated by the concepts of performing success using discursive strategies (Wagner and Wodak 2006); identity construction through bilingual strategies, including code-switching (Pavlenko 2001, 2003; Pavlenko and Piller 2001; Blackledge 2001; Blackledge and Pavlenko 2001; Gardner-Chloros 2009) and the idea of *double bind*: female professionals resisting patriarchal gender ideologies (Litosseliti 2014).

3 Methodology

I have approached this investigation on gendered professional identity construction among bilingual Russian female teachers/translators in the UK from the perspective of *narrative inquiry* and *narrative-in-interaction* (Bamberg and Georgakopoulou 2008; Barkhuizen et al. 2014). I use narrative inquiry and small story analysis (Georgakopoulou 2006; Bamberg 1997, 2006, 2011, 2014; Bamberg and Georgakopoulou 2008; De Fina and Georgakopoulou 2015), in combination with a case study approach to the narrative of a bilingual Russian female teacher/translator, as a strategy to extract the most trustworthy and essential data in order to answer the following research questions:

- What aspects of gendered professional identity emerge from the small stories and how does the identity shift from dilemmatic to agentive?
- What are the dominant discourses present in the narrative? Does the participant-narrator align to them or resist them through the narrative and what linguistic resources are used to make identity claims?

While acknowledging the broader body of research into narrative inquiry (e.g. Barkhuizen 2014; De Fina and Georgakopoulou 2015, among others), my focus is on gendered identity construction through reflective storytelling (Benson 2014). I choose small story analysis as a tool for highlighting dilemmatic identity construction (Bamberg 2011) through social interaction between the participant-narrator and the researcher (Georgakopoulou 2006). The analysis of a small story allows for better scrutiny of inconsistencies and ambiguities, which might appear in the participant's narrative. In other words, small story framework is most relevant for deconstructing identity as multiple and contradictory, as it gives us the opportunity to interrogate identity formation at the given time and space with the given interlocutor.

I have applied principles of self-reflexivity (Goldstein 2001) to the analysis of data and brought my own personal and professional experience to the investigation in order to reveal dominant discourses and ideologies that underlie the social issues that the participant-narrator and the researcher may raise (De Fina 2013). My self-reflexive stance and membership of the researched community give me a deeper understanding and empathy of its members' life trajectories, allowing for a greater agency in co-constructing their stories. As Riessman (2015) points out, this strategy lends research credibility and validity.

However, as a researcher, I am also conscious of the risks of imposing my own pre-conceived ideologies to the interpretation of the data. To avoid this, I have been careful to use self-reflection (De Fina and Georgakopoulou 2008) by creating what Baxter (2003) calls a polyphonic effect between the voices of the researcher and the researched. Through sharing similar biographical data with the participant-narrator, the researcher's agency comes to the fore of the analysis and becomes auto-biographical due to a high level of emotional and intellectual engagement in co-creating a story (Ellis and Bochner 2016; Wortham 2000).

I choose a positioning analysis framework, as applied by Davies and Harre (1990), because it gives an opportunity to analyse small stories as acts of gendered identity performance (Butler 1990) at a given time and space: the participant-narrator relates in a particular way to the story characters, the interlocutor and the global discourses at the moment of telling the story. The analysis has been carried out at three levels: at the first level I observe how the participant-narrator positions herself in relation to the characters within the story; at the second level I explore how the participant-narrator positions herself in relation to the interlocutor/researcher (myself) and at the third level I discover how the narrator positions herself in relation to dominant discourses or master narratives (Bamberg and Georgakopoulou 2008). I have involved discourse analysis to establish the ways identity is constructed discursively using linguistic strategies.

3.1 Data Collection

The qualitative data in this case study relates to an individual interview with Irina (not her real name) a professional Russian teacher/translator living in the UK. The interview was conducted in Russian at the request of the participant and recorded, transcribed and translated into English by the researcher. The interview lasted approximately two hours, with questions ranging from professional, family, immigration and institutional discourses. The focus was on small, fragmentary and scattered narrative (Archakis and Tsakona 2012), used both as a source of data and as an object of analysis (De Fina 2009). Irina's narrative is set within the professional discourse of teaching and translating with other discourses invoked: gender ideology, motherhood, immigration, work/life balance and professional success.

Irina's narrative was part of a previous larger-scale set of individual unstructured interviews I conducted with ten professional Russian teachers/translators in the UK for research purposes.

The ten participants geographically based in Sussex volunteered for the research. They share the following similar characteristics: they are self-employed Russian language teachers and/or translators based in Sussex; they are aged between 40 and 50 and immigrated to the UK ten or more years ago. They are *achieved bilinguals* (they have reached bilingual status as adults through education and socialisation) (Wei 2008). They are also educated to degree level and are married to British partners and have children. In addition, they are members of what Wenger (2010) defines as a community of practice, in this instance a community of Russian teachers and translators whose members are engaged in common activity through interactive shared practice of professional networking and support (Holmes and Meyerhoff 1999). This last characteristic is important for my analysis of the dilemmatic identity aspect—wanting to be part of the group and at the same time maintaining independence. Ethical consent was obtained from each participant and their names were changed for anonymity purposes.

3.2 Analysis and Interpretation of Data

This section presents the analysis of the data from an interview with Irina, the selected participant for this case study.

Irina arrived in the UK in 1997 from Russia. She has been married for 20 years to a British man and has two children of school age. She belongs to the community of self-employed Russian teachers and translators in Sussex who regularly collaborate professionally and socially via social media and in person. Irina is used as a "prototype" or example representative of the female Russian speaking teachers and translators' community in Sussex. My personal and professional background mirrors that of Irina with the only difference being the mode of employment—I have a full-time position at a university. However, I can relate to the part-time self-employed nature of Irina's job through my own professional story. We both have qualified teacher and translator status and identify ourselves as linguists, i.e. specialists in one or more foreign language. Therefore, the distinction between these two professional practices (teaching and translating) is not clearly defined within the context of the analysis due to the nature of Irina's work.

Irina's narrative is set within the discourse of her profession as a teacher and translator with other discourses also being invoked: gender, motherhood, immigration, work/life balance and professional success. She constructs her professional gendered identity chronologically through the narrative, outlining the most significant stages in her professional career through small stories.

3.2.1 Positioning Level 1: Positioning Against Story Actors

Irina begins the narrative by setting a scene of her initial steps towards building her career.

3 Language Teacher/Translator Gendered Identity Construction ...

When I arrived here, I did not know what to do, because English was my profession in Russia and when I arrived I did not immediately find my feet, but then I met an interpreter and she told me that here I can continue working as a translator or interpreter and a teacher of Russian, I just need to find a suitable position, get registered and so on. And so I became a translator and a freelance teacher of Russian.

The example shows that in relation to the character of the interpreter she met, Irina projects a dilemmatic agency (Bamberg 2011) positioning herself as initially lacking confidence and being confounded by a change of circumstances: the metaphor "did not find her feet" signals the difficulties she had to confront. The figure of an interpreter is brought in as an agentive involvement, marked via the coordinate "but then". The example demonstrates how the narrator's identity is constructed by the discourse of immigration (loss of professional confidence and security due to relocation to a foreign country) and by other actors (interpreter who agentively influenced Irina's professional choice).

As the narrative evolves, Irina positions herself more agentively: from becoming a registered translator to interpreter and teacher, then to business owner following the launch of her own website. In the example below "R" is researcher and "I" is Irina:

I: At first I did written translations, due to the fact that I sent my CVs to different agencies and for many years I had mainly written translations. And when I had another child and he grew up, I decided that I had the time now, even if not very much, to leave the house. First of all, it was important for my psyche—I had enough of sitting at home. It was very important. I still thought that with my qualifications I can only work as a translator or a teacher. On the one hand, it was too late to learn anything new, on the other hand, I did not know exactly what else I wanted to do. I did not feel like changing my life drastically. To learn another profession would have been expensive and would have required more time, but interpreting and tutoring jobs once or twice a month would have suited me. And so it happened that I decided to create my own website.

R: Yourself?

I: I only paid for setting up the website. I paid the web designer, created my own design, found the images, controlled the whole process, she only did three pages, then the site started growing, I started marketing it more, I started marketing my own site. I started working and now I have ten times more clients than I had before. It was important to create my own site and all the investments paid off, of course. Even at some point I had too much work. As one of my friends said, I should have started my agency at that point. I simply could not do it. It needed my attention. With an agency, it is a completely different story, one needs to work even more, more marketing and so on. Well, it was a good idea.

Irina projects herself as a logical person as reflected in the structure of the argumentative paragraph, which moves cohesively along a temporal sequence detailing the consequences of events, using subordinating conjunctions, connectors and contrasting phrases: "at first, due to the fact, and when, first of all, on the one hand, on the other hand, in principle, and so it happened". However, her claim about work being important for her psyche tells us about her dissatisfaction with the predominantly caregiving role and the need to add a professional role to the role of the mother, thus invoking a conflict between the discourses of motherhood and profession. The reiteration of "important" across two connecting clauses, with the addition of the intensifier "very" reinforces Irina's agentive positioning towards seeking employment in spite of motherhood constraints.

Irina's agentive stance is also revealed through elaboration on the success of her website: she constructs her identity as a cunning entrepreneur. She evaluates her success numerically: "I have ten times more clients now than I had before", "at some point I had too much work". She places emphasis on the fact that she created her website by herself by repeating this twice in one paragraph to highlight her positioning of independence and success.

The projection of success as a key topos of the narrative is contrasted with Irina's regret for not setting up her own translation and teaching agency, disclosing the lack of determination—"you would have needed to work more". Irina attributes greater agency to herself through the repetitive use of the first person pronoun. She minimises the agency of the web designer by numerically quantifying the latter's input in one sentence: "she only did three pages".

Up until this moment Irina's story has focused on positive aspects of her professional experience since she started her business. However, in the following critical incident, an interpreting assignment at the wedding of

3 Language Teacher/Translator Gendered Identity Construction …

a daughter of a wealthy Russian male client, she raises issues of discrimination in relation to her gendered professional identity.

> *R*: Were there any occasions when you had to suffer some humiliation?
> *I*: Yes there were. I come to my teaching and interpreting assignments now and sometimes I have to put the clients in their place. So, you don't know who your client is going to be and I had interpreted at weddings a few times. There was one wedding when I did not want to work as an interpreter any longer. Did not want to go out to do interpreting jobs. Because everything was paid by somebody's father—he was some oil magnate, as it turned out. So, his attitude was—"you are a woman, come only when you are called". That kind of attitude. No, it is rare now when you are not respected, when people are swine, so to speak. These are Russian clients, but a certain element, those who have a sea of money. And no culture.

In this account Irina constructs a strong and assertive gendered identity through the story of a discriminatory experience. This is achieved through the use of linguistic and discourse strategies, i.e. the use of idioms ("put someone in their place"). Her positioning against and her evaluation of the other character in the story, the father, is reinforced by the use of the passive, indefinite and non-personal expressions "some", "somebody's", as well as metaphors "the sea of money", epithets "people are swine" and comparisons which point out to the stereotypical character of a rich misogynistic man who pays the bills and is largely behind the scenes. The use of direct speech "come only when you are called" strengthens Irina's positioning as highly critical towards people with "that kind of attitude" and discriminatory gender ideology.

I co-construct Irina's story to highlight her positioning against the story characters and her dilemmatic agency—her professional fulfilment is restricted by both internal and external factors. Internally Irina is confounded by self-doubt expressed metaphorically "I did not find my feet", while externally Irina's professional identity is in conflict with her gendered identity as a mother and a caregiver. The repetition of "important", "I had enough of sitting at home" positions her agentively, at the same time, she is constrained by motherhood discourse—reference to the lack of time. Metaphorically Irina equates motherhood with home imprisonment "sitting at home", "leaving the house". However, her identity becomes stronger as she develops professionally—at the beginning of her career she needed external help and advice (the interpreter she met). Later in her narrative she minimises the role of a web designer numerically and emphasises her own agency through expression of ownership "my own", "controlled" and quantifiable success "ten times more", "too much". In another example we observe a similar development of her agentive stance in relation to her clients' unprofessional misogynistic behaviour: from "I did not want to work as an interpreter any longer" to "I have to put the clients in their place", "it is rare now when you are not respected". Irina's gendered identity is constructed agentively through the negative professional experience, resisting and challenging patriarchal discourse in the workplace.

3.2.2 Positioning Level 2: Positioning Against the Interlocutor

At level 2 positioning (self in relation to the audience) Irina perceives me as a colleague, collaborator and an empathetic figure, which is linguistically indexed through the use of first and second person plural forms when talking about her profession: "this is the type of job that we do". I express solidarity and understanding of the job that Irina does by rhetorically repeating the quantifying statement about the number of hours she had to work on one occasion, to which she reiterates "It was a very hard job", thus confirming the empathetic nature of the exchange.

Irina and I co-construct her identity as someone who gets stronger and wiser in the face of adversity. Our collaborative narrative leads to a new level of confidence in Irina's narration and a spontaneous switch to a different register. She illustrates the disdainful attitude of some of her clients towards her profession by revoking an anecdote from Russian history.

> *I*: Well, 300 years ago—it was documented in the archives—in all Russian military regiments there were horses, interpreters and other scum, who travelled with the Army.
> *R*: Scum?!

I: Well, it is understandable, we are helping, we offer services, but like any other profession—you hire a person, you need to respect her, I came with my particular skills, he would not have done without me. I reject some offers now. My profession taught me to hold my head high and I learned to respect myself more as a woman.
R: Yes, yes, yes.
I: And I feel that my character has become stronger.
R: Yes, this is good, this is good.
I: Good for my life and good for my children.

The switch to lower register (the word *scum*) is used to dramatise the narrative and to invoke further empathy from the interlocutor. This effect is achieved by contrasting the contemporary use of this word as emotively charged and vulgar and its historical meaning with non-offensive connotation. The dilemmatic agency of Irina's identity is displayed through the challenge of maintaining respect for her profession, which equated to "scum" 300 years ago. Her assertive stance with the emphatic use of metaphor "hold my head high" further reinforces her claim as a proud professional rejecting the portrayed negative professional discourse. Both Irina and I co-construct Irina's gendered identity as assertive, strong, self-respectful and good for her life and good for her children, by reiterating the adjectives "good", "strong" and echoing each other in affirmatives "yes, yes, yes". The extract also illuminates the relationship between professional and gendered aspects of Irina's identity—her professional experience has led to strengthening her agentive stance as a woman and a mother.

3.2.3 Positioning Level 3: Positioning Against Global Discourses

At level 3 positioning (in relation to dominant discourses) Irina's gendered identity is constructed by the discourse of motherhood and professional discourse.

R: We were talking about work, how do you manage to combine work, home, looking after children?
I: This is the beauty of my job: working for myself, I can control the volume of work and set my own deadlines. It is not that I have a luxury of choosing

> how much I work because I can afford it, it is because of the children. It is important for me to be there when they get home from school. There is nobody to help us here, so this job is convenient. Very convenient. Sometimes I think I am missing interaction with colleagues, but then I think what would I have done during the long summer holiday if I had a full-time job? We do not have any relatives here who could help.

She refers to the "beauty" of her job because of the flexibility. At the same time, she does not have the "luxury" of choice and misses the elements of a full-time job. She is also constrained by the lack of childcare help. Through this *double bind* professional gendered discourse, Irina positions herself in relation to the institutional childcare discourse implicitly stating that she cannot progress professionally due to the lack of childcare or its affordability (the mention of relatives). This demonstrates the dilemmatic nature of her identity of acting agentively as a professional (being in control of the volume of her work) yet being constrained by the discourse of motherhood.

Irina compares parenting ideology in Russia and in the UK and positions herself non-agentively towards what she considers to be *good parenting* discourse in the UK:

> Many mothers work "part time" here. So they can collect children from school. This is the way it is done here. Not like in Russia. In Russia children come home at 7 pm from afterschool clubs. I cannot judge whether it is good or bad. If I told them that in Russia it is customary for both parents to work full time, they would say it is "bad parenting", it would not suit them. By the same token, they don't like it that people wear fur in Russia – they think it is very bad. Different attitudes, different circumstances, all different.

Irina feels bound by a *bad parenting* discourse, the discourse of blame. She code switches to English for the lack of an exact equivalent in Russian. This use of bilingual strategy highlights what both interlocutors perceive to be the cultural difference between the two countries, which linguistically cannot be directly transferred. To emphasise this difference Irina draws the parallel with the attitude to wearing fur and reiterates the word "different" as the key in her positioning of conforming to the discourse

3 Language Teacher/Translator Gendered Identity Construction ... 59

of *good parenting*. On the one hand, Irina's dilemmatic agency of being different yet wanting to belong to the group is invoked through the use of third-person plural pronoun "they", "them", positioning her outside the group. On the other hand, she accepts "their" (the British culture) values of good and bad parenting as part of her cultural assimilation process: "this is the way it is done", "I cannot judge".

Irina's justification of her non-agentive positioning towards motherhood/parenting discourse is further illustrated by her relationship with her husband:

> My husband would like me to work and earn good money. But we cannot both work full time and look after children. This is not fair. Yesterday I had to work late, for example, so he had to come home, pick up the children, take them swimming, cook them dinner, all the rest of it. I can ask him to do this once a month, maximum once a fortnight, but not every day. This has never even been discussed. This is not expected of him.

Irina maintains her conformity to traditional Russian gender ideology where it is the norm for women to work a "double shift"—at home and in the office (Ashwin 2006): she does not think it is "fair" for her husband to do a *double shift*. Her stance towards gender ideology is dilemmatic—it is changing towards egalitarian (as explicitly stated in her attitude towards misogyny and discrimination in a professional situation), yet it stays the same within the family discourse: the changes "have never been discussed" and sharing childcare is "not expected of him" (her husband). The use of impersonal passive constructions emphasises Irina's lack of agency.

Another example of dilemmatic identity at work is Irina's positioning of being part of the Russian community by adhering to its traditional values and culture and at the same time disassociating herself from it. Irina constructs her identity as a professional teacher and translator in contrast to laypeople, thus identifying her positioning with that of the dominant professional discourse in the UK: her advanced qualifications and experience versus the lack of professionalism and skills of her competitors. Her dismissive attitude to the new competitors in the market is conveyed through the repetition of "those".

> Those people who now come to Britain: students, wives, Russian wives and so on… competition from those people, they are not very demanding of themselves – they have very low rates.

Her dilemmatic agency of being the same as others and being different is invoked through the dismissive use of "Russian wives". On the one hand, she contests and rejects essentialist gender ideology still prevalent in Russia through her explicit identity claims in the *wedding story* narrative (see positioning level 1). On the other hand, she maintains it by categorising this group of women "Russian wives" within a traditional gender framework—subservient to the husband, with no professional qualifications, but having to work as a result of a change of circumstances (Ashwin and Isupova 2018).

The complexity of Irina's stance on gender ideology and professional discourse is illustrated by the story of her teaching assignment with a female Russian client.

> It was a very hard job. I immediately understood all about her, she then apologised. Because she understood that I am a professional person.

At first, the client was dismissive of Irina's efforts and then, having seen her professional performance, apologised for her rudeness and engaged Irina in subsequent collaboration. On the one hand, Irina maintains her affiliation with the dominant discourse of the stereotypical perception of a particular Russian social class as people with lots of money and no culture. On the other hand, we can see the dilemmatic agency of constancy and change at work as illuminated by this small story. The keyword in her narrative is *understanding*, which is developed mutually between herself and the client through the course of the assignment: "I immediately understood all about her", "she understood that I am a professional". At the same time, this *understanding* is translated globally into Irina's understanding of people in general, developed through her professional career and her increased sense of tolerance. Linguistically her positioning is intensified through the use of metaphors:

You have to have an opportunity and a skill to understand them and understand why they behave the way they do, to be able to separate the wheat from the chaff. Well, she herself is not a very straightforward person. That is probably why she has so much in life, because she has such a tough character.

She departs from the idea of *rich equals rude* and evaluates her client as being complex, justifying her wealth by the toughness of her character. Irina positions herself in relation to the global social discourse as somebody who has become more understanding throughout the course of her career. By implication, this story also illuminates Irina's dilemmatic stance on gender ideology from traditionalist "Russian wives" to egalitarian—"the woman is tough, and I understand and respect her".

At level 3 positioning, Irina interactively co-constructs her professional gendered identity as dilemmatic and agentive at the same time. Her agentive stance towards professional discourse is being undermined by the discourse of *good and bad parenting*, the constraints of institutional childcare and traditional gender ideologies. Her lack of agency is evidenced linguistically: the use of third-person pronouns, reiteration of the word "different", use of impersonal constructions in relation to her husband sharing childcare duties. At the same time, she agentively positions herself against those who are unprofessional, thus highlighting her professional persona and her desire to differentiate from the certain elements of the Russian community. It is through professional discourse that Irina's stance towards traditional gender ideology is challenged by a successful female learner/client, which brings about a change in Irina's positioning—from antagonistic to understanding and respectful. The repetition of *understanding* in relation to the discourse of professional success strengthens Irina's progressive stance towards an egalitarian gender ideology.

4 Discussion

The analysis demonstrates the transformative force of the narrative in constructing gendered professional identity by bringing to the fore the dilemmatic agency of the narrator who conforms and at the same time resists the dominant professional and essentialist gender ideology through the course of small storytelling.

Positioning herself in relation to story actors, Irina uses agentive stance towards her career progression and professional success in the face of adversity arising from discriminatory experiences and the constraints of motherhood. The dilemmatic aspect of her identity as being agentive and constructed by others at the same time is invoked linguistically through vocabulary choice, the use of contrasting metaphors in reference to her career as a journey, motherhood as imprisonment and her misogynistic clients as "swine". As a researcher, I help co-construct Irina's identity through sharing my personal professional stories and triggering agency work through interactive remembering.

In relation to the interlocutor, Irina maintains strong in-group (Eckert and McConnell-Ginet 1992) identity of a cultured, knowledgeable, educated professional seeking and receiving empathy for her actions from the researcher, who is the member of the same community of practice. This stance is in opposition to the out-group of people who may not uphold the same values (the uncultured, rude, poorly educated class, as stated in Irina's narrative) but who belong to the same diaspora of Russian speakers living in the UK. Irina positions herself as culturally Russian, but disassociates herself from misogynistic elements of the Russian community. This positioning reflects the fragmented nature of the Russian speaking diaspora (Nikolko and Carment 2017). Irina's simultaneous membership in both local Russian and English-speaking communities further complicates her positioning towards discourse of motherhood, adopting the distinction between *good* and *bad* parenting. Irina's desire to maintain in-group identity, i.e. belonging to both sets of communities (Russian and British) puts her in a double bind. She is bound by the need to conform to *good parenting* discourse of prioritising family over career choices and by the traditional Russian *double shift* discourse, which suggests that a woman should have both professional and child caring responsibilities in equal measure (Ashwin 2006). Irina's dilemmatic identity of being part of the group and yet being unique is constructed linguistically by code-switching—the concept of *bad parenting* denotes the whole cultural layer shared by Irina and myself through our membership in the English-speaking community, however, this concept is non-existent in Russian language and culture.

Being bilingual, the narrator and the researcher do not just use Russian as a medium for communication, but use code-switching and emotively charged metaphors and epithets, attributed to Russian speech in particular, which makes the interaction unique. My sensitivity to bilingual resources helps reveal inconsistencies between explicit identity claims and identity constructed through small stories.

The narrative demonstrates the shift from dilemmatic to more agentive positioning, invoking the dilemmatic aspect of constancy and change in the move towards alignment with discourse of respectability and tolerance in Irina's professional world and egalitarian gender discourse. Irina's small stories illuminate the force of interactive narrative in identity construction in relation to the global gender and professional discourses.

5 Conclusion

This study represents a contribution to the under-researched area of small story analysis through the three-level positioning model (Bamberg 2006; Bamberg and Georgakopoulou 2008). It also gives an insight into aspects of gendered professional identity formation of the community of practice of Russian female teachers and translators in the UK, based on the narrated interaction between an individual and the researcher. Both, the participant and myself, the researcher, share membership of that community, their linguistic code values, memory and history. The study invokes the participant's dilemmatic agency (Bamberg 2011) of constancy and change, being the same as others and being different, as well as resisting and at the same time conforming to gender and professional ideologies through implicit and explicit identity claims, which are conveyed through discourse. The narrative, therefore, serves as an emancipatory tool, which has a transformative value for the individual.

As a reflective practitioner, who enquires about the professional gender identity of fellow Russian female teachers and translators, I compare the participant's story and experiences with mine, thus gaining access to deeper meaning and interpretation of all three levels of positioning in the stories, which unfold during interaction.

With this study, I also hope to add to the body of research on language teacher identity by giving voice to the underrepresented minority of Russian female teachers and translators in the UK and revealing their agentive and non-agentive positioning not only within their professional discourse but also within the discourses of motherhood, immigration, and gender ideology.

The limitation of the current small-scale study has the potential for increasing the sample of participants to carry out more interviews to elicit small stories, conduct ethnographic and autoethnographic observations in order to achieve a more in-depth and better understanding of professional gender identity construction through discursive practices.

References

Antaki, Charles, and Sue Widdicombe. 1998. *Identities and Talk*. London: Sage.

Archakis, Argiris, and Angelki Tzanne. 2005. Narrative Positioning and the Construction of Situated Identities. *Narrative Inquiry* 15: 267–291.

Archakis, Argiris, and Villy Tsakona. 2012. *The Narrative Construction of Identities in Critical Education*. London: Palgrave.

Ashwin, Sarah. 2006. Dealing with Devastation in Russia: Men and Women Compared. In *Adapting to Russia's New Labour Market: Gender and Employment Behaviour*, ed. Sarah Ashwin, 1–30. London: Routledge.

Ashwin, Sarah, and Olga Isupova. 2018. Anatomy of a Stalled Revolution. Processes of Reproduction and Change in Russian Women's Gender Ideologies. *Gender and Society* 32 (4): 441–468.

Bamberg, Michael. 1997. Positioning Between Structure and Performance. *Journal of Narrative and Life History* 7: 335–342.

Bamberg, Michael. 2006. Stories: Big or Small: Why Do We Care? *Narrative Inquiry* 16: 139–147.

Bamberg, Michael. 2011. Who Am I? Narration and Its Contribution to Self and Identity. *Theory and Psychology* 21: 3–24.

Bamberg, Michael. 2014. Identity and Narration. In *Handbook of Narratology*, ed. Hühn, Meister, Pier, and Schmid, 241–253. Berlin and Boston: Walter de Gruyter.

Bamberg, Michael, and Alexandra Georgakopoulou. 2008. Small Stories as a New Perspective in Narrative and Identity Analysis. *Text and Talk* 23: 377–396.

Barkhuizen, Gary. 2014. Narrative Research in Language Teaching and Learning. *Language Teaching* 47 (4): 450–466.
Barkhuizen, Gary, Phill Benson, and Alice Chik. 2014. *Narrative Inquiry in Language Teaching and Learning Research*. London: Routledge.
Baxter, Judith. 2003. *Positioning Gender in Discourse*. Basingstoke: Palgrave Macmillan.
Benson, Phil. 2014. Narrative Inquiry in Applied Linguistics Research. *Annual Review of Applied Linguistics* 34: 154–170.
Blackledge, Adrian. 2001. Complex Positioning: Women Negotiating Identity and Power in a Minority Urban Setting. In *Multilingualism, Second Language Learning and Gender*, ed. Aneta Pavlenko, Adrian Blackledge, Ingrid Piller, and Marya Teutsch-Dwyer, 35–77. Berlin: Mouton de Gruyter.
Blackledge, Adrian, and Aneta Pavlenko. 2001. Negotiation of Identities in Multilingual Contexts. *International Journal of Bilingualism* 5: 243–257.
Blommaert, Jan. 2005. *Discourse: A Critical Introduction*. Cambridge: Cambridge University Press.
Bucholtz, Mary, and Kira Hall. 2010. Locating Identity in Language. In *Language and Identity*, ed. Carmen Llamas and Dominic Watt, 18–29. Edinburgh: Edinburgh University Press.
Butler, Judith. 1990. *Gender Trouble, Feminism and the Subversion of Identity*. New York and London: Routledge.
Byford, Andy. 2012. The Russian Diaspora in International Relations: "Compatriots" in Britain. *Europe-Asia Studies* 64 (4): 715–735. https://doi.org/10.1080/09668136.2012.660764.
Canagarajah, Suresh, and Sandra Silberstein. 2012. Diaspora Identities and Language. *Journal of Language, Identity and Education* 11 (2): 81–84. https://doi.org/10.1080/15348458.2012.667296.
Coates, Jennifer. 2015. *Women, Men and Language: A Sociolinguistic Account of Gender Differences in Language*. New York and London: Routledge.
Davies, Bronwyn, and Rom Harre. 1990. Positioning: The Discursive Production of Selves. *Journal for the Theory of Social Behaviour* 20: 43–63.
De Fina, Anna. 2009. Narratives in Interview—The Case of Accounts: For an Interactional Approach to Narrative Genre. *Narrative Inquiry* 19 (2): 233–258.
De Fina, Anna. 2013. Positioning Level 3: Connecting Local Identity Displays to Macro Social Processes. *Narrative Inquiry* 23: 40–61.
De Fina, Anna, and Alexandra Georgakopoulou. 2008. Analysing Narratives as Practices. *Qualitative Research* 8: 379–387.

De Fina, Anna, and Alexandra Georgakopoulou. 2015. *The Handbook of Narrative Analysis.* New York: Wiley.

Eckert, Penelope, and Sally McConnell-Ginet. 1992. Think Practically and Look Locally: Language and Gender as Community-Based Practice. *Annual Review of Anthropology* 21: 461–490.

Ellis, Carolyn, and Arthur Bochner. 2016. *Evocative Autoethnography: Writing Lives and Telling Stories.* New York: Routledge.

Gardner-Chloros, Penelope. 2009. *Code Switching.* Cambridge: Cambridge University Press.

Georgakopoulou, Alexandra. 2006. Thinking Big with Small Stories in Narrative and Identity Analysis. *Narrative Inquiry* 16: 122–130.

Goldstein, Tara. 2001. Researching Women's Language Practices in Multilingual Work Places. In *Multilingualism, Second Language Learning, and Gender,* ed. Aneta Pavlenko Adrian Blackledge, Ingrid Piller, and Marya Teutsch-Dwyer, 77–103. Berlin: Mouton de Gruyter.

Gumperz, John. 1982. *Language and Social Identity.* Cambridge, MA: Cambridge University Press.

Holmes, Janet. 2005. Story-Telling at Work: A Complex Discursive Resource for Integrating Personal, Professional and Social Identities. *Discourse Studies* 7 (6): 671–700. https://doi.org/10.1177/1461445605055422.

Holmes, Janet, and Miriam Meyerhoff. 1999. The Community of Practice: Theories and Methodologies in Language and Gender Research. *Language in Society* 28: 173–183.

Holmes, Janet, and Stephanie Schnurr. 2006. "Doing Femininity" at Work: More Than Just Relational Practice. *Journal of Sociolinguistics* 10 (1): 31–51. https://doi.org/10.1111/j.1360-6441.2006.00316.

Isurin, Ludmila. 2011. *Russian Diaspora: Culture, Identity, and Language Change.* Contributions to the Sociology of Language. New York: Walter de Gruyter.

Janssens, Maddy, Tineke Cappellen, and Patrizia Zanoni. 2006. Successful Female Expatriates as Agents: Positioning Oneself Through Gender, Hierarchy and Culture. *Journal of World Business* 4: 133–148.

Johnson, Greer. 2006. The Discursive Construction of Teacher Identities in a Research Interview. *Studies in Interactional Sociolinguistics,* ed. Liliana Cabral Bastos, Maria do Carmo Leite de Oliveira 23: 212–321.

Juzwik, Mary, and Denise Ives. 2010. Small Stories as Resources for Performing Teacher Identity: Identity in Interaction in an Urban Language Arts Classroom. *Narrative Inquiry* 20: 37–61.

Kouritzin, Sandra. 2000. Immigrant Mothers Redefine Access to ESL Classes: Contradiction and Ambivalence. *Journal of Multilingual and Multicultural Development* 21 (1): 14–32. https://doi.org/10.1080/01434630008666391.

Litosseliti, Lia. 2014. *Gender and Language Theory and Practice*. London: Routledge.

Menard-Warwick, Julia. 2009. *Gendered Identities and Immigrant Language Learning*. Bristol: Multilingual Matters.

Mills, Jean. 2004. Mothers and Mother Tongue: Perspectives on Self-Construction by Mothers of Pakistani Heritage. In *Negotiation of Identities in Multilingual Contexts*, ed. Aneta Pavlenko and Adrian Blackledge, 161–192. Bristol: Multilingual Matters.

Mullany, Louise. 2010. Gendered Identities in the Professional Workplace: Negotiating the Glass Ceiling. In *Language and Identity*, ed. Carmen Llamas and Dominic Watt, 179–193. Edinburgh: Edinburgh University Press.

Myers-Scotton, Carol. 2005. *Multiple Voices: An Introduction to Bilingualism*. Michigan: Wiley.

Nikolko, Milana, and David Carment. 2017. *Post-Soviet Migration and Diasporas*. Migration, Diasporas and Citizenship. Cham, Switzerland: Springer.

Nunan, David, and Julie Choi. 2010. *Language and Culture: Reflective Narratives and the Emergence of Identity*. New York: Routledge.

Pavlenko, Aneta. 2001. Bilingualism, Gender, and Ideology. *International Journal of Bilingualism* 5: 117–151.

Pavlenko, Aneta. 2003. Eyewitness Memory in Late Bilinguals: Evidence for Discursive Relativity. *International Journal of Bilingualism* 7: 257–281.

Pavlenko, Aneta, and Bonny Norton. 2018. Imagined Communities, Identity, and English Language Learning. In *International Handbook of English Language Teaching*, ed. Jim Cummins and Chris Davidson, 669–680. Cham, Switzerland: Springer.

Pavlenko, Aneta, and Ingrid Piller. 2001. New Directions in the Study of Multilingualism, Second Language Learning and Gender. In *Multilingualism, Second Language Learning and Gender*, ed. Aneta Pavlenko, Adrian Blackledge, Ingrid Piller, and Marya Teutsch-Dwyer, 17–53. Berlin: Mouton de Gruyter.

Polanyi, Livia. 1995. Language Learning and Living Abroad: Stories from the Field. In *Second Language Acquisition in a Study Abroad Context*, ed. Barbara Freed, 271–291. Amsterdam: John Benjamins.

Riessman, Catherine. 2015. Entering the Hall of Mirrors: Reflexivity and Narrative Research. In *The Handbook of Narrative Analysis*, ed. Anna De Fina and Alexandra Georgakopoulou, 219–239. New York: Wiley.

Soreide, Gina. 2006. Narrative Construction of Teacher Identity: Positioning and Negotiation. *Teachers and Teaching: Theory and Practice* 12 (5): 527–547.

Wagner, Ina, and Ruth Wodak. 2006. Performing Success: Identifying Strategies of Self-Representation in Women's Biographical Narratives. *Discourse and Society* 17: 385–411.

Watson, Cate. 2007. Small Stories, Positioning Analysis, and the Doing of Professional Identities in Learning to Teach. *Narrative Inquiry* 17 (2): 371–389.

Wei, Li. 2008. Dimensions of Bilingualism. In *The Bilingualism Reader*, ed. Li Wei, 3–23. London and New York: Routledge.

Wenger, Etienne. 2010. Communities of Practice and Social Learning Systems: The Career of a Concept. In *Social Learning Systems and Communities of Practice*, ed. Chris Blackmore, 179–198. London: Springer.

Werbińska, Dorota. 2016. Language-Teacher Professional Identity: Focus on Discontinuities from the Perspective of Teacher Affiliation, Attachment and Autonomy. In *New Directions in Language Learning Psychology, SLL ad Teaching*, ed. Christina Gkonou, Dietmar Tatzl, and Sarah Mercer, 135–157. Cham, Switzerland: Springer.

Wortham, Stanton. 2000. Interactional Positioning and Narrative Self-Construction. *Narrative Inquiry* 10: 157–184.

4

"When I Am Teaching German, I Put on a Persona": Exploring Lived Experiences of Teaching a Foreign Language

Maria Luisa Pérez Cavana

1 Introduction

The following description by Brown (2007) shows the complexity and the multi-layered nature of language learning:

> Learning a second language is a long and complex undertaking. Your whole person is affected as you struggle to reach beyond the first language into a new language, a new culture, a new way of thinking, feeling and acting. Total commitment, total involvement, a total physical, intellectual, and emotional response are necessary to successfully send and receive messages in a second language. (Brown 2007, p. 1)

We could paraphrase Brown's quote for languages teaching arguing that teaching a foreign language is a complex undertaking where the *whole person*'s involvement is required: body, emotions and cognition. As a matter of

---

M. L. P. Cavana (✉)
Faculty of Wellbeing, Education and Language Studies, The Open University, Milton Keynes, UK
e-mail: Maria-Luisa.Perez-Cavana@open.ac.uk

© The Author(s) 2019
M. Gallardo (ed.), *Negotiating Identity in Modern Foreign Language Teaching*, https://doi.org/10.1007/978-3-030-27709-3_4

fact, this *whole person* involvement makes languages stand out from other teaching subjects, such as Geography or Maths where physical, emotional or cultural aspects might play a minor role, if any at all. In a similar way as learning a language, teaching a language presents specific challenges to teachers, in particular the physical involvement as required in the pronunciation and fluency; the emotional involvement, such as teachers' feelings in relation to the language or culture they teach; or responding to the students expectations regarding their language competence. In summary to be a language teacher is grounded in being able to "personify", enact and embody a language that often is not the mother tongue.

In this chapter, I will focus on describing how this language teachers' enacting unfolds as an embodied mode of experience.

This chapter uses phenomenology as a starting point of the study on the lived experiences of language teachers and as an analysis tool to investigate the structure of their experience.

Language teachers have been the object of numerous studies and research debates over the last decades and this has produced a significant amount of knowledge and ongoing debates. On the one hand, sociocultural and poststructuralist studies have established the complexity and multiplicity of language teachers' identities. On the other hand, the debate around the Native Speaker (NS) versus Non-Native Speaker (NNS) is still open and a dominant reference in Second Language Acquisition (SLA) research. Most studies however have focused on language teachers as objects of investigation and not on their experiences as subjects.

There is also an emerging trend around the phenomenon of languages learning from a humanistic perspective (Ros i Solé 2016) that considers the *whole person* approach as a way to convey the complexity and multi-layered experience of languages learning. Within this context, phenomenology, and in particular the exploration into the lived experience of language (*Spracherleben*), has been considered both as a relevant and as an under-researched approach (Busch 2015). This research gap is particularly noteworthy in relation to language teachers.

Within this context the questions I wanted to explore were: What is it like to teach a language that is not your mother tongue? How is the sense of self when teaching a foreign language? How is their embodied self? How the language teacher-self does relate with their "normal" self?

This chapter aims to make a contribution into this under-researched field investigating the lived experiences of two languages teachers using phenomenology as starting point. The data are qualitative and rich gathered from in-depth interviews. The analysis uses phenomenological tools and reflections to uncover the structure of human existence.

1.1 Positioning the Study in the Literature

From the point of view of SLA research, sociolinguistics and the wide field of foreign language teaching, the topic of language teachers' identity has emerged over three decades and has been object of a significant number of studies.

Of particular relevance for language teachers is the discussion about the Native Speaker versus Non-Native Speakers (NS-NNS). This debate was initiated by Medgyes (1994) (who coined the terms), and Braine (1999). These terms express the view that the native speaker is the norm towards which language learners should strive to emulate (Ricento 2005). Davies (2004) explains in relation to this view that there are two main approaches: the linguistic view, which sees the native speaker as the "repository and guardian of the true language", and the social view, which sees the native speaker as "the standard setter" (Davies 2004, p. 448).

Although the dichotomy NS-NNS has been heavily criticized as a myth (Paikeday 1985) and as an Anglo-centric construct (Moussu and Llurda 2008), it continues to be part of the norms, perceptions and expectations around language teachers and is still widely used (Arva and Medgyes 2000; Pachler et al. 2007; McNamara 1991; Shin 2008). It also plays a significant role regarding perceptions of professional competence of language teachers, as Murdoch puts it: "language proficiency will always represent the bedrock of their professional confidence" (Murdoch 1994, p. 254). The students' preferences for native language speakers has been demonstrated in some studies (Lasagabaster and Sierra 2005) as well as the self-doubt of non-native language teachers (Arva and Medgyes 2000; Hayes 2009). However, the claim that NS teachers are better teachers than NNSs, and that NNSs are deficient in terms of linguistic and cultural authority has been questioned in different studies (Matsumoto 2018; Atamturk et al. 2018). In his comprehensive review of the NS-NNS debate, Alan Davies concludes that the term NS "remains ambiguous" as it is both "myth and reality" (Davies 2004, p. 431).

The debate around NS-NNS is closely related with the broader research area of language teacher identity. As this paper focuses on lived experiences of language teachers, and on their self or selves as part of their lifeworld, it can be situated within this current broad field of research.

What follows is a short overview of current debates around the identity of teachers, in particular of language teachers.

There has been an increasing interest in researching the topic of teacher identity over the last two decades, as well as a growing emphasis on the role of emotions, passion, commitment and courage in teaching (Akkerman and Meijer 2011; Beauchamp and Thomas 2009). Many researchers have attempted to define teacher identity, and although there is not a widely accepted definition, there are some common characteristics that many scholars seem to consider fundamental to teacher identity from a post structuralist point of view (Beauchamp and Thomas 2009). These are: multiplicity of identities, the discontinuity of identities and the social nature of identity. One main focus of research within this field has been the identity of newly qualified language teachers (Ruohotie-Lyhty 2013; Trent and DeCoursey 2011; Kanno and Stuart 2011; Hallman 2015). Another main line of research has been the colonial legacy of NNS teachers (Case 2004; Cho 2014; Trent and DeCoursey 2011; Reis 2015; Canagarajah 2012). From the point of view of the theoretical approaches around language teacher identity, although there is not a single coherent theoretical approach, the poststructuralist perspective in different variants seems to be the predominant one (Varghese et al. 2009; Morgan 2004; Norton and Toohey 2011).

If we consider the main characteristics described above for teacher identity in general, similar central features have been used to describe language teachers' identity: "(I)dentity is not a fixed, stable, unitary, and internally coherent phenomenon but is multiple, shifting, and in conflict" (Varghese et al. 2009, p. 22).

From the review on language teachers identity research it emerges that the majority of the studies remain at the theorizing level, either social identity theory or theory of situated learning (Varghese et al. 2009). Even the studies which have approached language teachers' identity from a narrative inquiry have a strong theorizing focus on sociocultural theory (Tsui 2007; Ruohotie-Lyhty 2013) to study the development of professional teacher identity over a period of time.

This emphasis on theoretical approaches to languages teachers shows the need to explore other perspectives such the lived experience of language teachers, which this chapter aims to address.

2   Method

The main interest of this study was to investigate the subjective experience of teaching a foreign language. It draws from the identified under-researched phenomenon of how teaching a language impacts on the teacher's sense of self, from the point of view of the lived experience. For this reason phenomenology as a research method was chosen.

The phenomenological method draws from the work of philosophers such as Husserl, Heidegger or Merleau-Ponty who investigated the things themselves in their appearing (Merleau-Ponty 1962). The main principle of Phenomenology is to examine every topic getting back to the conditions found in of our experience as expressed in Husserl's phenomenological dictum: "to the things themselves" (Husserl 1950, p. 6). By this he meant that phenomenology should base its study on "the way things are experienced rather than various extraneous concerns which might simply obscure and distort what is to be understood" (Gallagher and Zahavi 2012, p. 6).

The focus of phenomenology is the way things appear to us through experience, and the aim of phenomenological research is to provide a rich textured description of lived experience (Finlay 2008). Phenomenology uses the term *lifeworld* and it involves a way to describe the world as experienced, as lived, rather than a world separated from the people experiencing it (Horton-Salway 2007).

Phenomenology as a qualitative human science research method seems to offer a uniquely ideal approach to study the taken-for-granted experience of teaching a language. Phenomenology starts with wonder, with having a fresh look at everyday objects and activities as if it was the first time we saw them. It is a reflection that problematizes "everydayness" and taken-for-granted ways of thinking (Ravn 2016). Thus it will enable a new, fresh look into the lived experience of language teachers.

2.1 Participants

The purpose of this study was to generate rich descriptions of language teaching experiences. To gather the data, I carried out in-depth interviews with two participants. They were both very experienced British language teachers: one bilingual (English-French) with German as an additional language, and the other was a NNS teacher of French. The study was conducted in accordance with the British Psychological Society (BPS) code of Ethics. In terms of how these were applied within the proposed research this refers to: respect to the individuals, being aware of my own competence, being responsible to avoid any harm to participants and to myself and being fair and honest.

The participants were asked for their written consent and they were informed about their right to withdraw at any time. In order to ensure confidentiality and anonymity, the names used in this paper—John Carpenter and Claire Woods—are not the real names and some personal details have been omitted.

The participants were chosen following a maximum variation sampling (Langdridge 2007). This means that the researcher tries to find participants who have a common experience, but with a wide variation of demographic characteristics. The table below provides the key differences in several relevant personal characteristics of Claire and John (Table 1).

The participants were interviewed separately for thirty to forty minutes. The interviews were recorded and transcribed.

Table 1 Participants' details

Claire	John
Female	Male
Under 45	Over 50
Secondary education, face-to-face	Higher education, distance education
Bilingual French/English: teaching French and German	Not bilingual teaching French

The interview questions were designed following the phenomenological approach and following the recommendations of M. Englander for a phenomenological interview (Englander 2012). I asked the participants for a description of teaching a language, for example a concrete experience or situation they could recall. The subsequent questions followed the responses of the interviewee with focus on the phenomenon being researched. While I was open to their responses and their experiences, I also kept in mind the focus on my research which was their lived experiences as language teachers. Therefore, my questions tried to elicit as many concrete descriptions of their experiences as possible.

To reflect on my role as a researcher using this method. I considered the following about the phenomenological method. I was aware of the importance of self-awareness in doing this type of investigation and I put into practice as much as I could the *epoché*, this means, bracketing my own understanding, my own background and my own involvement.

I developed an attitude of refraining, at least initially, from importing external frameworks and setting aside judgements about the phenomenon (Finlay 2009). Obviously bracketing can be achieved only to a certain extent, and in my case, as I am a language teacher it is impossible to put aside my experiences and knowledge. However, I think that the phenomenological method enabled me to be open and see the phenomenon—in my case, the experiences of language teachers—in a new way. When I processed and analysed the interviews, the findings were for me unexpectedly new and some of them intriguing, suggesting my position in this study as insider-outsider (Milligan 2016).

2.2 Analysis

In the analysis I followed the phenomenology approach as portrayed by (Giorgi 1985). Giorgi uses a Husserlian-inspired approach and provides detailed guidelines for researching psychological topics that can also be applied to educational phenomenon. It involves (Giorgi and Giorgi 2008; Willig 2008):

1. The collection of concrete descriptions of the phenomenon from participants;

2. The researcher's adoption of the phenomenological attitude;
3. An impressionistic reading of each description to gain a sense of familiarity with the whole;
4. The in-depth re-reading of the description to identify "meaning units", which capture specific aspects of the whole;
5. Identifying and making explicit the significance for each meaning unit; and
6. The production and articulation of a general description of the structure(s) of the experience.

Although the analysis starts with descriptive phenomenology, the final stages of the analysis also include elements of interpretative and existentialist phenomenology. That involves the context, intention and meaning of the text, as well as looking for a general understanding of what it means to be human, using for example reflections from the work of Sartre or Merleau-Ponty. Following Finlay (2009) I consider the division between descriptive and interpretative analysis as part of a continuum.

For phenomenologists there is the debate around the focus of their research (Finlay 2009): Is it the focus on the essential and general structures or of a phenomenon (eidetic)? Or is it to explain individual experience (idiographic)? Although the approach of this paper is strongly ideographic exploring how teaching a language is experienced by individuals, I also adopted a middle view as suggested by Halling (2008), firstly looking at particular experience; secondly considering the themes common to the phenomenon and thirdly looking at philosophical and universal aspects of being human. Following Halling's approach I aimed to move back and forth between experience and abstraction as presented in the following sections.

3 Findings

3.1 A Male Non-native French Higher Education Lecturer

John is a very experienced teacher of French. He has an excellent level of French but he is aware that he is not a native speaker.

3.1.1 A Fictitious Identity?

In the interview John described a situation during an intensive French course where students were complaining about not having a native speaker teacher, he said: "and I am not a native French speaker, so I consider myself included in that critics, so that is quite destabilizing as a teacher".

After feeling questioned by what he thought was a "false perception on their part". He decided to adopt a French identity throughout the course, he changed his British name for a French one. The students were convinced that he was a native French teacher:

> so what I did was to adopt a French identity, (…) I changed my name on my name badge that we all wore and I translated my name literally from John Carpenter to Jean Charpentier which is a direct translation, and I told my colleagues at the beginning of the two week period to only refer to this name and not to my normal name, and it had a dramatic consequence.

The *dramatic consecuence* he is referring to, was significant for him as well as for his students.

For him because what started as a game became part of his reality and of the way he perceived himself:

> (…) little by little I felt it changing my own identity as in much as I had then to try and sustain the pretence of being French and not being British and it is difficult to pinpoint exactly what it does to you internally, but I was aware that I somehow portrayed a different personality.

With his new identity as Jean Charpentier, John remembers: "I think the first time I did it, I was a little bit self-conscious about it and was aware and wondered whether it was convincing and how quickly that would be found out, so there was a sense of cheating or being a fraud or not being genuine".

At the beginning John/Jean had the feeling that he was representing a fictitious identity, even feeling that he was cheating or being a fraud. However, this was related to the possibility that students could "find out the truth", more than anything else.

John/Jean on the other side, was aware of the reasons why he did that: "it was for the teaching, and it had a real purpose to it". It was to have more credibility for his student, to meet their expectations and their believes: the idea that a good language teacher has to be a native speaker.

John/Jean gave the students what they wanted: a native speaker teacher. But what does it mean? To have a French name? To have an excellent command of the language? None of the students doubted that John/Jean was a native speaker. In fact as the students found out at the end of the course that John/Jean was British they could not believe it and had difficulties to process this revelation. John/Jean recalls: "when the students found out that I was not a native speaker they were quite shocked and they had to make, just for the last two hours of the last day, they had to adjust their perceptions to me back to 'oh he is actually British' and some of them had great difficulty doing that and some of the were not persuaded by it initially, and so I reasoned from that, I must have got into it and projected some sort of Frenchness".

It is interesting that when students found out, they had "to adjust their perceptions", said John/Jean. I wonder in which way? Did they see him as a different person? Did he sound different? Less French? Did they see him as a worse teacher? Did they have to question all that they had learned from him? In terms of the students' perceptions, I can only speculate about their perceptions in a somewhat absurd situation in which they had to question what they had experienced over two weeks, namely that his French teacher, turned out not to be French.

3.1.2 Projecting Some Sort of Frenchness

In relation of John's/Jean's sense of self while he was acting as Jean, while being conscious of his fictitious identity, he also recognized that part of him was genuinely feeling French and "thinking" French. He spoke about projecting "some sort of Frenchness", he described: "being involved in teaching French now and again for ten years and spending a lot of time in France and using French virtually every day has had an influence on me anyway, and there are times for example, when I can't find words in English or I find I am dreaming in French" or even when he talked in French without noticing, he described one of those situations "I was confused and thought, oh where am I? And what language should I speak? So you do internalise things to such a degree, so sometimes it can just throw your compass a little bit".

There is no clear cut for John/Jean about his feeling British or French, or his language (French or English), sometimes he does not know, until he heard someone speaking in a language and then he adjusts to the context.

In terms of how this experience was for him, he clearly enjoyed it. For John having a fictitious identity was a "liberating experience", even if he felt he was cheating or being a fraud: "I got used to it and it was fun, I enjoyed it, it was adopting a slightly different personality and (…) the overriding feeling was (…) it was amusing more than anything".

Having the possibility, the choice to project different personalities, not to be constraint to a single one was experienced as a liberating feeling.

3.1.3 Being More Than What the Other Sees

The category "Selfhood" in phenomenology is used to account for a structural feature of conscious experience, and it has to do with the person's sense of agency, the feeling of their own presence and voice in a situation (Ashworth 2003). The self is actually completely interwoven with our links with others and provided by interaction with others. In their reflections on social forms of self-consciousness, Gallagher and Zahavi (2016) acknowledge that the "I" can become aware of itself through the eyes of other people: I might frame my awareness of myself from the perspective of others, trying to see myself as they see me. Within this attitude, the judgements that I make about myself are constrained by social expectations and cultural values (Gallagher and Zahavi 2016). In the case of John's experience, it is the interaction with the others (his students) what makes him aware of himself—as "deficient", non-native French teacher, this means that his sense of self is radically challenged and questioned. This type of interaction can be considered as an "other-mediated form(s) of self-experience" (Zahavi 2012). A clear example of this form of self-experience can be found in the reflections of Sartre in the third part of

"Being and Nothingness" in what he describes "Le pour-autri": Being for the others.

According to Sartre, self-consciousness (he exemplifies this in relation to shame) presupposes the intervention of the other, that is, the self of which I am ashamed. My public persona did not exist prior to my encounter with the other, it was brought about by this encounter. To feel shame is to accept the other's evaluation; it is to identify with the object that the other looks at and judges. In being ashamed I accept and acknowledge the judgement of the other. Sartre states: "(…) I need the mediation of the Other in order to be what I am" (Sartre 2003, p. 312). Commenting on this passage Dan Zahavi explains Sartre's position with the sentence: "I *am* the way the other sees me, and I am nothing but that" (Zahavi 2014, p. 213).

A closer analysis of John's/Jean's situation reveals that Sartre's approach does not quite work for him. Rather his action adopting a different identity puts him in a position to say: "I am (both) the way the other sees me, and *more than that*". This means, instead of being just constrained by others, the experience is liberating and empowering: it opens an array of possibilities, such as:

> "I am what you think I am" (I am like a NS of French, you cannot tell the difference)
>
> "I am not what you think I am" (I am actually British, not a NS of French)
>
> "I am what I think I am not" (I do feel French, I project "Frenchness")
>
> "I am not what I think I am" (I am not a deficient teacher, I am not only British)

John's display of a fictitious identity reveals the multi-layered aspects of the self where the terms "fictitious" or "real" do not mean anything. Also the terms NS, NNS, in John's experience lose the solidity they appear to have in current debates and teachers' and students' expectations. They reveal themselves as volatile, unsubstantiated constructs that appear or disappear depending on the context and situation.

3.2 A Female Bilingual (French/English) Secondary Teacher with German as an Additional Language

The lived experiences of Claire teaching a language are characterized by fluidity and interdependence of the three languages/cultures: English, French and German and the impossibility to provide a static, or stable account of any of them, her feeling more enacting or inhabiting a language depends on the circumstances, the students and the context.

3.2.1 In the Middle-In Between

Claire clearly feels her role of a language teacher as a mediating person: "I think when I teach German I am a bit of an intermediary between the English student and the German language and culture", "I am facilitating them to get nearer to a different culture, to a different language" "I feel like an intermediary I want to persuade the children I am teaching that this is fantastic, that this is really good". When I asked Claire about where she positions herself when explaining something about the French or German culture (inside/outside) her response was "Ah…in the middle I think (…) in the middle, neither in one or the other" (neither British nor German).

The role of an intermediary is difficult to grasp and to explain: "neither here, nor there".

The position of an intermediary resonates with the reflections of Simone Weil in relation with the Greek term *Metaxu (in- between-ness)*, something that both separate and connect us. She exemplifies this with the image of two prisoners whose cells adjoin communicate with each other by knocking on the wall: "The wall is the thing which separates them but it also their means of communication" (Weil 2004, p. 145).

Clare as an intermediary feels both separation and connection of her students with the language and culture she is teaching. She has a double function being the same as them/being different from them.

When I asked about to position herself in relation to being British or French, she is unable to give a clear answer "Obviously being bilingual French is part of me, but I don't feel…I still feel very English… I still feel like a person from outside looking into (outside the culture) I don't feel either one or the other, I don't feel French or German, but when I teach I do".

3.2.2 I Put on a Persona

One recurring theme in Claire's interview is the experience of being someone different, creating a persona, pretending, in a word, enacting a different person when she teaches.

Talking about her experiences teaching German she said:

> "You have to be like a different person, don't you?" And she further describes her experience of teaching a language as having a different identity; she says: "when I am teaching, when I am speaking German I feel I'm having a persona, I don't think I pretend to be a German in particular, but I feel like a German expert, as a teacher of German as opposed to myself" (…)

> Part of your own character is there, it has to be, doesn't it, but you also project something. I think all teachers do that, don't they? I think that if you are teaching a language, I think you project something that you think will typify a German person, or if I am doing a French lesson, I would use the expression 'oh la la', not because I think that French people would say that, but because it is attached to the persona 'being a French person' or being a French teacher.

When asked about what she means when she says "persona", Claire answers: "What I mean…when they see me, they don't see me like Claire Woods (*Her name*) but they see me like a German teacher, they say Frau Woods, or in French they say: Madame Woods" when asked about how this experience feels, she answers: "I feel quite empowered, because I know I am the expert…(…) I think having a persona is quite liberating, isn't it? It enables you to be more creative".

Being a language teacher for Claire has a fundamental ambiguity of being/and not being herself at the same time: to be herself, she has to be someone different. This being someone different emerges in the interplay of herself, the pupils and the social/cultural context. To illustrate and analyse this I will use the phenomenological concept of *intersubjectivity*, which, since Husserl, has been object of systematic and extensive discussions among phenomenologists. Intersubjectivity is a relation between subjects and includes an investigation of the first-person perspective. Intersubjectivity requires a simultaneous analysis of the relationship between subjectivity and world. That means that "the three dimensions *self*, *other* and *world* belong together, they reciprocally illuminate one another, and can only be fully understood in their interconnection" (Zahavi 2019, p. 88). Claire's responses and actions in relation of her lived experiences as a language teacher are indeed not only connected to the situation and the others—her pupils—but they only emerge in interconnection. At one point in the interview Claire said that she felt British, but when I asked her: "Hundred per cent?" she answered "Well, except if somebody says something about France or Germany, or French or German, and then I would become an intermediary again".

Her embodied self/selves also emerge in the interaction: her voice, her gestures depend on the language she is teaching, as well as on the type of learners: "I speak a lot lower when I speak German, lower, not the volume but the pitch, I have a deeper voice in German and I have a higher voice in French" She also talks about a body feeling more "airy" when she speaks French.

3.2.3 Feeling Protective

Claire says in her interview that she feels protective in relation to the culture and to the language she is teaching, if someone says something against the French or German culture or language, she will defend them: "I do defend them as well, for example if they say 'why do they use such a long word, it is ridiculous' and I would say, 'well, you know that is really clever'. I do that…I can feel quite defensive, I suppose".

Talking about a German film (Das Leben der anderen), Claire feels angry when her students cannot appreciate or understand how good the film is: "(…) it's a brilliant film. They were saying, they didn't get it and I felt very cross with them, I said, *you silly boy*, again is purely German. I couldn't be anything else, and again I feel very much…very protective". In her role as intermediary she oscillates from one side to the other, connecting her pupils with the other side/the other culture and language.

4 Discussion

Ashworth (2003) stresses the ideographic, that means individual, focus of phenomenological research and that the possibility of a "coherent ideographic description" of each interviewee is the immediate finding of the research (Ashworth et al. 2003, p. 273).

However, as mentioned before, I followed Halling's approach when looking at common themes and more general and universal topics in Claire's and John's experiences as language teachers.

The purpose of this study was to explore the lived experiences of languages teachers, and in particular their sense of self. The analysis of the data gathered through the in-depth interview has revealed some aspects of the life world of language teachers which I will present in the following.

One essential part of their experience of being a language teacher was associated with being someone else: "putting a persona, having a fictitious identity, pretending". This apparent contradiction was however not a sort of alienation, rather they had the sense that "being someone else" was their way of being authentic, of being themselves. What sounds like a clear contradiction was lived in their experiences as "liberating", "empowering" and "creative".

They accounted for multiple selves depending on the context: a British-self, in "normal life" not in an educational setting, a French-self when teaching French, an intermediary when teaching British pupils, the protective-German-self when British people critizcized the German culture, the patriotic self when teaching the French culture, etc. However those multiple selves did not appear as solid coexisting identities, but as a fluid movement, as a continuous changing depending on the context. Although there was a clear interplay between of self-others and world, there was still a strong sense of agency, of choice, of creativity in their being-in-their-world as language teachers.

The role of intermediary also emerged as a fundamental feature of their lived experience as language teachers. This role expresses, on the one hand, an ambiguity of locus, of their position: "in between", "not here, not there"; on the other hand it reveals both connection and distance. Their efforts to connect students with another language and culture also reveal that what is given is distance, ignorance and disconnection.

In relation to the debate of the NS-NNS their experiences seem to confirm Davies (2004) statement that the notion of NS is both myth and reality. In the case of John, it was reality as part of the students' beliefs that they projected into him, it was myth as John/Jean showed that the distinction had no real substance whatsoever. From a more philosophical reflection John's self-awareness can be considered other-mediated experience of the self, as described by Sartre, however his experience revealed a stronger sense of agency, choice and creativity.

When we look into the findings in relation to current research about teacher identity and in particular to language teacher identity, the results offer some more nuanced insights into the view of language teachers' identity as multiple and shifting, as stated by Varghese et al. (2009). More than multiple well-defined conflictual identities, the experience of the language teachers in this study seems to reveal a self that is in itself fluid, moving, changing, creative, contradictory and ambiguous. This fluid self seems to be also more in line with an emerging new paradigm of language learning where the learner is seen as a continuous, multiple and fractured self (Ros i Solé 2016).

Other new insights that have been unveiled in this study is how contradictions seem to be harmonized in their experience: being someone else, being in between, being and not being NS and how the self-awareness of those contradictions are experienced *erlebt* as energizing: "fun", "amusing", as "liberating", "empowering" and "creative".

5 Conclusion

The phenomenological approach allowed me to look into the lifeworld of language teachers from the perspective of the teachers as subjects, not only as object of study. Although this study focused on two individual experiences, some themes have been identified and explored that seem to be part of the phenomenon investigated, the lived experiences of language teachers.

Being a language teacher revealed itself in its contradictory nature, where those contradictions are experienced as harmonized and energizing. In particular the need to project a *persona* or a *fictitious identity* was at the centre of the lifeworld of being a language teacher.

It has also manifested in its role as intermediary, mediating between connexion and distance, interpreting between languages, cultures and individuals.

These insights are valuable contributions for the investigation of the life world of language teachers, yet they are just some glimpses of one possible way of looking at it.

As Husserl points out, all phenomena and objects invite us to explore further:

> There is still more to see here, turn me so you can see all my sides, let your gaze run through me, draw closer to me, open me up, divide me up; keep on looking me over again and again, turning me to see all sides. You will get to know me like this, all that I am, all my surface qualities, all my inner sensible qualities. (Husserl 2001, p. 41)

Following this spirit, this study may invite and inspire other researchers to further looking into the lifeworld of language teachers.

References

Akkerman, Sanne F., and Paulien C. Meijer. 2011. A Dialogical Approach to Conceptualizing Teacher Identity. *Teaching and Teacher Education* 27: 308–319.

Arva, Valeria, and Péter Medgyes. 2000. Native and Non-native Teachers in the Classroom. *System* 28 (3): 355–372.

Ashworth, Peter. 2003. An Approach to Phenomenological Psychology: The Contingencies of the Lifeworld. *Journal of Phenomenological Psychology* 34 (2): 145–156.

Ashworth, Peter, Madeleine Freewood, and Ranald Macdonald. 2003. The Student Lifeworld and the Meanings of Plagiarism. *Journal of Phenomenological Psychology* 34 (2): 257–278.

Atamturk, Nurdan, Hakan Atamturk, and Celen Dimililer. 2018. Native Speaker Dichotomy: Stakeholders' Preferences and Perceptions of Native and Non-native Speaking English Language Teachers. *South African Journal of Education* 38 (1). https://doi.org/10.15700/saje.v38n1a1384.

Beauchamp, Catherine, and Lynn Thomas. 2009. Understanding Teacher Identity: An Overview of Issues in the Literature and Implications for Teacher Education. *Cambridge Journal of Education* 39 (2): 175–189.

Braine, George (ed.). 1999. *Non-native Educators in English Language Teaching*. Mahwah, NJ: Erlbaum.

Brown, H. Douglas. 2007. *Principles of Language Learning and Teaching*. White Plains and New York: Pearson.

Busch, Brigitta. 2015. Linguistic Repertoire and *Spracherleben*, the Lived Experience of Language. Working Papers in Urban Language & Literacies. Paper 148. King's College London, London.

Canagarajah, Suresh. 2012. Styling One's Own in the Sri Lankan Tamil Diaspora: Implications for Language and Ethnicity. *Journal of Language, Identity & Education* 11 (2): 124–135.

Case, Rod E. 2004. Forging Ahead into New Social Networks and Looking Back to Past Social Identities: A Case Study of a Foreign-Born English as a Second Language Teacher in the United States. *Urban Education* 39 (2): 125–148.

Cho, Hyesun. 2014. 'It's Very Complicated': Exploring Heritage Language Identity with Heritage Language Teachers in a Teacher Preparation Program. *Language and Education* 28 (2): 181–195.

Davies, Alan. 2004. The Native Speaker in Applied Linguistics. In *Handbook of Applied Linguistics*, ed. Alan Davies and Catherine Elder. Wiley. ProQuest Ebook Central. https://ebookcentral.proquest.com/lib/open/detail.action?docID=214151.

Englander, Magnus. 2012. The Interview: Data Collection in Descriptive Phenomenological Human Scientific Research. *Journal of Phenomenological Psychology* 43: 13–35.

Finlay, Linda. 2008. Introducing Phenomenological Research. http://www.linda.finlay.com/introducingphenomenomologicalresearch.doc. Accessed 19 April 2012.

Finlay, Linda. 2009. Debating Phenomenological Research Methods. *Phenomenology and Practice* 3: 6–25.

Gallagher, Shaun, and Dan Zahavi. 2012. *The Phenomenological Mind*. London and New York: Routledge.
Gallagher, Shaun, and Dan Zahavi. 2016. Phenomenological Approaches to Self-Consciousness. In *The Stanford Encyclopedia of Philosophy*, ed. Edward N. Zalta, Winter 2016 Edition. https://plato.stanford.edu/cgibin/encyclopedia/archinfo.cgi?entry=self-consciousness-phenomenological. Accessed 25 June 2017.
Giorgi, Amedeo. 1985. Sketch of a Psychological Phenomenological Method. In *Phenomenology and Psychological Research*, ed. Amedio Giorgi. Pittsburgh, PA: Duquesne University Press.
Giorgi, Amedeo, and Babro Giorgi. 2008. Phenomenological Psychology. In *The SAGE Handbook of Qualitative Research in Psychology*, ed. Carla Willig Carla and Wendy Stainton-Rogers. London: Sage.
Halling, Steen. 2008. *Intimacy, Transcendence and Psychology: Closeness and Openness in Everyday Life*. New York: Palgrave Macmillan.
Hallman, Heidi L. 2015. Teacher Identity as Dialogic Response: A Bakhtinian Perspective. In *Advances and Current Trends in Language, Teacher Identity Research*, ed. Yin Ling Cheung, Selim Ben Said, and Kwangkhyun Park. London: Routledge.
Hayes, David. 2009. Non-native English-Speaking Teachers, Context and English Language Teaching. *System* 37 (1): 1–11.
Horton-Salway, Mary. 2007. *Social Psychology: Critical Perspectives on Self and Others*. DD307 Project Booklet. Milton Keynes: The Open University.
Husserl, Edmund. 1950. *Cartesianische Meditationen und Pariser Vorträge*. Husserliana I. The Hague: Martinus Nijhoff.
Husserl, Edmund. 2001 [1917/1918]. *Die 'Bernauer Manuskripte' über das Zeitbewußtsein*. Husserliana 33. Dordrecht: Kluwer Academic.
Kanno, Yasuko, and Christian Stuart. 2011. Learning to Become a Second Language Teacher: Identities-in-Practice. *Modern Language Journal* 95 (2): 236–252.
Langdridge, Darren. 2007. *Phenomenological Psychology: Theory, Research and Method*. Harlow: Pearson.
Lasagabaster, David, and Juan Manuel Sierra. 2005. What Do Students Think About the Pros and Cons of Having a Native Speaker Teacher? In *Non-native Language Teachers: Perceptions, Challenges and Contributions to the Profession*, ed. Enric Llurda. New York: Springer.

Matsumoto, Yumi. 2018. Teachers' Identities as 'Non-native' Speakers: Do They Matter in English as a Lingua Franca interactions? In *Criticality, Teacher Identity, and (In)equity in English Language Teaching: Issues and Implications*, ed. Bedretti Yazan and Nathaniel Rudolph. Cham: Springer.

McNamara, David. 1991. Subject Knowledge and Its Application: Problems and Possibilities for Teacher Educators. *The Journal of Education for Teaching* 17 (2): 113–128.

Medgyes, Péter. 1994. *The Non-native Teacher*. London: Macmillan.

Merleau-Ponty, Maurice. 1962. *Phenomenology of Perception*. London: Routledge and Kegan Paul (Original, 1945).

Milligan, Lizzi. 2016. Insider-Outsider-Inbetweener? Researcher Positioning, Participative Methods and Cross-Cultural Educational Research. *Compare* 46 (2): 235–250. https://doi.org/10.1080/03057925.2014.928510.

Morgan, Brian. 2004. Teacher Identity as Pedagogy: Towards a Field-Internal Conceptualisation in Bilingual and Second Language Education. *Bilingual Education and Bilingualism* 7 (2 and 3): 172–188.

Morgan, Brian, and Matthew Clarke. 2011. Identity in Second Language Teaching and Learning. In *Handbook of Research in Second Language Teaching and Learning*, ed. Eli Hinkel. Abingdon: Routledge.

Moussu, Lucie, and Enric Llurda. 2008. Non-native English-Speaking English Language Teachers: History and Research. *Language Teaching* 41 (3): 315–348.

Murdoch, Georg. 1994. Language Development Provision in Teacher Training Curricula. *The ELT Journal* 48 (3): 253–265.

Norton, Bonny, and Kelleen Toohey. 2011. Identity, Language Learning, and Social Change. *Language Teaching* 44 (4): 412–446.

Pachler, Norbert, Michael Evans, and Shirley Lawes. 2007. *Modern Foreign Languages: Teaching School Subjects 11–19*. Oxford: Routledge.

Paikeday, Thomas M. 1985. *The Native Speaker Is Dead!* Toronto: Paikeday Publishing Inc.

Ravn, Susanne. 2016. Phenomenological Analysis in Sport and Exercise. In *Routledge Handbook of Qualitative Research in Sport and Exercise*, eds. Brett Smith and Andrew C. Sparkes. London and New York: Routledge.

Reis, Davi. 2015. Making Sense of Emotions in NNEST's Professional Identities and Agency. In *Advances and Current Trends in Language Teacher Identity Research*, ed. Yin Ling Cheung, Selim Ben Said, and Kwangkhyun Park. London: Routledge.

Ricento, Thomas. 2005. Considerations of Identity in L2 Learning. In *Handbook of Research in Second Language Teaching and Learning*, ed. Eli Hinkel. Retrieved from http://ebookcentral.proquest.com. Accessed 18 April 2019.

Ros i Solé, Cristina. 2016. *The Private World of the Language Learner*. London: Palgrave Macmillan. ProQuest Ebook Central. https://ebookcentral.proquest.com/lib/open/detail.action?docID=4746999. Accessed 19 March 2019.

Ruohotie-Lyhty, Maria. 2013. Struggling for a Professional Identity: Two Newly Qualified Language Teachers' Identity Narratives During the First Years at Work. *Teaching and Teacher Education* 30: 120–129.

Sachs, Judyth. 2005. Teacher Education and the Development of Professional Identity: Learning to Be a Teacher. In *Connecting Policy and Practice: Challenges for Teaching and Learning in Schools and Universities*, ed. Pam Denicolo and Michael Kompf, 5–21. Oxford: Routledge.

Sartre, Jean-Paul. 2003 [1956]. *Being and Nothingness*. London and New York: Routledge.

Shin, Sarah J. 2008. Preparing Non-native English-Speaking ESL Teachers. *Teacher Development* 12 (1): 57–65.

Trent, John, and Matthew DeCoursey. 2011. Crossing Boundaries and Constructing Identities: The Experiences of Early Career Mainland Chinese English Language Teachers in Hong Kong. *Asia-Pacific Journal of Teacher Education* 39 (1): 65–78.

Tsui, Amy B.M. 2007. Complexities of Identity Formation: A Narrative Inquiry of an EFL Teacher. *TESOL Quarterly* 41 (4): 657–680.

Varghese, Manka, Brian Morgan, Bill Johnston, and Kimberly A. Johnson. 2009. Theorizing Language Teacher Identity: Three Perspectives and Beyond. *Journal of Language, Identity & Education* 4 (1): 21–44.

Weil, Simone. 2004 [1947]. *Gravity and Grace*, trans. E. Crawford and M. von der Ruhr. London and New York: Routledge.

Willig, Carla. 2008. *Introducing Qualitative Research in Psychology*. Maidenhead: Open University Press.

Yin Ling, Cheung, Selim Ben Said, and Kwangkhyun Park. 2015. *Advances and Current Trends in Language Teacher Identity Research*. London: Routledge.

Zahavi, Dan. 2012. Self, Consciousness, and Shame. In *The Oxford Handbook of Contemporary Phenomenology*, ed. Dan Zahavi. Oxford: Oxford University Press.

Zahavi, Dan. 2014. *Self and Other: Exploring Subjectivity, Empathy and Shame*. Oxford: Oxford University Press.

Zahavi, Dan. 2019. *Phenomenology: The Basics*. London and New York: Routledge.

5

Becoming a Language Professional in Higher Education: A Psychosocial Case Study

Donata Puntil

1 Introduction

This chapter is an overview of a pilot study conducted in 2018 as part of a Doctorate in Education. It focuses on the complex and intertwined correlation between personal and professional instances in the trajectory of language professionals in the context of British Higher Education (HE). The three participants of this investigation are mainly referred to as *language professionals* throughout the chapter, rather than language teachers, although at times these definitions are interchanged. The focus on *professionals* reflects the emphasis of this study on the participants' journey into *professionalization* in the field of language teaching. In addition, particular attention is given to the interaction between past and present in the process of professional identity formation in which fantasies of the past are constantly negotiated at unconscious, individual and social level, as highlighted by Bainbridge and West (2012). Personal and emotional aspects

---

D. Puntil (✉)
King's College London, London, UK
e-mail: donata.puntil@kcl.ac.uk

of teachers' investment in change, in their agency in professional growth and in their relationship to knowledge in their discipline also represent a key focus of this research in line with a *psychosocial* approach to research in education (Frosh 2010).

The choice to position this study within a *psychosocial* framework is closely linked to my own professional background and to my personal journey since, besides being a language educator, I am also a qualified psychoanalytic psychotherapist, member of the British Psychoanalytic Council. The professional background in psychoanalytic psychotherapy represents a strong aspect of my own professional identity and informs the ontological and epistemological framework of this research, as well as the methodological choices employed for the study.

The three main research questions underpinning the study are as follows:

1. How is the professional identity of HE language teachers constructed?
2. What is the role of personal critical incidents in language teachers' professional journeys?
3. What is language teachers' relationship to knowledge, to the taught subject?

The methodology used for this study is auto/biographical narratives framed within a case study context (Yin 2009) within a qualitative insider researcher framework (Hellawell 2006) aiming at emphasizing the validity and legitimation of participants' individual voices (De Fina and Georgakopoulou 2013) in the narrative process.

Written, oral and visual narratives are analysed within a thematic framework; the psychoanalytical perspective, following the *psychosocial* approach of the study, supports the formulation of themes and of critical instances in teachers' personal and professional accounts, paying particular attention to the discursive mode of the narration, to contradictions, changes of tone, avoidances, silences that might shed light to psychodynamic unconscious defences towards anxiety-provoking instances (Frosh 2010; Hollway and Jefferson 2013). In addition, the psychoanalytical stance brings a further dimension to the analysis of autobiographical narratives, as outlined by De Fina and Georgakopoulou (2013), since it places its focus not only on the *told* story, but also and mostly on the *untold*, on what is implied and referred to, but not explicitly narrated.

The context in which this study takes place is a Modern Language Centre (MLC) within the UK university in which I also work holding a senior position. The choice to situate this research within the same department I belong to is closely related to my professional role within that department where I am responsible for training and staff development. Within this context, I progressively reflected on the impact personal trajectories have on professional pathways and how they represent important motivational factors in the journey into professionalization. Within the context of UK higher education, Language Centres are often marginalized in the academic discourse since they are usually positioned outside the mainstream research-based frameworks and consequently the voice of language teachers is often considered peripheral in the academic discourse (Worton 2009). As a language professional myself and as a language educator, I am aware that this reality might have a negative impact on teachers' motivation and interest in further professional development, potentially undermining their professionalism and professionalization and closing up new opportunities for career progression.

Despite this demotivational reality, the language professionals I closely work with, including myself, are profoundly engaged and committed to their professional role, therefore one of the main aims of this study is to investigate the personal motives beyond the professional choices in order to give voice and legitimization to those under-represented stories. There is also an assumption that the engagement in the research process might promote participants' self-reflection on their agency in professional change and transformation and might empower them to embark in new personal and/or professional projects, as emphasized by West and Merrill (2009).

The following paragraphs outline the theoretical framework underpinning the study and describe in detail the methodology that has been employed to collect and analyse data within an auto/biographical perspective, followed by a final discussion on the outcomes of the study.

2 Theoretical Framework

2.1 On Nomadic Identity: A Post-structuralist Approach

The study presented in this chapter is mainly aligned within a post-structuralist approach to knowing and to experience with particular reference to authors like Deleuze and Guattari (1987, 1994, 2000), Giddens (1991), Braidotti (2011a, 2014) and Bauman (2000) who underpin the research questions and shed light into my investigation into human life.

I particularly refer to Deleuze and Guattari's (1987) notion of time as non-linear, as circular and fragmented and to their consideration of time as *becoming*. In their main body of work *Capitalism and Schizophrenia* (2000) the authors clearly refer to Bergson's concept of time as a universal non-linear feature and as a dimension that is structured along the coexistence of different *durations*, different *becoming* that coexist and juxtapose in a non-linear sequence of events. Their consideration of time as *becoming*, is closely related to the notion of memory as both a conscious and unconscious, fragmented recollection of un-sequential events. The authors describe memory as multiplicity, as an involuntary and creative *rhizome*, as an *assemblage*, as an act of recollecting deterritorialized events. In line with their philosophy, I also refer to Braidotti (2011a, b, 2014) notion of *nomadism*, considered not only as a physical displacement between different territories, but also as an existential positioning between different internal representations of one's identity.

In the last two decades, there has been a shift within the context of Second Language Acquisition (SLA) research moving towards an interdisciplinary conception of language learning and teaching referring to post-structural socio-cultural theories and practices. We could consider the seminal articles by Norton (1995, 1997, 2000, 2010, 2013), Pavlenko (2001, 2006, 2007), and Pavlenko and Blackledge (2004) as the turning points in SLA research towards a post-structuralist paradigm by which research on language learning started to shift towards identity as the core of investigation. This shift of SLA research on identity had also an impact on investigating language teachers as critical participants in the process of professional identity formation (Morgan 2004; Varghese et al. 2005; Tsui 2007;

De Costa and Norton 2017; Barkhuizen 2017; Miller et al. 2017; Wolff and De Costa 2017; Zheng 2017; Mercer and Kostoulas 2018). This position places language teachers as agentic in their professional self-negotiation crossing borders between languages, cultures, social contexts and professional paradigms and considers these passages as having profound effects on one owns' perception of oneself and on professional practices.

The study discussed in this chapter aligns within this epistemological shift in SLA towards post-structuralism while presenting at the same time a key innovative aspect in its *psychosocial* framing (Frosh 2010; Bainbridge 2018; Holloway and Jefferson 2013) employing psychoanalytically informed positioning and methodological tools to question conscious and unconscious factors at the centre of teachers' personal and professional trajectories.

At present, there are only few studies that employ tools of investigation towards a psychoanalytical stance (Block 2007; Mansfield 2000; Morgan and Clarke 2011). By drawing on post-Kleinian object-relation psychoanalytical theories (Klein 1963, 1975; Winnicott 1971, 1975; Bion 1959, 1962), this investigation challenges binary notions of bi-culturalism, arguing that language teachers not only navigate in between different territories constantly reconstructing their professional identity depending on the context they operate within, but also come to terms with complex and non-linear notions of identity and diversity within themselves, being mediators of cultural and linguistic change within their identity formation (Kristeva 1991; Coffey 2013).

2.2 On Becoming a Language Educational Professional

While engaging with the work of the post-structuralist thinkers mentioned above and particularly with Braidotti (2011a, b, 2018) and Deleuze and Guattari (1987) who underpin my ontological positioning, I progressively reflected on my nomadic journey as a language learner, educator and researcher. I therefore started to acknowledge that this study begun unofficially forty years ago when I was eight-years-old and had my first direct experience of being in a language class. I was fascinated and mesmerized by the English language teacher. I wanted to become a language professional. While immersed in the research described in this chapter, I came progressively to realize that it is this nomadic dialogue with myself that I am carrying on with this study, a dialogue I started many years ago; a research that begun, before it officially begun, as many researches do, and that makes me aware that I have always been in the middle of it.

I grew up in a small village in the Dolomites in North Italy, an area which is very close to Austria and Slovenia, linguistically very rich and mixed, hosting few communities of minority languages. Being exposed since a young age to linguistic diversity, to code switching and to complex intercultural experiences, played a significant role in my perception of languages as part of one's own identity and as pathway to a professional journey. The professional trajectory that characterized my development as a language teacher, and later on as a language educator, is closely related to these early experiences, to an ongoing internal dialogue with my past, as well as to rational and career-driven decisions. I can now confidently state that in my nomadic experience of life abroad, I decided to become a language professional mainly to maintain that contact with my origins, with my mother-tongue, with my *internal objects*, considered in psychoanalytical terms, as the key figures who had an impact on my personal and professional choices (Klein 1963).

As previously stated, the interaction between past and present in professional trajectories is the main focus of this study. As Goodson argues "definitions of our professional location and of our career direction can only be arrived at by detailed understanding of people's lives. Studies of professional life and patterns of professional development must address these dimension of the personal" (2003, p. 61). In these words, as alongside his entire body of work on teachers' lives, Goodson highlights the relevance of *critical incidents*, as crucial events in teachers' lives that can affect career choices and professional practices. He endorses a shift in education research from investigating *teacher-as-practice* to researching *teacher-as-person* (2003, p. 60). The same stance is taken by Hargreaves (1994, 1998, 2000, 2001) who advocates for a shift of perspective in research on teacher development from practice-based to the realm of the personal and of the emotional. Both Goodson and Hargreaves claim that teachers' *life cycle*, determined by professional and personal choices, is an important aspect of professional development and that it should play a central role in educational research.

Based on these assumptions, I chose to position my study within a *psychosocial* epistemological paradigm as a suitable underpinning frame to represent the interrelation between personal and professional in the unfolding of language teachers' nomadic stories of professionalization.

2.3 On Professional Identity Formation: A Psychosocial Perspective

Holloway and Jefferson (2013), in their innovative methodological approach to social research based on a psychoanalytical framework, define the inter-relation between intra and intersubjectivity in the analysis of participants' data as *psychosocial*:

> [...] tracking this relationship relies on a particular view of the research subject: one whose inner word is not simply a reflection of the outer world, not a cognitively driven accommodation of it. Rather, we intend to argue for the need to posit research subjects whose inner words cannot be understood without knowledge of their experiences in the world, and whose experiences of the world cannot be understood without knowledge of the way in which their inner words allow them to experience the outer world. This research subject cannot be known except through another subject; in this case the researcher. The name we give to such subjects is psychosocial [...]. (2013, pp. 3–4)

Holloway and Jefferson (2013) use the term *psychosocial*, as does Frosh (2010), to describe the application of psychoanalytical thinking to social and educational contexts and to frame the analysis of data as the interplay of participants' conscious and unconscious motives, emphasizing the insider position of the researcher:

> Psychoanalytically inclined researchers start from the position that unconscious processes infiltrate the narrative accounts given by research participants, so that interpretative strategies aimed at uncovering these unconscious processes will be needed. [...] This renders psychoanalysis as usefully explaining the way in which external events become incorporated 'into' the psyche or self, notably through concepts such introjection and identification. (2010, p. 200)

In psychoanalytically framed research, the emphasis is placed on the agency of the subject, on its internal world and on the relationship between researcher and participants in the meaning-making narration of events, without disregarding the reality of external circumstances in context. Within this perspective, the use of psychoanalysis as a methodological tool can enrich data analysis by offering a *thickening* and in-depth interpretative understanding of data, particularly in relation to personal narratives.

The notion of *becoming*, referring back to Deleuze and Guattari and to Braidotti, is also central to psychoanalytical inquiry, in which early and subsequent experiences are constantly intertwined in a multiplicity of levels in which present, past and future are dynamically interconnected. Klein (1975), Winnicott (1971), and Bion (1962) described in different ways the early relationship between infant and mother as the outset for the adult relationship to knowledge and to learning. In Bion's view, the baby capacity of thinking and learning is closely related to the mother's *reverie*, viewed as her containing capacity to process the infant's instinctive, irrational thoughts and to give meaning to them. The capacity to think (Bion 1962), to learn and to relate to other human beings, is deeply rooted in early relationships to significant others. Winnicott's (1971) view on playing as a creative meaning-making act, can also be considered as an expression of learning and of personal development. Every step within the journey into education could be considered, in Winnicottian terms, as a transitional process, as a step into growth, independence and empowerment (Salzberger-Wittenberg et al. 1983).

Professional lives, including the ones investigated within this research, can therefore be considered as act of *becoming*, as life-long and life-deep processes involving the relationship to learning, to emotional investment, to the meaning of choices and to the value of motivations, as outlined by

Bainbridge and West (2012) and by Hunt and West (2006). The framing of this study within a *psychosocial* perspective employing psychoanalytical tools of investigation considers participants as agents in their meaning-making choices into professional journeys and views their trajectories into learning and becoming professionals as transformative, embodied and emotional process in which phantasies, dreams, fears and conflicts play a central role (Britzman 2009; Youell 2006).

3 Methodology

As previously outlined, this study employs auto/biographical narratives as physical and symbolic spaces of self-reflection and as co-operative meaning-making investigative tools where knowledge is co-constructed between researcher and participants (Formenti 2017; Hollway and Jefferson 2013; West and Merrill 2009).

The use of narrative methodology is mainly based on Bruner's (1986, 1987, 1990, 2002) account of self-narratives as discursive constructions allowing individuals to organize and to represent concepts of themselves. Within this perspective, narrative inquiry is referred to as an act of co-construction (Bamberg 1997; Riessman 2003), drawing from Bakhtin (1981) notion of the dialogic self. Narrating one's life is therefore not only viewed as a re-telling of past events, but as an act of identity making in the here and now, as a dialogic text in its *becoming* in which past, present and future are all contained in the act of narration (Brockmeier 2000).

Narratives are key tools of investigation also within psychoanalytical theories and clinical practice where the act of narrating is considered as an act of identity-making in its own right. In the encounter between patient and therapist, the here and now within the therapeutic encounter holds the same value as past events narrated through accounts of memory and is investigated within the parameters of transference and countertransference interactions. In narratives, as well as in psychoanalysis, critical instances and turning points in one's account of one's life are considered crucial points of investigation invested with symbolic meaning (Bruner 2001). The analysis of turning points should allow to distinguish what is *normal* from what is *extraordinary* within the account of one's life; the extraordinary events are usually interpreted as agents of change, as it emerges in the data collected for this study and outlined in following paragraphs (Hollway and Jefferson 2013; West & Merrill 2009).

3.1 Data Collection

Data collected and analysed in this study are based on the auto/biographical accounts of three participants within the department described in previous paragraphs, as well as on my reflective diary and on my psychoanalytic dialogue with a clinical supervisor, as outlined in the following sections of this chapter.

The participants described below chose a fictional name to represent themselves within this study, as outlined in Table 1.

The data collection took place during three months in 2018 and was divided into five stages: a first stage in which participants wrote a short account of their professional life following an open question. The written autobiographical accounts were followed by a second stage in which unstructured interviews were conducted. Participants were asked to bring either an object, or/and a picture, to the interview as a representation of themselves as language professionals. Asking participants to bring on object/photo to the interviews is based on Winnicott (1975) and on Bollas (2009) psychoanalytic consideration that "an evocative object" might trigger new self-negotiations and might allow participants to engage in different emotional discourses about their professional selves.

The interviews were conducted using free association psychoanalytical techniques, by which participants were guided as little as possible, allowing space and time for free associations to emerge as part of the narration. Hollway and Jefferson (2013) define this approach as Free Association Narrative Interview (FANI). My own countertransference experience as a researcher during the interview was considered as part of the data. Transference and countertransference are key concepts within the psychoanalytical encounter; they represent the relationship between analyst and patient and within a *psychosocial* framework they shape the relationship

Table 1 Participants' demographic data

Participants	Age	Gender	Ethnic background	Nationality	Languages	Type of employment	Length of employment
Alia	50–59	F	Middle Eastern	British	Arabic English French	Full-time	15 years
Priya	40–49	F	South-Asian/Indian	Indian	Hindi English Urdu Spanish Sanskrit (read) Harijavani (read) Punjabi (receptive) Gudjuratu (") Dogri (") Bangla (")	Hourly-paid	4.5 years
Lila	50–59	F	Latin-American	Argentinian	Spanish Galician English Italian	Full-time	17 years

between researcher and participants based on the notion that: "Psychoanalytic exploration of fieldwork pays particular attention to […] how unconscious processes structure relations between researcher, subject and data gathered" (Hunt 1989, p. 9).

The third stage of the data collection process was a second interview with participants in which the researcher engaged them in a cartography activity (Braidotti 2011a, b). Participants were sent in advance the written transcript of their interview and the cartography activity was based on them drawing their life trajectory and extracting key themes from their own narratives. The activity's main aim was to actively engage participants in the data validation and interpretation and to give them agency and ownership in the research process.

The fourth stage consisted of a group meeting in which all three participants were involved in a reflecting writing activity on the research process and on their position within it.

Stage five represents my on-going reflective activity consisting of keeping a diary to annotate field-notes, thoughts, emotions and flow of events during the research process in order to promote reflectivity (Bryman 2016). In line with psychoanalytical clinical practice, I decided to have a clinical supervisor, besides my Doctorate academic supervisors, in order to monitor my emotional and personal responses to the research process, with a particular focus on my relationship to participants, following Frosh (2010) and Hollway and Jefferson (2013) *psychosocial* approach.

Table 2 visualizes the main stages of data collection.

3.2 Data Analysis

Written, oral and visual narrative data were analysed within a narrative methodological perspective (Smiths and Watson 2010) focusing on the concept of life as a journey and on its reconstruction through the narrative process. The analysis also focused on transference and countertransference dynamics, as highlighted by Blanchard-Laville and Chaussecourt:

> […] the clinical approach values the subjects' subjective engagement and the effects of this in terms, for instance, of the countertransference effect

5 Becoming a Language Professional in Higher Education …   103

Table 2 Stages of the data collection

Stages	Description	Aims
Stage 1	Short questionnaires and written biographical accounts	To elicit demographic data and to prompt a first stage of self-reflection and of biographical data collection
Stage 2	Unstructured, free associative interviews (about 1 hr each) based on the written account and prompted by a participant's object/photo	To expand on biographical data with a focus on personal instances
Stage 3	Cartography activity	To validate researcher's data analysis and to include participants in the data interpretation
Stage 4	Group meeting and writing activity	To include participants in the research process and to reflect on the research methodology
Stage 5 (ongoing)	Researcher's reflectivity: • Field notes • Diary keeping • Clinical supervision	To promote an on-going self-reflective process in all stages of the research

on the researcher. This subjective engagement provides a useful resource for building important knowledge. The subjectivity of the researcher is completely integrated as part of the investigation: it is 'grist to the mill' for studying psychic phenomena between people. (2012, p. 55)

Table 3 outlines the eight key themes that have been identified in relation to the participants' autobiographical accounts.

Further to the above eight themes, the following three narrative categories were taken into consideration while analysing data (Table 4).

A proforma was conceptualized for each participant, following the model suggested by West and Merrill (2009) and by Hollway and Jefferson (2013), and a participant's portrait in which the researcher annotated demographic data, first impressions, thoughts and interview dynamics immediately after the interviews, paying particular attention to countertransference reflections and to the emergence of unconscious manifestations.

Table 3 Main themes in the narrative accounts

Themes	Description
1. Family	Both in relation to the family of origins, as well as the a newly-created family in a different context from the country of origin
2. Professional journey—relationship to the subject	In terms of education and professional training both in the country of origin and in other contexts and relationship to knowledge
3. Critical incidents	Described by the narrator as events that had an impact on their life and professional choices
4. Significant others	Identified as key important people/mentors that had an impact on the participants' life and personal trajectories
5. Values	Life and professional values identified as important by the participants in their life and professional practices
6. Languages	Described by participants as having an impact on their self-representation
7. Journey	Described by participants both in terms of spatial and symbolic journeys that had an impact on their identity formation and professional life
8. Relationship to students/colleagues/institution	Expressed by participants as crucial in their pedagogical practices and in their professional identity

4 Discussion

The three vignettes below are an account of my reflections based on the thematic analysis of the participants' written, oral and visual narratives, combined with the participants' self-reflections and with my personal notes.

Table 4 Narrative categories

Categories	Description
a. Setting and transference instances	In terms of the physical setting of the interview and the relationship between participant and researcher—unconscious aspects are also taken into consideration
b. Narrative mode	Considered as the narrative voice and other relevant extra-linguistic features
c. Researcher's reflexivity—countertransference instances	Based on field notes, reflective diary and auto/biographical thinking—unconscious projective processes might also be considered

4.1 Participant 1: Teaching as a Second Life

Alia is a Middle East woman aged between 50 and 59. During the interview she seems fully in control of the situation, very confident and outspoken in her answers with a very assertive narrative tone. Her narrative voice is clearly in the first person, with full ownership of her statements. Alia lived in different places throughout her life due to her husband working situation, mainly in the Middle East where she successfully worked in management and moved to UK in her late thirties to follow her daughter's education. When in England, she started to engage with the possibility to become a teacher of Arabic. Her husband seems to have been the major influence in her first steps towards a second career; throughout her narrative he is portrayed as a key figure in her decision-making processes, together with other members of her family. Her husband's death, as described in the interview, represented a critical incident in her personal life and a decisive turning point in her professional trajectory. The object Alia brought to the interview was a photo with her extended family; a photo Alia is describing to me with pride and emotion, highlighting the multicultural and multilingual traits that characterize her family. When asked who were the important others in her professional life, Alia mentions her husband, her mother, her daughter and her step-daughter.

The gender-generational discourse seems to be central in Alia's perception of herself as a language teacher, particularly in her relation to what she defines as being her 'teaching mission', that of deconstructing western stereotypes about Middle Eastern women:

> […] I am a girl from the Middle-East. An Arab girl from the Middle-East. And on its own it carries a rather stigma if you put it on its own a Muslim Arab girl, that in itself is a stigma. And for me I am carrying the flag of a modern, Muslim, Arab Girl who is breaking the norm and doing something to improve the image of that person and this is something very dear to my heart.

Teaching her native language is very clearly a mission for Alia, not only a profession. It is something deeply embedded in her identity as a Middle Eastern woman with "deep, resilient roots". When asked about her initial decision to start teaching, she replied that "it was sheer accident"; an accident that changed completely her life: "I think it's a discovery and I was lucky that teaching found me. I didn't find teaching, the teaching job has found me. […] it was a second life". Alia seems to be very proud of her capacity to have embraced this *second life* and to have subsequently trained as a language professional, stating that "it is still a learning journey".

In the cartography activity Alia drew a tree described as having strong and deep roots, a tree that is ever-green and keeps blossoming, a tree from the Middle East with, at its core, notions of growth, resilience, change and transformation through learning and teaching. When asked about the interviewing stages and about her participation into the study, she said it was "overwhelming ….reading yourself…it's like re-discovering yourself […] the questions make you think…so you suddenly start to look at yourself as an outsider…".

4.2 Participant 2: A Tutor Is for Life

Priya is originally from India; her age is in the range of 40–49. She moved to UK in 2007 to pursue her studies in art. She is a mixed-media artist; in India she graduated in art and languages, studying also literature and linguistics. She speaks many Indian languages and dialects, besides English and Spanish and she states that languages are very important in the formation of her identity. Significant others in her personal and professional life are female figures in her family, who transmitted the passion for reading, studying and for teaching. Priya seems to be very proud in telling her grandmother's story and the fact she was graduated, which was an exceptional reality in India in her generation. There is a strong sense of pride that permeates Priya's narrative of learning and later on of teaching. Priya came to teach languages later in her life, after she moved to UK where she met her husband who, in her words, encouraged her to teach Hindi.

Priya seems to be very proud of her journey into teaching, although many times in her narration she states that "it was a challenging experience". From Priya's narration, it slowly emerges that teaching is invested with deep personal and professional values stemming mainly from the cultural and social position teachers are related to in India, which resonates of sacred and almost religious connotations:

> A. Yes, very, very important I think and it comes from my culture, because in my culture a tutor and your student relationship is almost sacred [...].
> Q. Yes…
> A. It's considered really, really high. So that's why students have loads of respect for teachers, for tutors. [...]

The association of teaching to *something sacred*, something precious not only in religious terms, is a recurrent theme in Priya's narration, highlighting the value she attributes to her professional life and to what it stands for. Priya's narrative is characterized by a developing sense of ownership and pride in her teaching profession, accompanied by an increasing confidence and passion for teaching, which slowly emerges to play a central role in her identity formation: "It's for life. A tutor is for life". And later on in her interview: "[...] So, and then you realise that and when you teach and there are good results it gives you a boost…. [...]… like a sanctuary, yes…."

The photo Priya brought to the interview, is a picture depicting her students in India; a picture at first glance I thought represented her family. Through her narrative it emerges that language teaching means something more than being a "good teacher"; it is invested with personal meanings that resonate her personal transformative story of being a woman from India who moved from the security of her cultural and social background to new territories and new possibilities: "[…] teaching in this country has given me a lot as a person, I think that, and it has also created another entire new identity for me, in a way […]". Moving to UK seems to represent for Priya a critical incident that had important consequences for her professional development, since it is in UK that she met her husband and started embracing the idea of re-training as a language teacher.

Her drawing in the cartography activity was that of a ladder with strong large foundations, moving upwards towards new possibilities. In the drawing Priya used words in different languages, placing her Hindi identity as a woman at the base of the ladder and her migration to UK as a central step into the ladder.

When asked about her participation in the research process, she stated it was an "introspective experience".

4.3 Participant 3: Teaching as a Social Act

Lila is a Latin-American woman aged between 50 and 59. She is a very experienced teacher with more than twenty years' experience in teaching English and Spanish both in UK and in Latin-America. She seems to be quite confident and outspoken during the interview, with a clear sense of ownership of her teaching profession and of pride in her achievements as a language teacher. As for the previous two participants, teaching for her started almost by chance when she was in her early twenties and moved to London following her boyfriend. In London she worked in a volunteering project with Latin-American refugees. She describes this project as being very interesting and rewarding, although emotionally demanding. In her narrative there is a strong sense of identification with the fragility and displacement of refugees.

The identification with students is a recurrent element throughout her narrative, as if by identifying with them she is in a certain way defending herself from her own sense of fragility and displacement. Lila's personal and professional history is characterized, in her narrative, by a sense of struggle, of resilience, of complex migration between countries and by challenging personal circumstances that had a profound impact on her professional choices.

After her first three years in UK, Lila moved back to her original country where she worked in primary schools. Lila decided later to move back to UK. It seems that this period represents a crucial event in her personal life and a turning point also in her professional career, by which she seems to have come to terms with her professional identity as a language teacher:

> […] definitely (assertive tone of voice)….absolutely….in terms of professional identity, that's my identity…because there are many things that I like, I do a little bit, but the identity it's that of a language teacher….

Lila remained to live and work in UK and she is still very committed and engaged with the teaching profession, above all with the social and political implications related to teaching her native language. Teaching Spanish represents for Lila the possibility to keep a close contact with her native language and country. By projecting aspects of her own identity and personal history into her teaching practices, Lila seems to have come to terms with her sense of loss and of displacement that characterized her life experiences of migration:

> I really think it makes a difference when you teach your own language…definitely…yes, because it's about …it's also about your identity…it's everything…it's the stereotypes, the culture, you are part of that in the class, so you are… 'the real thing' (laughs)….

Throughout her interview, Lila refers very often to teaching as a safe place to be, as a position where she can go when feeling down and when unsure of where she belongs to, as if teaching her native language offers her a reconnection with her sense of identity and of belonging, opening new possibilities of self-negotiation: "so yes, in difficult times it gave me sense of, you know, to have a responsibility into my life, a place where to go to…". We can clearly see that teaching for Lila, as for the two previous participants, is not just a professional practice, but it is an expression of her identity, an activity that reconnects her with her cultural and linguistic belonging, with her experience of migration and of coming to terms with an internal process of transformation. In the cartography activity, Lila drew a winding road with many turning points, with images of change, endurance and transformation; she also placed some key figures alongside this journey. Her participation in the research, was referred to as interesting, overwhelming and introspective.

5 Conclusion

Based on the analysis of the data described in previous paragraphs, this study gives evidence of language professional journeys into teaching as characterized by complex personal dynamics of migration and negotiation of identities in new cultural and linguistic landscapes and by a clear sense of personal investment in the teaching profession. As suggested by Block (2003, 2007, 2014), we can see that professional choices, are very clearly intertwined with personal lives and with critical incidents, like in the case of the three participants, in which loss of important people and migration to new countries, determined personal and professional turning points. In the case of the second participant, particularly the migration into a new country with a different cultural and social framework, seemed to represent the major step into a re-negotiation of her professional identity into new paradigms.

The process of *becoming* for all three participants seems to resonate Deleuze and Guattari (1987) and Braidotti (2011a, b, 2014) post-structuralist view of the subject as multiple, *nomadic*, fragmented and in constant re-negotiation of their lifestyles and believes among a variety of options. Data emerging from this study also seem to substantiate Giddens (1991) and Baumann (2000) definition of *ontological insecurity* as characteristic of the post-modern era, in which key central figures seem to represent stable points of reference in the precariousness of *liquid modernity*. This view refers back to psychoanalytical theories and in particular to Winnicott's believes stating that the foundation of human subjectivity and of a sense of security at the basis of human development and learning, are generated by the trust invested in *caretakers* and by the progressive presence of secure and stable *transitional objects*.

We can clearly see from the data collected in this study, that the presence of key secure figures in the participants' personal lives, had a determinant effect on their stories of migration and on their professional choices. In addition, we can see that teaching *the mother-tongue* clearly represents something much more than just teaching a subject; it is an act invested with profound personal meanings, with cultural, social and moral values that are embedded in past experiences. We could consider that teaching the first language, *the mother-tongue*, like in my personal and professional biography, is a sort of Winnicottian *transitional space*, in which participants seem to project aspects of their self-identity, of their personal stories of migration in order to keep a connection with their original physical and symbolic place of belonging and of security, with their *mother-land*. Teaching one own's language seems to be a place for self-negotiation.

The data analysis clearly indicates that language teaching is indeed *identity at work* and that the journey into *becoming a language professional* is characterized by nomadic experiences of transformation (Braidotti 2011a, b) and by a complex interaction between conscious and unconscious fantasies between the margins of the personal and of the professional. The *nomadic* and *psychosocial* approach to language teachers' trajectories, allowed space to non-linear thinking, to be attentive to disruptive elements in the narrative discourse of people's lives, to consider unconscious elements in the unfolding of experiences and to give space to the circular dimension of time in teachers' accounts of themselves. This approach also allowed me to reflect on my own diasporic journey into the uncertainty and non-linearity of becoming a language professional and a researcher. In this way, *nomadology*, besides being an ontological framework of reference, also becomes a methodology, that, particularly through the cartographic activity, empowered participants to visually and physically represent their complex and fragmented personal and professional journeys in a disruptive and unconventional way.

Learning and developing as a language professional, do not seem to follow linear and predicted trajectories into knowledge and professional life, particularly those language journeys linked to nomadic and diasporic experiences of migration and of life in liminal zone of proximity. The narrative accounts co-constructed with participants seem to give voice to scattered and fragmented experiences of transformation in which personal and professional knowledge are intertwined, connected and interrelated in a non-linear *assemblage* of occurrences and circumstances that define the multiplicity of the self. Learning and becoming a language professional seems to be a *rhizomatic*, non-linear journey across boundaries and across time and space.

The findings of this initial study will be further developed and new data will be collected for the completion of the Doctorate in Education and will hopefully contribute to a larger debate on language teachers' identities with the aim to gear training opportunities towards more holistic approaches. The outcomes of this study also indicate that the *psychosocial* methodological framework informed by a psychoanalytical stance towards data collection and analysis, can be considered as a valid investigative tool to provide in-depth data analysis in relation to research on identity. We can also conclude that a consenting engagement in a research project articulated within a psychoanalytical framework, might, like therapy itself, make participants, including the researcher, more aware of their inner conflicts to learning and to professionalization and might potentially initiate transformative journeys, as outlined by Bainbridge and West (2012).

References

Bainbridge, Alan. 2018. *On Becoming an Educational Professional: A Psychosocial Exploration of Developing an Educational Professional Practice*. Basingstoke: Palgrave Macmillan.

Bainbridge, Alan, and Linden West. 2012. *Minding a Gap, Psychoanalysis and Education*. London: Karnac.

Bakhtin, Mikhail. 1981. *The Dialogic Imagination: Four Essays by M. M. Bakhtin*. Austin, TX: University of Texas Press.

Bamberg, Michael. 1997. *Narrative Development*. Mahwah, NJ: Lawrence Erlbaum.

Barkhuizen, Gary. 2017. Investigating Language Tutor Social Inclusion Identities. *The Modern Language Journal* 101 (1): 61–75.

Bauman, Zygmund. 2000. *Liquid Modernity*. Cambridge: Polity Press.

Bion, Wilfred. 1959. *Experiences in Groups*. New York, NY: Basic Books.

Bion, Wilfred. 1962. *Learning from Experience*. London: Heimann.

Blanchard-Lanville, Claudine, and Philippe Chaussecourte. 2012. A Psychoanalytically Oriented Clinical Approach in Education Science'. In *Minding a Gap,*

Psychoanalysis and Education, ed. Alan Bainbridge and Linden West, 51–63. London: Karnac.
Block, David. 2003. *The Social Turn in Second Language Acquisition.* Edinburgh: Edinburgh University Press.
Block, David. 2007. The Rise of Identity in SLA Research, Post Firth and Wagner (1997). *The Modern Language Journal* 91 (5): 863–876.
Block, David. 2014. *Second Language Identities,* 2nd ed. London: Bloomsbury.
Bollas, Christopher. 2009. *The Evocative Object World.* New York: Routledge.
Braidotti, Rosi. 2014. Writing as a Nomadic Subject. *Comparative Critical Studies* 11 (2–3): 163–184.
Braidotti, Rosi. 2011a. *Nomadic Subjects: Embodiment and Sexual Difference in Contemporary Feminist Theory,* 2nd ed. New York: Columbia University Press.
Braidotti, Rosi. 2011b. *Nomadic Theory: The Portable Lisa Braidotti.* New York: Colombia University Press.
Braidotti, Rosi. 2018. A Theoretical Framework for the Critical Posthumanities. *Theory, Culture, Society,* 1–31.
Britzman, Deborah. 2009. *The Very Thought of Education: Psychoanalysis and the Impossible Profession.* Albany, NY: State University of New York Press.
Brockmeier, Jens. 2000. Autobiographical Time. *Narrative Inquiry* 10: 51–73.
Bruner, Jerome. 1986. *Actual Minds, Possible Worlds.* Cambridge, MA: Harvard University Press.
Bruner, Jerome. 1987. Life as Narrative. *Social Research* 54 (1): 11–32.
Bruner, Jerome. 1990. *Acts of Meaning.* Cambridge, MA: Harvard University Press.
Bruner, Jerome. 2001. Self-Making and World-Making. In *Narrative and Identity: Studies in Autobiography, Self and Culture,* ed. J. Brockmeier and D. Carbaugh, 25–37. Amsterdam & Philadelphia: John Benjamins.
Bruner, Jerome. 2002. *Making Stories, Law, Literature, Life.* Cambridge Massachusetts: Harvard University Press.
Bryman, Alan. 2016. *Social Research Methods,* 5th ed. Oxford: Oxford University Press.
Coffey, Simon. 2013. Strangehood and Intercultural Subjectivity. *Language and Intercultural Communication* 13 (3): 266–282.
De Costa, Peter, and Bonny Norton. 2017. Introduction: Identity, Transdisciplinarity, and the Good Language Teacher. *The Modern Language Journal* 101: 3–14.
De Fina, Anna, and Alexandra Georgakopoulou. 2013. *Analyzing Narrative, Discourse and Sociolingusitic Perspective.* Cambridge: Cambridge University Press.

Deleuze, Gilles, and Felix Guattari. 1987. *A Thousand Plateaus: Capitalism and Schizophrenia*. Minneapolis: University of Minnesota Press.
Deleuze, Gilles, and Felix Guattari. 1994. *What Is Philosophy?* New York: Columbia University Press.
Deleuze, Gilles, and Felix Guattari. 2000. *Anti-Oedipus: Capitalism and Schizophrenia*. Minneapolis: University of Minnesota Press.
Formenti, Laura. 2017. *Formazione e Trasformazione. Un Modello Complesso.* Milano: Raffaello Cortina.
Frosh, Stephen. 2010. *Psychoanalysis Outside the Clinic, Interventions in Psychosocial Studies*. London: Palgrave Macmillan.
Giddens, Antony. 1991. *Modernity and Self-Identity: Self and Society in the Late Modern Age*. Stanford, CA: Stanford University Press.
Goodson, Ivor. 2003. *Professional Knowledge, Professional Lives*. Maidenhead: Open University Press.
Hargreaves, Andy. 1994. *Changing Teachers, Changing Times, Teachers' Work and Culture in Postmodern Times*. London: Continuum.
Hargreaves, Andy. 1998. The Emotional Practice of Teaching. *Teaching and Teacher Education* 14 (8): 835–854.
Hargreaves, Andy. 2000. Four Ages of Professionalism and Professional Learning. *Teachers and Teaching: Theory and Practice* 6 (2): 151–182.
Hargreaves, Andy. 2001. The Emotional Geographies of Teaching. *Teachers College Record* 103 (6): 1056–1080.
Hellawell, David. 2006. Inside Out: Analysis of the Insider Outsider Concept as a Heuristic Device to Develop Reflexivity in Students Doing Qualitative Research. *Teaching in Higher Education* 11 (4): 483–494.
Hollway, Wendy, and Tony Jefferson. 2013. *Doing Qualitative Research Differently: A Psychosocial Approach*. London: Sage.
Hunt, Celia. 1989. *Psychoanalytic Aspects of Fieldwork*. University Paper Series on Qualitative Research Methods, 18. Newbury Park, CA: Sage.
Hunt, Celia, and Linden West. 2006. Learning in a Border Country: Using Psychodynamic Ideas in Teaching and Learning. *Studies in the Education of Adults* 38 (2): 160–177.
Klein, Melanie. 1963. *Envy and Gratitude and Other Works, 1946–1963*. New York: Delacorte Press/Seymour Laurence.
Klein, Melanie. 1975. *Love, Guilt and Reparation and Other Works, 1921–1945*. New York: Free Press.
Kristeva, Julia. 1991. *Strangers to Ourselves*. New York: Columbia University Press.
Mansfield, Nick. 2000. *Subjectivity: Theories of the Self from Freud to Haraway*. St Leonards: Allen & Unwin.

Mercer, Sarah, and Achilleas Kostoulas. 2018. *Language Teacher Psychology*. Bristol: Multilingual Matters.

Miller, Elizabeth R., Brian Morgan, and Adriana L. Medina. 2017. Exploring Language Teacher Identity Work as Ethical Formation. *The Modern Language Journal* 101 (1): 91–105.

Morgan, Brian. 2004. Teacher Identity as Pedagogy: Towards a Field-Internal Conceptualization in Bilingual and Second Language Education. *Bilingual Education and Bilingualism* 7 (2 and 3): 172–188.

Morgan, Brian, and Clarke Matthew. 2011. Identity in Second Language Teaching and Learning. In *Handbook of Research in Second Language Teaching and Learning*, ed. Eli Hinkel, 817–836. New York: Routledge.

Norton, Bonny. 1995. Social Identity, Investment, and Language Learning. *TESOL Quarterly* 29 (1): 9–31.

Norton, Bonny. 1997. Language, Identity and the Ownership of English. *TESOL Quarterly* 31 (3): 409–429.

Norton, Bonny. 2000. *Identity and Language Learning: Gender, Ethnicity and Educational Change*. Harlow, UK: Pearson Education/Longman.

Norton, Bonny. 2010. Language and Identity. In *Sociolinguistics and Language Education*, ed. Nancy Hornberger and Sandra Lee McKay, 349–369. Bristol: Multilingual Matters.

Norton, Bonny, and Brian Morgan. 2013. *Poststructuralism: In Encyclopedia of Applied Linguistics*. Oxford: Wiley-Blackwell.

Pavlenko, Aneta. 2001. In the World of the Tradition, I Was Unimagined: Negotiation of Identities in Cross-Cultural Autobiographies. *International Journal of Bilingualism* 5: 317–344.

Pavlenko, Aneta. 2006. *Bilingual Minds*. London: Multilingual Matters.

Pavlenko, Aneta. 2007. Autobiographic Narratives as Data in Applied Linguistics. *Applied Linguistics* 28 (2): 163–188.

Pavlenko, Aneta, and Adrian Blackledge. 2004. *Negotiation of Identities in Multilingual Contexts*. Clevedon: Mulitlingual Matters.

Riessman, Catherine K. 2003. *Narrative Analysis*. London and Newbury Park, CA: Sage.

Salzberger-Wittenberg, Isca, Elsie Osborne, and Gianna Williams. 1983. *The Emotional Experience of Learning and Teaching*. London: Karnac.

Smiths, Sidonie, and Julia Watson. 2010. *Reading Autobiography: A Guide for Interpreting Life Narratives*. Minneapolis: University of Minnesota Press.

Tsui, Amy. 2007. Complexities of Identity Formation: A Narrative Inquiry of an EFL Teacher. *TESOL Quarterly* 41 (4): 657–680.

Varghese, Manka, Brian Morgan, Bill Johnston, and Kimberly Johnson. 2005. Theorizing Language Teacher Identity: Three Perspectives and Beyond. *Journal of Language, Identity and Education* 4: 21–44.

West, Linden, and Barbara Merrill. 2009. *Using Biographical Methods in Social Research*. London: Sage.

Winnicott, Donald W. 1971. *Playing and Reality*. London: Routledge.

Winnicott, Donald W. 1975. *Transitional Objects and Transitional Phenomena: Through Pediatrics to Psycho-Analysis*. New York: Basic Books.

Wolff, Dominik, and Peter De Costa. 2017. Expanding the Language Teacher Identity Landscape: An Investigation of the Emotions and Strategies of a NNEST. *The Modern Language Journal* 101 (1): 76–90.

Worton, Michael. 2009. *Review of Modern Foreign Language Provision in Higher Education in England*. Higher Education Funding Council for England. https://webarchive.nationalarchives.gov.uk/20180319114655/; http://www.hefce.ac.uk/data/year/2009/Review,of,Modern,Foreign,Languages,provision,in,higher,education,in,England/. Accessed 12 November 2018.

Yin, Robert K. 2009. *Case Study Research: Designs and Methods*, 4th ed. London: Sage.

Youell, Biddy. 2006. *The Learning Relationship: Psychoanalytic Thinking in Education*. London: Karnac.

Zheng, Xuan. 2017. Translingual Identity as Pedagogy: International Teaching Assistants of English College Composition Classrooms. *The Modern Language Journal* 101 (S1): 29–44.

6

Modern Language Teacher Identity Formation Through Engagement with Exploratory Practice: The Future Will Tell

Assia Slimani-Rolls

1 Introduction

In this chapter, I explore the formation of the professional identity of a group of modern language teachers (MLTs) as practitioner researchers (PRs) through the narratives that they wrote following their voluntary participation in a longitudinal (2014–2016) Language Practitioner Research (LPR) project that I co-directed (Slimani-Rolls and Kiely 2018). The aim of this project was to enable the participating teachers to implement the principled framework of Exploratory Practice (EP) in their classrooms. EP is a form of practitioner research (PR) designed to empower language teachers and learners to develop a better understanding of their practice (Allwright and Bailey 1991; Allwright 2003; Allwright and Hanks 2009). These narratives were published in Slimani-Rolls and Kiely (2018) as part of the dissemination of the project outcomes.

A. Slimani-Rolls (✉)
Regent's University London, London, UK
e-mail: Rollsa@REGENTS.ac.uk

This chapter contains three sections reporting firstly on the precarious environment in which MLTs in English universities exercise their profession; providing secondly an account of the LPR project which used EP and whose advocates have put it forward as an innovative approach for continuing professional development (CPD) and finally analysing and discussing teacher identity formation from the published narratives that the MLTs wrote to make sense of their EP lived experience.

The narratives are situated in the context of teaching modern languages in higher education (HE) sector which regulates the profession in English universities, and in the institutional context of the LPR project whose aim is to introduce EP to MLTs. The project and the analysis of the teachers' narratives are informed by the sociocultural theory of learning (Lantolf 2000; Lantolf and Poehner 2008; Johnson 2006; Johnson and Golombek 2002) and identity formation within Communities of Practice (CoP) (Wenger 1998).

2 Teaching Modern Languages in HE

In a review on the health of MLs in HE in England, Worton (2009), unveiled the fractured environment in which MLTs operate. This review casts light on the existing tensions between the University ML Departments who 'define themselves as teaching language through content and culture' and the Language Centres and Institution-Wide Language Provision (IWLP) which are 'erroneously perceived as teaching only language skills' (ibid., p. 4). The review reported that MLTs in the Language Centres/IWLP are often depicted as non-academic, non-research active and mere service providers of everyday language learning (ibid., p. 26). In reality, however, they teach languages for specific purposes providing a high level of content on culture and society, business, politics, law, medicine and other disciplines (ibid., p. 29). Indeed, an IWLP annual survey by the University Council of Modern Languages and the Association of University Language Centres (Campbell et al. 2016) confirmed that most of their MLTs hold relevant teaching qualifications at Diploma, Master or Doctorate level and possessed considerable professional experience (2016, p. 2). Nevertheless, IWLP remain, to this day, supported by many hourly paid staff working in vulnerable contract employment with limited or no access to development opportunities which are otherwise accessible to staff in the ML Departments (2016, pp. 11–13).

To the absence of professional recognition, casualisation of work conditions and scarce staff development opportunities, the declining ML student recruitment caused by some language policies, as we shall see below, has impacted on the A-Level student numbers creating major complications that marred the overall MLTs' professional experiences. As expressed by Swarbrick (2002) 'no post-16 pupils, so no graduates, so no teachers' (2002, p. 12) causing the closure of some ML departments (Malpass 2014, p. 2). Hence, less demand for MLs studies means less demand for teachers and this will be evidenced, below, by the working contracts of the LPR project ML participants.

It is undeniable that the expansion of English as a lingua franca has played a role in the apathy that is shown to learning MLs (Lo Bianco and Slaughter 2009; Graddol 2006), but not only this. Policymaking is blamed by many to have hampered seriously the growth of ML learning since compulsory language learning by 14-year-old pupils was abolished under a labour government in 2004 (Lanvers and Coleman 2017). This decision, explains Worton (2009), has effectively sent the message that many students will not study MLs and has, in some way, demotivated universities from planning ahead for the development of MLs as they would normally do for other disciplines. Worton contends that there has been insufficient 'joined up' thinking (ibid., p. 14) across the educational language sector about the role of MLs over the last two decades or so. This long oversight led to weaknesses in teaching and curricula throughout the sector including life-long programmes (Tinsley and Board 2016; Holmes 2014).

Watt (2004) calls for the 'urgent need for properly trained quality language teachers to deliver a coherent modern foreign language syllabus starting in the primary school sector and continuing throughout the education system' (2004, p. 66). Pauwels (2011) calls for innovative language curricula and use of research-informed teaching in HE. In this respect, Macaro et al. (2016), and Macaro (2003) urge MLTs' to engage in research activities. However, a literature review about research engagement in ELT concludes that 'teacher research remains largely a minority activity' (Borg 2010, p. 391). This statement is shown further to be representative of the MLTs research situation (Marsden and Kasprowicz 2017). The reasons for this widespread phenomenon are well documented in Hanks (2017) and Borg (2010, p. 409) among many others. Lack of time, research skills, access to and support for research as well as lack of mutual interest that teachers and university researchers show to each other's work are only some of the reasons that loom large in reports on language teachers' lack of research activity.

Surely the decline in the take up of ML learning, the lack of peer and institutional support and prospects must impact on MLTs' development, and ultimately on how they perceive their professional identity. In this regard, two definitions are relevant to the context of the MLTs of this chapter. The first is from Varghese (2006) who defines teacher professional identities 'in terms of *the influences on teachers* (added emphasis), how individuals see themselves, and how they enact their profession in their settings' (2006, p. 212). The second is from Norton (2000) who defines identity as 'how a person understands his or her relationship to the world, how that relationship is constructed across time and space, and how that person understands *possibilities for the future*' (added emphasis) (2000, p. 5). As we shall find in this chapter, prospects, possibilities for the future, emotions, influences on and agency of teachers are intertwined and play their part in teacher identity formation. Furthermore, Gee (2000–2001) notes that 'identity is connected not to the internal states but to *performances* (added emphasis) in society' (2000–2001, p. 99). However, as seen above, teachers' engagement in research is scarce. Indeed, Tavakoli (2015) argues that the 'segregation between the two communities [of teachers and researchers] is related to the limited mutual engagement, absence of a joint enterprise, and lack of a shared repertoire between them' (2015, p. 37). Hence, the relevance of working as a research project leader with teachers in order to empower them to understand and implement in their classroom EP which is proposed to bridge the gap between teachers and researchers.

3   Exploratory Practice (EP) as a Distinctive Form of Practitioner Research (PR)

EP belongs to the PR family together with reflective practice (Farrell 2007) and action research (Burns 2005) to cite only these because they are known to many readers.[1] EP distinguishes itself by its principled framework that guides teachers and their learners to investigate together puzzles or teaching concerns about their classroom environment. Examples of these puzzles are 'why aren't the students interested in my teaching?' (Slimani-Rolls and Kiely 2014); 'why are particular tasks, and not others, recommended by researchers?' and 'why doesn't group work proceed in the classroom as planned?' Through puzzling, EP embraces 'why' as the deeper rationale for research to inspire teachers to understand their professional context. Puzzle investigations are led by a set of principles that constitute the backbone of EP as explained below.

1. 'Quality of life' for language teachers and learners is the most appropriate central concern for practitioner research in our field.
2. Working primarily to understand the 'quality of life', as it is experienced by language learners and teachers, is more important than, and logically prior to, seeking in any way to improve it.
3. Everybody needs to be involved in the work for understanding.
4. The work needs to serve to bring people together.
5. The work needs to be conducted in a spirit of mutual development.
6. Working for understanding is necessarily a continuous enterprise.
7. Integrating the work for understanding fully into existing curricular practices is a way of minimising the burden and maximising sustainability. (Allwright and Hanks 2009, pp. 149–154)

Principle 1 prioritises the classroom participants' quality of life (QoL) in order to sustain trust, respect, confidence, self-esteem and self-efficacy in ways that bind people in their interactions with one another. Such interactions are held to promote the participants' social and emotional well-being and are more likely to stimulate the advancement of quality of work. In other words, it is the QoL that leads the way to quality of work (Gieve and Miller 2006). Principle 2 recommends that the search for understanding the QoL as lived by the participants should happen prior to any attempt at bringing change because understanding is 'prerequisite to intelligent decision-making' (Allwright and Hanks 2009, p. 152).

Principles 3, 4 and 5 of collegiality and inclusivity for mutual development are about enhancing the 'power of working together' (Miller and Cunha 2009, p. 217). EP puts the emphasis on bringing together all those who can invest in the enterprise of understanding classroom practice, not least the learners who are seen as co-partners. Indeed, Worton (2009) has shown above how detrimental is the separation between staff in the Language Departments and Language Centers/IWLP working in silos rather than together using each other's resources for their mutual development.

Principles 6 and 7 propose that teachers integrate the search for understanding into their everyday teaching activity, so that this search becomes part of teaching and not extra to it. Using their own familiar pedagogic activities as investigative tools or Potentially Exploitable Pedagogic Activities (PEPAs) would enable them to investigate their classrooms sustainably through, for instance, brainstorming sessions, pair/group work and class discussion, interviews, dialogic feedback, posters, surveys and so on. Hence, EP provides opportunities 'to articulate an epistemology of practice that characterises teachers as legitimate knowers' (Johnson and Golombek 2002, p. 3).

EP principles chime with sociocultural theories of learning (Lantolf 2000; Lantolf and Poehner 2008) which highlight that 'what teachers know and how they use their knowledge in classrooms are highly interpretative and contingent on knowledge of *self* (added emphasis), students, curricula and setting' (Johnson and Golombek 2002, p. 2), a knowledge that they have experienced in their own situated practice (Lave and Wenger 1991). Hence, EP calls for teachers to use resources which are constitutive of their professional identity.

Prior to moving to the final section, I present the LPR project methodology which sets itself as a background for this chapter providing an account of how I acted as a project leader, researcher and mentor to guide the teachers' engagement with EP and, as a result, provide them with the opportunity to narrate their EP experiences from which I shall explore the formation of their professional identity.

4 LPR Project Methodology: The Researcher and the Researched

To facilitate teachers' engagement in research, I invited language teachers from my university to join this project. Six volunteered, three ELTs and three MLTs teaching languages for business purposes at undergraduate level. It is important to stress that while the ELTs were employed full-time, the MLTs were on fractional and hourly paid contracts highlighting the precariousness of the ML teaching profession that was mentioned earlier.

I engaged in 'empowering research' (Cameron et al. 1992) given the relationship that I developed between myself as the researcher and the practitioners as researched. The project was carried out '*on, for* and *with*' them (ibid., p. 22). I made the research goals explicit explaining that my role consisted of guiding them to investigate their chosen puzzles. I facilitated the sharing of knowledge among ourselves by creating collaboration, dialogue and trust through enhancing the EP principles of 'collegiality' and 'inclusivity'. Three strategies were used to scaffold everyone's efforts. First, I encouraged the participants to undertake peer observation of teaching (POT) with each other to create conversations about their teaching. Second, I offered one-to-one mentoring sessions to each of the practitioners in response to their request for help with their investigations. These sessions helped to demystify research and empower them to focus on reflecting on their practice as they live it daily. As one of the participants contends [d]iscussions with the internal lead became deeper as trust emerged and our relationship evolved to a point where I felt more of an insider in the process' (Banister 2018, p. 147) Finally, to heighten further the 'open, interactive and dialogic' methodology (ibid., p. 23), we agreed to meet, every six weeks, to express understandings and misunderstandings discussed during the POT, and those that happened during the mentoring sessions that the teachers felt were valuable to bring to the forum. Hence, opportunities for partnerships and collaborations developed allowing the group members to gel and grow into a community created over time by the sustained pursuit of a joint enterprise, mutual engagement and shared repertoire (Wenger 1998). This collegiality was demonstrated by one of the ELTs who explained that 'the broader impact of this project on me as a teacher is that I have gained a sense of raised professional esteem and have formed stronger collegial bonds with the group members. In fact, working together [...] allowed me to see that the puzzles we each brought to the project were actually issues which had been important to each of us as teachers. However, what took our discussions beyond the usual staffroom exchanges [...] was having experienced research-practitioners leading explorations into the literature and the students' perspectives' (Houghton 2018, p. 164). Learning collectively how to use EP, the teachers have ensured a route for their socialisation through the appropriation of relevant academics' behaviours and discourse conventions in their pursuit of sharing my enterprise of understanding how EP works in the classroom. In Gee's words, they gained access to the 'ways of thinking, acting and believing' (2005, p. 7) allowing their identity as PRs to be enacted and also ascribed to the learners with whom they negotiated their puzzle elucidation.

The practitioners sustained their efforts throughout 2014–2016 fostering for themselves personal, social and professional developments (Slimani-Rolls and Kiely 2018) that space constraints prevent us from discussing here. Witnessing the benefits that they derived, I invited them to write narratives about their lived experiences (2016–2017) in order for them to deepen their sense making (Johnson and Golombek 2011) of EP and share their insights given the scarcity of PR activities. These narratives were published in Slimani-Rolls and Kiely (2018) and so ethical considerations were addressed and consent forms signed. As such, the MLTs are referred to, by their names, as authors, when quoting from their narratives which constitute the topic of the next and final section of this chapter.

5   Modern Language Teachers' Narratives

Language teacher identity represents an emerging field. The interpretive social paradigms in theories of sociocultural learning mentioned earlier in reference to EP 'have an interest in identity, agency, discourse, diversity, social interaction, local context and lived experience' (Miller 2009, p. 172). This section aims to bring insights from identity theory (Wenger 1998) and identity definitions (Norton 2000; Varghese 2006), as said earlier, to explain the formation of MLTs' professional identity in their attempts to develop as PRs.

Narratives are research methods used to search for teacher identity arguing that their strength lies in that they capture experiences as they happen 'in the midst' of the complexity of classroom life (Clandinin and Connelly 2000, p. 63). As such, narratives have the potential to bring 'new meaning and significance to the work of teachers within their own professional landscapes' (Johnson and Golombek 2006, p. 3). They are used here as a lens to explore the MLTs' professional identity formation during their EP journey.

Wenger (1998) proposes a dual process of 'identification' and 'negotiability of meaning' to understand the complex processes of identity formation. Identification is defined as the investment of the self in building modes of belonging which become constitutive of our identities. Wenger explains that while engaging in practice allows individuals to find out how they can participate in activities and develop the competences that are required, relating to others gives individuals a sense of who they are. From this perspective, identification is participative, relational and experiential. It is also reificative when individuals identify or are being identified to socially organised groups or roles. As to the negotiability of meaning, it determines the extent to which individuals are competent and able to commit to shape the meaning in which they are invested. This notion is essential to identity formation because meanings are achieved in the process of participation and they contribute to the definitions of events, actions, symbols, concepts, ideas which are important within the social configuration to which one is aiming to belong. Another notion that is relevant to this chapter is the concept of *trajectories*. Wenger explains that identity in practice develops out of interactions between participation and reification leading him to consider that identity 'is not an object, but a constant becoming […], as we go through a succession of forms of participation, our identities form trajectories [which have] a coherence through time that connects the past, the present and the future' (1998, pp. 153–154).

Further to Wenger, Zembylas (2003) asserts emotions in teacher identity construction as primarily 'affective and is dependent upon power and agency, i.e., power is understood as forming the identity and providing the very condition of its trajectory' (2003, p. 213). Indeed, both power relations and agency played part in motivating the MLTs' participation in the LPR project. The institutional demands of engaging in research and scholarship were instrumental in having the project funded which, as a result, stimulated the teachers' participation. Examining a set of articles on recognising and realising teachers' professional agency, Edwards (2015) was surprised not to find the dialectic of person and practice mentioned in this literature given the teachers' sensitivity to the environments in which they worked and how these contributed to how they were or were not able to exhibit agency. She explained that 'paying attention to the demands that teachers recognise and respond to in the dialectic of person and practice may produce further useful insights' (2015, p. 781) as we shall see later.

5.1 The ML Participants

The three MLTs teach Italian, French and Spanish. The teachers of French and Spanish are experienced teachers employed on fractional contracts. They have worked over fifteen years in the institution where the EP project took place. They contributed, while on their EP journey, to creating new language programmes in response to the institutional demand of widening language tuition across the campus to fight against the decline of ML learning. The situation of the teacher of Italian is different. She is an experienced teacher but is an hourly paid visiting lecturer who studies for a Ph.D. and teaches undergraduate students in another university as well as privately in an international company. Although this chapter is about MLTs, there will be, when relevant, references to the ELTs as all six practitioners worked collaboratively throughout the EP enterprise.

5.2 Methodology

It is worthwhile to remind the reader that, except for the Italian teacher, the participants are neophyte researchers and writers. To facilitate therefore the re-storying of their narratives, I invited them to brainstorm, as a group, the major stages that they underwent to elucidate their puzzles during 2014–2016. This strategy responded also to the book reviewers who requested a similar format across the six narratives. Several headings emerged under which the teachers' accounts were constructed: (1) introduction; (2) search for understanding, (a) puzzle identification, (b) rationale for the chosen investigative method(s), (c) data collection, (d) data analysis; (3) understanding and discussion; (4) reflection into the EP processes and the way forward. A word limit was estimated by the group for each of these sections which were debated in terms of their content. For instance, a theme that was brought up was the identity perspectives whereby the reflection about the self as teacher and as researcher has emerged as a logical topic to raise together with teachers' beliefs and perceptions of research; compatibility of teaching and research; professional trajectory regarding the role of research in their professional life; the role of writing and publication including the researcher role: being a novice, or not being novice and being treated like one. it is important here to emphasise that the suggestion of writing the narratives came up at the end of the project when I realised that the teachers had embraced the EP enterprise. Indeed, one the participants asserted that 'EP offered tangible benefits and enhanced understanding, sustaining my interest to the degree that I worried about having a 'research hole' in my professional life as the project's end neared (Banister 2018, p. 149). Extending the project to enable the writing up of the narratives was, on the one hand, welcomed by the participants but, on the other hand, some felt apprehensive about what to write about. In this sense the participants needed to be supported and their memory jogged so they could confidently engage with the new experience of writing.

Apart from this editorial directive which led to the participants and project leader to discuss together the layout of the narratives, the participants re-storied their experiences freely. I focussed mostly on ensuring clarity of language and quest for substantiating frequent claims such as 'I was so impressed by the students' level of contributions' and 'the discussion went very well'. The aim was to encourage them to see their narrative as embedded within the sociocultural and sociohistorical contexts of what constitutes an impressive contribution and a successful discussion and so on. It took between 9 and 11 months for the narratives to be constructed

(2016–2017) as no time abatement was provided for the teachers to compose their narratives.

5.3 Data Analysis

The data analysis was conducted as follows: first, I read the narratives while attempting to identify commonalities and idiosyncrasies in the teachers' reactions to the implementation of the EP principles. Then, I identified the EP principles which the MLTs found particularly challenging and traced how they engaged in the practice through developing effective PEPAs and involving the students as partners allowing them to identify themselves and be identified by others as PRs. Early in this process, I opted to report in detail on the analysis of the narrative of one ML teacher, Michelle Rawson (2018) who caught my attention when, considering her professional identity. She concluded that 'I regard myself more as a teacher than a researcher' (p. 102). Strikingly, two of the ELT teachers manifested their identity differently. One explained that '[d]isseminating my research helped me to identify a legitimate aspect to my professional identity. Presenting and publishing consolidate the notion of a researcher dimension to identity in a way which personally I would find hard to achieve through reflective practice alone' (Banister 2018, p. 149). The other asserted that 'the project enabled me to reshape and establish my new identity of 'research practitioner' thus boosting my teacher self-efficacy beliefs' (Goral 2018, p. 182). Hence, it was important to establish the circumstances which incited the ML teacher to make such a statement. Space constraints preclude detailed analyses of all three ML narratives. However, quotes from the two other MLTs' and the ELTs' narratives are provided when helpful to the data analysis.

5.4 Teachers' Early Encounter with Exploratory Practice (EP)

The following excerpt depicts, one of the ELTs, Marianna Goral (2018) reporting on her early encounter with EP. It is typical of the six participants' reactions in the initial stages of their participative identification demonstrating the shock that engaging with EP had initially had on the reconstruction of their teacher identity.

> I was so concerned about finding the 'right puzzle': Would my puzzle be worth researching and would there be enough substance to it? Would this research truly make a difference in my own classroom pedagogy and would the notion of simply 'understanding' something rather than going down the route of problem-solving satisfy my learners and me? How would my learners cope with research being implemented in their class time? Furthermore, I was not sure if I would be able to marry my 'day job' and the LTR Project: Would I be able to balance two years of research and the demands that come with it, along with my existing workload and other commitments? Would I be able to strike a healthy balance and avoid burn out? EP professes that implementation of … (PEPAs) allows for research to take place at the same time as teaching but what about all my other work commitments, would I be able to align these with my research? (2018, p. 170)

Similarly, to Marianna, the participants felt vulnerable and destabilised, at first, in their attempts to work with EP. In this regard, Zembylas (2003) explains that teacher identity 'requires the connection of emotions with self-knowledge' (2003, p. 213). Indeed, the mentoring sessions indicated that their confidence was shaken. However, while Zembylas contends that vulnerability can have a double impact causing emotional turmoil and isolation, he recognises that it can also lead to transformation once teachers achieve a better understanding of their surroundings and make appropriate adjustments to suit the new circumstances. Teacher emotions can be 'sites for transformation or resistance' and play a major part in their identity and agency (Zembylas 2005, p. 214). In this case, the community of practice set up by the teachers and the project leaders has protected them from isolation and vulnerability and has, as we see later, provided them with the means of reifying their identity.

The MLTs did not, however, encounter difficulties with all the EP principles. The teacher of French, Michelle Rawson (2018) reported that:

> Not surprisingly this [EP] commitment to a collegial approach was a key motivation for my joining … the project. (2018, p. 92)

While the teacher of Spanish, Esther Lecumberri (2018) illustrated more amply that:

> The focus on understanding and improving the quality of life of both learners and teachers … encouraged me to participate … Promoting collegiality by bringing teachers together was another reason to embrace the project, which afforded opportunities to collaborate with colleagues, and benefit from a mentor's guidance to develop my research skills. (2018, p. 106)

Indeed, Wenger contends that 'surviving together is a viable enterprise […] in the quest for a viable identity' (1998, p. 6) that is of value to the institution and to higher education in general. Their agency in understanding EP and developing rapport with each other and with myself as their mentor have supported them in their identity reconstruction as PRs.

Although discussed at the outset of the project, learner inclusivity and use of PEPAs seemed to be at odds with the participants' teaching approaches. Michelle explained:

> Although I have always involved my students in class discussion, I initially had some difficulty in seeing them as co-partners … due to the way I myself had been taught to regard the teacher as dispenser of knowledge and students as recipients. (2018, p. 93)

In other words, there is a limit to the learner's integration in the classroom processes beyond the discussions and group work as routinely practiced. Furthermore, the ELT teacher, Chris Banister (2018), asserted frankly, I doubted whether my learners would be sufficiently motivated to engage deeply with classroom research (2018, p. 147). Hence, both principles of PEPAs as research tools and learners as partners have challenged epistemologically the teachers and it took them well over a year before they managed to rethink and implement these two EP principles. As indicated earlier, the mentoring sessions and group discussions played an important role in instilling confidence and trust in the teachers to rethink their teaching routine. The CoP in which they evolved fuelled their sense of self-esteem and self-efficacy, maintained their willingness to research themselves and their surroundings and contributed to fine tuning their efforts while venturing into unfamiliar territories. Michelle became gradually more adventurous looking at the classroom context and the students through a different lens noting that:

> A slightly different focus was used in each phase of the project … to explore the student's views and 'dig' deeper into their thoughts and feelings as well as to review and refine my search for understanding as it evolves from one phase to the next… I used a group discussion when I first shared my puzzle with the students. Did they think that the use of Italian had a negative impact on learning French? This was something I had not done before asking students about their views on an aspect of their learning. I normally expect students to follow the plan or the agenda I have set … I knew I would be 'less in control' of the direction the conversation was going to take. (2018, pp. 93–94)

After all, Michelle used the same old technique of group discussion but, this time, she no longer saw its purpose limited to practising only curricular activities. She used discussion as a research instrument to vehicle a serious conversation for the students to express real-life concerns, feelings and thoughts that mattered to them and their peers. Why do they use their mother tongue rather than practice the target language is a serious question for the teacher's sense of professional identity? She exercised her agency to find ways of investigating this frustrating issue together with the students in ways that resonate with them as mature individuals 'capable of taking learning seriously' (Allwright and Hanks 2009, p. 15).

> Overall, I felt that they were happy, even proud to be part of the 'puzzle'. A couple of them stated that they really enjoyed being treated as mature and responsible learners and not 'primary school' students. They claimed that it was refreshing to be able to freely express their views; to find that their opinions mattered, and feel trusted and feel taken seriously … With hindsight, I felt that this discussion was vital in opening up a channel of communication to talk and to see their contribution valued. (2018, p. 94)

Emotions are central to teaching (Hargreaves 1998; Zembylas 2003). In this regard, the students' emotional reactions to Michelle's adjusted practice have enhanced her sense of identity as a professional as she facilitated meaningful exchanges between herself and the students and between the students themselves. Emotional experiences as well as relationships change when teachers get to know their students better. Not only has Michelle risen to the challenge of viewing PEPAs as research tools and learners as co-partners, she gained also, as a result, a renewed interest in and respect for the students' views. She has actually 'lived' the understanding that 'teaching is, above all, about relationships and that building good rapport with students is vital' (2018, p. 94). According to Palmer (1998), Michelle demonstrated 'capacity for connectedness' (p. 13) by reconfiguring a classroom discussion into a novel research instrument to reify her professional identity.

While Michelle's puzzle was about the students' use of their mother tongue, Esther's was about why they employed their mobile phones in disruptive ways. She could simply apply the ban that the university had put on the use of these devices but she 'chose to care' (O'Connor 2008; Hargreaves 1998) because she knows that banning their use would deprive them from employing them usefully as cameras, dictionaries, information providers and recorders. Instead, Esther opted for the inclusive approach to negotiate a more accommodating use of these devices rather than impose a unilateral ban; thus, demonstrating the idea that teachers' emotions guide the formation of their identities (Nias 1986; Zembylas 2003).

With the students' permission, Esther created a PEPA by videoing one of her lessons to demonstrate the distraction that these mobile phones can cause. Encouraged by the students' recognition that they can be divisive, Esther developed a survey to address the likely impact of these devices on the students' concentration and participation, the extent of the participants' responsibility to keep them at bay and the value of the University policy. Esther explains below why she felt that she was successful in her endeavour.

> I believe that the decision to allow mobile phones in class should arise from mutual understanding and agreement, not from a frustration position of powerlessness and uncertainty about who should make decisions. Open

exploration in the classroom of the contexts of, reasons for, and consequences of phone uses is a strategy that can influence the overall atmosphere in the classroom in a positive way and avoid the negative impact of controlling and banning the use of mobile phones. (2018, p. 114)

Zembylas (2003) contends that the connection between teacher identity and emotions is the result of agency and is determined by the individuals to reflect on their professional actions (2003, pp. 224–225). The experiences that both MLTs have lived with their students cast light on the confidence and professionalism with which they have embraced their CPD and evolved their practice. Such development is more likely to fit in with their professional identity as they remained at the heart of this process-oriented enterprise working on their own agenda rather than a pre-established schedule.

6 Discussion

Following Wenger's theory of identity (1998), the MLTs' narratives showed that they engaged with two important sources of identity formation: they recognised that they possess the competence that their community values, and that their professional identity has been reified beyond their legitimate peripheral participation. Indeed, they wrote about their feelings of excitement and exhilaration following their contribution in institutional, national and international events whereby they have been given legitimacy of access to practice. In Wenger's views, 'identity in practice is a layering of events of participation and reification by which our experience and its social interpretation inform each other' (1998, p. 151).

Among the many actions and events that have reified their identity as professionals was the LPR project recognition as 'an example of excellent practice in recent British educational research/scholarship' by the organising committee of the Annual Conference of the British Educational Research Association (BERA, Leeds University, 2016) in which some of the participants have contributed. Subsequently, BERA invited the practitioners to represent them at the Annual Conference of the American Educational Research Association (AERA, Texas, 2017). Although for funding reasons, they could not all participate in the BERA/AERA events, the invitation itself gave a tremendous boost to their sense of professional identity. It is, indeed, worth mentioning here that it was never the aim of the project to encourage the practitioners to disseminate externally as this was well beyond the project leaders' initial expectations. One realises only too well the challenges that making one's work public could present. I could not, however, reject the practitioners' request for support with the development of potential conference abstracts. Doubts on their forthcoming achievements would only nullify the work that I did as their mentor to make accessible their search for understanding. I could only open up yet another facet for their development. Their perseverance in voluntarily disseminating their work demonstrates commitment to their professional growth and highlight their dormant capabilities.

The three MLTs agreed that the EP experience was, in their own words, '*inspiring*', '*exhilarating*', '*rewarding*' and '*empowering*'. While they commented amply on the gains that they derived from their EP experience, they also reported on the challenges that they have confronted including those of disseminating their work. Michelle argued that 'there is always a difficult balance between the institutional requirements of the job and the new vision of EP which is not always facilitated by the working conditions' (2018, p. 102). Esther recognised that 'time and dedication are required' (2018, p. 115). Anna confirmed also the pressure of time but mostly focussed on analysing the principles and how she implemented in her practice.

On balance, Michelle focussed on 'the attention already need[ed] to be given to other activities as a teacher (for instance, developing modules to be taught across the University to encourage more students to learn foreign languages, and organising cultural events)' (2018, p. 102). Indeed, Michelle is reminding us that the efforts of elucidating teaching puzzles could appear rather demanding against the decline in the interest that characterises ML studies. 'EP clearly has value, but the teaching environment may not always facilitate it' and she sees herself 'more of a teacher than a researcher' (p. 102). Yet, further along the line, she adds 'I found presenting the understandings of my puzzle […] an enriching and enlightening experience. Although it was stressful, it was also exhilarating as the feedback […] from the audience was very encouraging' (p. 102).

On the one hand, Michelle's experiences are competing in the midst of the past, where language programmes had to be created to bring new students, the present where the EP and institutional needs have to be balanced and the future which depends on what can currently be done to improve it. Michelle's identity is visibly impacted upon by the past and the present which are influencing the way she perceives the future. On the other hand, Esther ventured into the future remarking that the teaching concerns that she noticed during her endeavours '*could* (added emphasis) become potential puzzles to explore in the future' (2018, p. 116). Being a developing researcher with varied prospects of working in HE, Anna seemed to have decidedly adopted the mentor's suggestion that 'the next stage of the project would focus on involving actively the learners in phrasing and investigating their own puzzles' (2018, p. 131). Indeed, Anna is taking in her stride the idea that there will be a next phase to the project which consists of working with the learners themselves. It is extremely relevant to refer here to Wenger (1998) who explains that as trajectories '[…] our identities incorporate the past and the future in the very process of negotiating the present' (1998, p. 155).

Varghese's (2006) definition of identity in terms of *the influences on teachers*, referred to earlier on, is compatible with the MLTs' accounts under discussion. Embodied in EP, the influences of others through the LPR project have been invaluable. As indicated earlier, teachers relate to students and identities are relational. EP has opened up options that are taken forward in different ways—as teachers, as researchers/academics—but always within an expanded sense of identity although the influences are not limited only to those exerted by EP and the project set-up. The precarious professional situation of MLTs in HE is omnipresent and continues to overshadow their professional lives.

Identity is also about 'how a person understands possibilities for the future' (Norton 2000, p. 5). The efforts of implementing EP might look heavy against the backdrop of the declining interest in MLs. However, it depends on how the future manifests itself through the improvements to the ML situation that HE institutions, the British Council, British Academy, business associations and others are trying to bring. More recently, a framework proposal from the All-Party Parliamentary Group on Modern languages has put forward a National Recovery Programme 'of strategic objectives [to be] implemented by the professionals and practitioners [...] to achieve a step change in the UK's languages capability' (2019, March 4). It depends, therefore, on what the future brings. If the student recruitment improves then the EP framework would be instrumental in helping a strong return of ML studies across the educational sector and the construction of a better quality of life for teachers and students alike, as stated earlier.

7 Conclusion

EP values have been embraced and its benefits reaped. All the participating teachers noted the way the project gave them a confidence and sense of personal growth, while in turn enabled exploration, optimism and innovation. Marianna's illustrative excerpt clearly indicated that identities are constructed in the midst of 'tension between our investment in the various forms of belonging and our ability to negotiate the meanings that matter in those contexts' (Wenger 1998, p. 188). Engaging in practice, as the participating MLTs did, is a compelling form of identification because it involved investing themselves in what they did and in the relationships that they developed.

Times have changed since the late 1980s and early 1990s in which Block (2000) reported as having failed to support ML teachers in Language Centres to undertake action research projects. Back then, research and scholarship were not in teachers' professional contracts, nor were teachers mentored to engage with research. Currently, the future looks promising. Much work is being developed by various professional bodies and institutions to improve ML uptake and MLTs professional development. An example of this is the IATEFL Research Special Interest Group (Smith et al. 2016) which strives to devise accessible ways for language teachers to make their work public in manageable ways.

Note

1. For a deeper discussion on similarities, differences and distinctive philosophical underpinnings between members of the PR family, see Hanks (2017, pp. 23–31).

References

All-Party Parliamentary Group on Modern Languages National Recovery Programme for Languages. http://bit.ly/LanguagesRecoveryProgramme2019. Accessed 18 March 2019.

Allwright, Dick. 2003. A Brief Guide to Exploratory Practice: Rethinking Practitioners Research in Language Teaching. *Language Teaching Research* 7 (2): 109–111.

Allwright, Dick, and Kathleen M. Bailey. 1991. *Focus on the Language Classroom: An Introduction to Classroom Research for Language Teachers.* Cambridge and New York: Cambridge University Press.

Allwright, Dick, and Judith Hanks. 2009. *The Developing Language Learner: An Introduction to Exploratory Practice.* Basingstoke: Palgrave Macmillan.

Banister, Chris. 2018. Rebuilding Practitioner Self-Efficacy Through Learner Feedback. In *Exploratory Practice for Continuing Professional Development: An Innovative Approach for Language Teachers*, Assia Slimani-Rolls and Richard Kiely, 135–151. London: Palgrave Macmillan.

Block, David. 2000. Revisiting the Gap Between SLA Researchers and Language Teachers. *Links & Letters* 7: 129–143.

Borg, Simon. 2010. Language Teacher Research Engagement. *Language Teaching* 43 (4): 391–429.

Burns, Anne. 2005. Action Research: An Evolving Paradigm? *Language Teaching* 38: 57–74.

Cameron, Deborah, Elizabeth Frazer, Penelope Harvey, Ben Rampton, and Kay Richardson. 1992. *Researching Language: Issues of Power and Method.* London: Routledge.

Campbell, Caroline, Chiara Cirillo, Mark Critchley. 2016. UCML-AULC Survey of Institution-Wide Language Provision in Universities in the UK (2015–2016). Accessed 12 November 2018. http://www.ucl.ac.uk/languages-education/he-languages.

Clandinin, D. Jean, and F. Michael Connelly. 2000. Teachers' Professional Knowledge Landscapes: Secrete, Sacred, and Cover Stories. In *Teachers' Professional Knowledge Landscapes*, ed. F. Michael Connelly and D. Jean Clandinin, 1–15. New York: Teachers College Press.

Edwards, Anne. 2015. Recognising and Realising Teachers' Professional Agency. *Teachers and Teaching* 21 (6): 779–784.

Farrell, Thomas S. C. 2007. *Reflective Language Teaching: From Research to Practice.* London: Continuum.

Gee, James Paul. 2000–2001. Identity as an Analytic Lens for Research in Education. *Review of Research in Education* 25: 99–125.

Gee, James Paul. 2005. *An Introduction to Discourse Analysis: Theory and Method.* New York: Routledge.

Gieve, Simon, and Ines K. Miller. 2006. *Understanding the Language Classroom.* Basingstoke: Palgrave Macmillan.

Goral, Mariana. 2018. Insight into Learner Generated Materials. In *Exploratory Practice for Continuing Professional Development: An Innovative Approach for Language Teachers*, ed. Assia Slimani-Rolls and Kiely Richard, 169–183. London: Palgrave Macmillan.

Graddol, David. 2006. *English Next.* London: British Council.

Hanks, Judith. 2017. *Exploratory Practice in Language Teaching: Puzzling About Principles and Practices.* London: Palgrave Macmillan.

Hargreaves, Andy. 1998. The Emotional Practice of Teaching. *Teaching and Teacher Education* 14 (8): 835–854.

Holmes, Bernardette. 2014. *Born Global.* British Academy. https://www.thebritishacademy.ac.uk/born-global. Accessed October 2018.

Houghton, John. 2018. Gaining Deeper Understanding of Teaching Speaking Skills from Collaborative Inquiry. In *Exploratory Practice for Continuing Professional Development: An Innovative Approach for Language Teachers*, ed. Assia Slimani-Rolls and Kiely Richard. London: Palgrave Macmillan.

Johnson, Karen E. 2006. The Sociocultural Turn and Its Challenges for Second Language Teacher Education. *TESOL Quarterly* 40 (1): 235–257.

Johnson, Karen E., and Paula R. Golombek. 2011. The Transformative Power of Narrative in Second Language Teacher Education. *TESOL Quarterly* 45 (3): 486–509.

Johnson, Karen E., and Paula R. Golombek. 2002. *Teachers' Narrative Inquiry as Professional Development.* Cambridge: Cambridge University Press.

Lantolf, James P. 2000. *Sociocultural Theory and Second Language Learning.* Oxford: Oxford University Press.

Lantolf, James P., and Matthew E. Poehner. 2008. *Sociocultural Theory and the Teaching of Second Languages*. London: Equinox.

Lanvers, Ursula, and James A. Coleman. 2017. The UK Language Learning Crisis in the Public Media: A Critical Analysis. *Language Learning Journal* 45 (1): 3–25. https://doi.org/10.1080/09571736.2013.830639.

Lave, Jean, and Etienne Wenger. 1991. *Situated Learning: Legitimate Peripheral Participation*. Cambridge, UK: Cambridge University Press.

Lecumberri, Esther. 2018. Mobile Phones in My Language Classroom: A Cause for Concern or a Source of Communication. In *Exploratory Practice for Continuing Professional Development: An Innovative Approach for Language Teachers*, ed. Assia Slimani-Rolls and Richard Kiely, 105–117. London: Palgrave Macmillan.

Lo Bianco, Joseph, and Yvette Slaughter. 2009. *Australian Education Review: Second Language Australian Schooling*. Camberwell: ACER Australian Council for Educational Research.

Macaro, Ernesto. 2003. Second Language Teachers as Second Language Researchers. *The Language Learning Journal* 27 (1): 43–51.

Macaro, Ernesto, Suzanne Graham, and Robert Woore. 2016. *Improving Language Foreign Language Teaching: Towards a Research-Based Curriculum and Pedagogy*. Abingdon: Routledge.

Marsden, Emma, and Rowena Kasprowicz. 2017. Foreign Language Educators' Exposure to Research: Reported Experiences, Exposure Via Citations, and a Proposal for Action. *The Modern Language Journal* 17: 1–30. https://doi.org/10.1111/modl.12426.

Miller, Jennifer. 2009. Teacher Identity. In *The Cambridge Guide to Second Language Teacher Education*, ed. Anne Burns and Jack Richards, 172–181. Cambridge: Cambridge University Press.

Miller, Ines K., & I.A. Cunha Maria. 2009. The 'Web of Life of the Rio de Janeiro Exploratory Practice Group. In *The Developing Language Learner: An Introduction to Exploratory Practice*, ed. Dick Allwright and Judith Hanks, 216–234. Basingstoke: Palgrave Macmillan.

Malpass, Debra. 2014. The Decline in Uptake of a-Level Modern Foreign Languages: Literature Review: A Review of Modern Foreign Languages at A Level—A* Grade and Low Take Up. Published by the Joint Council for qualifications. Available from http://www.jcq.org.uk/media-centre/news-releases/mfl-review-press-notice. Accessed 20 March 2019.

Nias, Jennifer. 1986. *Teacher Socialisation: The Individual in the System*. Waurn Ponds, VIC: Deakin University Press.

Norton, Bonny. 2000. *Identity and Language Learning: Gender, Ethnicity and Educational Change*. London: Longman.

O'Connor, Kate E. 2008. "You Choose to Care": Teachers, Emotions and Professional Identities. *Teaching and Teacher Education: An International Journal of Research and Studies* 2 (1): 117–126.

Palmer, Parker J. 1998. *The Courage to Teach*. San Francisco: Jossey-Bass.

Pauwels, Anne. 2011. Future Directions for the Learning of Languages in Universities: Challenges and Opportunities. *Language Learning Journal* 39 (2): 247–257.

Rawson, Michelle. 2018. Using the Mother Tongue in the Language Classroom. In *Exploratory Practice for Continuing Professional Development: An Innovative Approach for Language Teachers*, ed. Assia Slimani-Rolls and Richard Kiely, 91–103. London: Palgrave Macmillan.

Slimani-Rolls, Assia, and Richard Kiely. 2014. 'We Are the Change We Seek': Developing Teachers' Understanding of Their Classroom Practice. *Innovations in Education and Teaching International* 51 (4): 425–435.

Slimani-Rolls, Assia, and Richard Kiely. 2018. *Exploratory Practice for Continuing Professional Development: An Innovative Approach for Language Teachers*. London: Palgrave Macmillan.

Smith, Richard, Paula Rebolledo, Deborah Bullock, Andrea Robles López. 2016. '*By* Teachers *for* Teachers': Innovative, Teacher-Friendly Publishing of Practitioner Research. *English Language Teacher Education and Development (ELTED) Journal* 20: 116–125.

Swarbrick, Ann. 2002. *Teaching Modern Foreign Languages in Secondary Schools: A Reader*. Abingdon: Routledge.

Tinsley, Teresa, and Kathryn Board. 2016. *Language Trends 2015/16: The State of Language Learning in Primary and Secondary Schools in England*. London, Berkshire: British Council, Education Development Trust.

Tavakoli, Parvaneh. 2015. Connecting Research and Practice in TESOL: A Community of Practice Perspective. *RELC Journal* 46 (1): 37–52.

Varghese, Manka. 2006. Bilingual Teachers-in-the-Making in Urbantown. *Journal of Multilingual and Multicultural Development* 27 (3): 211–224.

Watts, Catherine. 2004. Some Reasons for the Decline in Numbers of MFL Students at Degree Level. *Language Learning Journal* 29: 59–67.

Wenger, Etienne. 1998. *Communities of Practice: Learning, Meaning and Identity*. Cambridge: Cambridge University Press.

Worton, Michael. 2009. Review of the Health of Modern Foreign Languages (MFL) in English Higher Education. http://www.hefce.ac.uk/media/hefce1/pubs/hefce/2009/0941/09_41.pdf. Accessed 24 September 2018.

Zembylas, Michalinos. 2003. Interrogating 'Teacher Identity': Emotion, Resistance, and Self-Formation. *Educational Theory* 53: 107–127. https://doi.org/10.1111/j.1741-5446.2003.00107.x.

Zembylas, Michalinos. 2005. Emotions and Teacher Identity: A Poststructural Perspective. *Teacher and Teaching: Theory and Practice* 9: 214–238. https://doi.org/10.1080/13540600309378.

7

How a Community of Practice Shapes a Modern Foreign Language Teacher's Views of Herself as a Teacher over Time and Space: A Biographical Case Study

Christina Richardson

1 Introduction

Much recent literature on language teaching and learning has foregrounded the importance of understanding identity in promoting effective language learning (Norton and Toohey 2011). Similarly, within teacher education, the value of identity research has been acknowledged not only in the process of teacher-learning and development (Beauchamp and Thomas 2009; Norton 2017; Pennington and Richards 2016; Varghese et al. 2005) but also increasingly in the retention of teachers in the profession (Morrison 2013). In order to develop professionally, in the sense of taking responsibility for their own professional development, it is increasingly recognised that teachers need to develop agency (Toom et al. 2015) to navigate the school Modern Foreign Language (MFL) subject domain, a site of seemingly unresolvable debates on issues that concern teachers such as the role of grammar and the use of the target language (Swarbrick

C. Richardson (✉)
King's College London, London, UK
e-mail: christina.l.richardson@kcl.ac.uk

2002). Agency is defined in Pyhältö et al. (2015) as the "capability of intentional and responsible management of new learning at both individual and community levels" (2015, p. 813).

This chapter, with the author's professional background as a language teacher educator within a higher education institution setting, seeks to gain insights into how language teacher identity develops over time and how factors such as communities of practice (Wenger 1998, 2010) and affiliations (Werbińska 2016; Pennington 2015) shape that development. The concept of a community of practice (CoP), originally developed in relation to a social theory of learning (Lave and Wenger 1991; Wenger 1998), is widely contested in terms of nature, scale and applicability (Hodkinson and Hodkinson 2004). Hodkinson and Hodkinson's own work in this area whilst focusing on CoPs in relation to school teachers' learning in the workplace is, however, useful here in providing discussion and analyses of similar secondary school contexts to my own. The definition of CoP that most resonates with my own conceptualisation and context is that of Wenger's work (1998), which sees a CoP as a social learning system. This view recognises identity formation as part of learning, stressing the importance of learning as becoming (Wenger 1998), a focus that is central to this chapter. I use the term "affiliation", following Werbińska (2016, p. 137), to refer to "the individual's willingness to become a language teacher and desire for recognition as a legitimate member of the teaching community". I also refer to disciplinary affiliations more loosely to refer to associations or connections, for example, within Applied Linguistics.

My interest in the influence of these factors stems from my professional engagement as a teacher educator with research and practice in relation to the process of becoming a teacher and consequently in the construction of language teacher identity. As Werbińska (2016) points out, becoming a teacher is an ongoing process: the formal learning of the initial teacher training is a phase, albeit an important one, in the shaping and development of teachers and identity formation is implicated in the process.

At a time where within the UK school system there is an increasing sense of crisis about teacher retention as recognised by the Public Accounts Committee report "Training and Developing the Teaching Workforce" (2018), an exploration of the relationship between teacher identity and teacher retention from an Initial Teacher Education perspective is both timely and pertinent. Understanding how teachers work and learn together and their perceptions of themselves at different stages of their careers is increasingly important when considering how best to equip teachers for their careers and for retaining teachers longer term.

The language teaching context of the research presented here is that of a teacher of French and German working in the secondary school sector. Within MFL teaching specifically, the national picture in England is frequently presented as a far from positive one (Lanvers and Coleman 2017; Tinsley and Dolezal 2018), a factor that may impact on teacher recruitment and retention. Of particular concern, as highlighted in Tinsley and Dolezal's survey of language trends (ibid.), have been the declining levels of participation in the study of MFL, particularly French and German since the removal of the compulsory study of MFL for 14 to 16-year olds, together with the introduction of more challenging examinations. However, a recent government initiative announced by the current schools standards minister (Speck 2019) creating a Centre of Excellence at York University and nine specialist language hubs in schools, is set to attempt to boost the teaching of modern languages in schools.

Having sketched the background to this chapter, I now provide an overview of the structure of the chapter. This chapter is organised in the following way: first, I present an account of the theoretical underpinnings of the conceptualisation of language teacher identity that is pertinent to this chapter. Subsequently, I introduce the study and discuss the research methodology and present the analysis and discussion of the case study data.

2 Theoretical Framework

In this section, I explore the complex notion of teacher identity and highlight the central features of language teacher identity. I draw on sociocultural theory on communities of practice as reflected in the seminal work of Lave and Wenger (1991), Wenger (1998), and Hodkinson and Hodkinson (2004) to look at the relationship between communities of practice, learning and identity. I begin by exploring the notion of language teacher identity.

2.1 Understanding Language Teacher Identity

It is widely agreed that teacher identity is a complex and multifaceted construct (Beauchamp and Thomas 2009; Beijaard et al. 2004), a concept that remains challenging to define and one which may also represent a site of struggle (Norton 2000). Day et al. (2007) working within the UK school context maintain quite simply that teacher identity is the way in which teachers define themselves to themselves and others and is different from teacher role. Research into teacher identity (Beijaard et al. 2004; Pennington and Richards 2016; Varghese et al. 2005 amongst others) has consistently identified two features of identity. First, teacher identity is constructed over time, evolving throughout a teacher's career. Longitudinal studies such as early work on professional development phases (Huberman 1995) and variation in teachers' effectiveness in different professional life phases (Day et al. 2007) have offered some insight into generic patterns in teacher development. However, as Steadman points out:

> In the making of the teacher, there is no endpoint of perfection at the end of a linear pathway or on completion of an apprenticeship: the practice of learning to teach is an ongoing process, marked by uneven development (2018, p. 6).

Second, teacher identity is situated (Pennington and Richards 2016) and develops through a process of interaction with others (Cooper and Olson 1996). The social and cultural environment plays a crucial role in shaping teacher identity and may further be reflected in "affinity groups", which share according to Gee (2000, p. 105): "allegiance to, access to and participation in specific practices" or in affiliations to a particular professional community (Werbińska 2016). Pollard et al.'s work (2019) within the UK school context highlights the influence of teaching colleagues both in the immediate school environment and beyond and the benefits in relation to school effectiveness of communities of practice (Lave and Wenger 1991) where teachers are also learners.

The views of teacher identity discussed above are particularly pertinent to the focus and context of this research. Firstly, the nature and structural organisation of classroom teaching in UK schools is such that teachers rarely work in isolation as they are frequently part of a subject department where teachers of the same subject have opportunities to work closely with other colleagues. Consideration of the influence of CoPs is, therefore, particularly relevant. Secondly, Day and colleagues' work (2007) and later work reported in Day and Gu (2010), whilst not specifically looking at language teacher identity, is situated within the same UK school context as my study. Furthermore, it involved exploration of teachers' professional identity as part of their longitudinal studies of teachers' lives.

Whilst the above discussion has highlighted features of teacher identity, which may apply across different subject teaching contexts, it is important in this case study of an MFL teacher to consider research literature that looks more specifically at language teacher identity. Building on Richards' work (2010) which identified core areas of competence and expertise in language teaching, Pennington and Richards (2016) reconceptualised and developed these competences in relation to language teacher identity. Of interest here, are the notions of *language-related identity*, *disciplinary identity* and *membership of a CoP*. Language teachers need to have not only the linguistic knowledge but also the skills to communicate easily with those who have little knowledge of the language (Pennington and Richards 2016). According to Pennington (2015), a language teacher's identity is best built upon a foundation not only of specific linguistic and curriculum knowledge but also on broader knowledge of the content of the field (for example, in Applied Linguistics) gained through formal education. In the context of MFL teaching in the secondary school setting that is the focus of the chapter, consideration of language-related identity in relation to their linguistic knowledge is particularly important: teachers' confidence and competence in the target language have long been part of the debate over the use of target language in MFL classrooms (Macaro 2000).

It has been increasingly argued (Sharkey 2004; Pennington and Richards 2016) that teachers should not only possess practical and theoretical knowledge but should also be producers of knowledge, developing personal understandings of teaching (Borg 2006) that include beliefs, principles and theories. These understandings underpin teacher maxims (Richards 2006) or sets of working principles which reflect how teachers' identity develops over time (Pennington and Richards 2016) and how teachers' knowledge and theorising evolve.

What I have sought to emphasise here is that teachers develop their identities individually within a timeframe but always within a context, of which there are many not only the CoP, but also the wider educational community and society as a whole.

2.2 Identity Formation Through Situated Learning: The Subject Department as Community of Practice

An aspect of a language teacher's identity that has been considered by researchers is the teacher's connection to one or more of the communities of practice. Exploring the formation of identity through situated learning has been the focus of seminal work by Lave and Wenger (1991) and Wenger (1998), Wenger et al. (2002) amongst others. Wenger (1998, p. 149) emphasises the link between identity and practice, seeing the two as "mirror-images of one another" and argues that identity is shaped by communities of practice. Beauchamp and Thomas (2009, p. 180) also explain that "by participating in a community of professionals a teacher is subject to the influences of this community on identity development". Within the secondary school setting, the subject department in this case the MFL department, grouping together teachers of the same discipline, often forms this community of practitioners (Dimmock and Lee 2000; Visscher and Witziers 2004). However, within these departmental groups there may be associations between practitioners who embrace similar practices and share similar approaches (Gee 2000). Hodkinson and Hodkinson (2003) draw on Bourdieu's notions of *habitus* (1984) and *dispositions* (Bourdieu and Wacquant 1992), emphasising that a person's dispositions evolve over the course of a learner's "learning career" (Bloomer and Hodkinson 2000). The above theories which highlight the situated nature of learning provide a useful framework for exploring identities in practice and identity (trans)formation in practice.

2.3 Development of School MFL Teacher Identity over Time

The dynamic and continually evolving nature of teacher identity has been highlighted in earlier discussion as a central characteristic of identity. I cite Norton's definition of identity here as it emphasises identity construction across both time and space. Norton (2013, p. 4) defines identity as "the way a person understands his or her relationship with the world, how that relationship is constructed across time and space, and how that person understands possibilities for the future". Here she recognises the way in which identity may shift over time, but she also sees both teacher agency and social structures as central to identity formation. This definition is particularly resonant with the context of my study which draws on an MFL teacher's reflections on her identity over time and in different teaching contexts.

In understanding how identity develops over time, it is helpful to consider how individual and institutional identity work together and how these identify shift as teachers progress in their careers. This career progression is recognised to be unpredictable, full of uncertainty and non-linear (Gatti 2016), a view that resonates with research into professional life phases (Day 2012) and seminal research by Huberman (1993, 1995) who argued that the process of career development is filled "with plateaux, discontinuities, regressions, spurts and dead ends" (Huberman 1995, p. 196).

New teachers typically present an institutionally-sanctioned, traditional, teacher-led identity in their early career as their "default identity" according to Richards (2006, p. 16) This *safe* style is one which new teachers might readily assume as they recognise the more traditional style as providing a recognised structure for a class to be delivered and managed effectively. As teachers become more confident they may move away from this default teacher identity to a more authentic and personal identity (Richards 2006). Shifts in identity may continue to occur throughout a teacher's career, according to Pennington and Richards (2016), when teachers feel under pressure to deliver content for exams, where they have concerns about behaviour management, the introduction of new teaching methods or experience a lack of confidence in the target language (Richards 2006). This section has highlighted the unevenness of identity development; however, it is worthy of note that opportunities for ongoing professional development together with early promotion may enhance the teacher's sense of identity and belonging as I discuss in Sect. 3.

3 The Study

This chapter originates in research conducted as part of my doctoral study (Richardson 2011) which looked at inclusive practice in teaching Modern Foreign Languages in mainstream schools with a focus on students with dyslexia. Whilst not explicitly looking at teacher identity, the initial study revealed that subject communities of practice were highly influential in shaping teachers' knowledge, beliefs and understanding of MFL teaching. This chapter develops the study by providing a biographical case study of Maria, a teacher of French and German at School X, one of the participant schools at the time the initial research was undertaken. In line with British Educational Research Association (BERA) ethical research guidelines all participant schools and names were anonymised, and any identifying features of the school were not referenced.

Taking a biographical case study approach (Barkhuizen et al. 2014), building on the author's doctoral research, in this chapter I explore the development of Maria's identity as a teacher of MFL in relation to the environmental and social influences of her school setting. Maria, an experienced Modern Languages teacher, worked from 2000 to 2008 in a secondary school. She gained her teaching qualification and moved to School X in 2000, becoming Head of the MFL department in 2001. She took a break from MFL teaching to have a family but continued to be involved in education as a sports coach from 2013 but also pursuing further studies in language education.

The general research questions (RQs) underpinning this chapter are as follows:

RQ1. How does Maria see herself as an MFL teacher?
RQ2. What contextual factors shape her sense of professional identify over time and space?

3.1 Methodology

This research takes a biographical case study approach (Barkhuizen et al. 2014). According to these authors, biographical case studies are studies of individuals in which data are elicited from the participants and written up as narrative accounts. Such accounts may be followed by further analysis mirroring Tsui's study (2007) of the career of an EFL teacher in China. A biographical case study was chosen for two main reasons: first, biographical case studies, as a form of narrative enquiry, allow for the exploration of personal accounts of experience and are means of giving a voice to teachers and gaining insight into their interpretations of those lived experiences. The most resonant characteristic of narrative enquiry for this study is that it allows for exploration of language teacher identity over time and in multiple settings and contexts (Barkhuizen et al. 2014). Time and space are key considerations in this research as I seek to explore the development and shaping of Maria's identity over a period of eighteen years and in different contexts.

Data were collected from the case study participant, Maria, in an in-depth semi-structured interview, with a view to exploring her professional trajectory over time and space and how her views of herself as a teacher might have changed as she moved between different teaching contexts since I first interviewed her for my doctoral research in 2002.

According to Charmaz (2003, p. 312) qualitative interviewing: "provides an open-ended, in-depth exploration of an aspect of life about which the interviewee has substantial experience, often combined with considerable insight". Interviewing as a data-collection technique is widely used in social sciences (Alshenqeeti 2014) for the following purposes: firstly, to gain information relating to specified research objectives; secondly, to test hypotheses or to suggest new ones; thirdly, as validation of other methods by providing more in-depth information or throwing light on unexpected results.

3.2 Data Analysis

The approach I have taken in the process of analysis of data draws on the analytic-inductive techniques, which are used within the *naturalistic* or *interpretivist* paradigm for the analysis of interview and observation data (Goetz and LeCompte 1981). These techniques, Analytic Induction (Znaniecki 1934) and the Constant Comparative method (Glaser and Strauss 1967), begin with the data themselves and then through inductive reasoning lead to the development of theoretical categories. They both involve scanning and categorising data.

The interview data were transcribed and then coded (Charmaz 2003). In line with the Constant Comparative Approach, the interview data were examined closely, line-by-line and labelled with a term or category, in an attempt to find a term that "distils events and meanings without losing their essential properties" (Charmaz 2003, p. 320). The key themes that emerged were as follows: experiencing self-doubt, valuing family support, encountering new methods, consolidating practices, making connections, viewing language as performance, valuing humour. These themes are addressed under the relevant Professional Development Phase (Ewing and Manuel 2005) heading in the next section.

4 Analysis of Findings and Discussion

To give a sense of identity development over time, the data are presented according to an adapted version of critical phases identified in teachers developing professionalism (Ewing and Manuel 2005). Pollard et al. (2019) explain that the sense of commitment and value sets with which many teachers begin their careers are validated as professional characteristics with time but that this trajectory of professional development frequently involves conflicts between the desire to be a teacher and practical challenges. Most teachers can resolve these conflicts and develop a sense of professional identity, frequently experiencing similar stages as they develop a "more confident professionalism" (ibid., p. 10). These stages move from "Early expectations; facing early challenge", through "Early days of first appointment", "consolidating pedagogical content knowledge" to "building a professional identity and voice" (Ewing and Manuel 2005). Maria's career trajectory is neither smooth nor linear (Gatti 2016) and does not fit neatly with Ewing and Manuel's phases (2005), but using the critical phases shown below allows for discussion of the development of Maria's identity as she moves in, out and across different phases. Ewing and Manuel's phases have been adapted to reflect Maria's trajectory and Phases 2 and 3 have been merged and re-named.

4.1 Phase 1: Early Expectations: Facing Early Challenges When in Training

The first phase to emerge as critical for Maria was her first training placement where she experienced what Werbińska (2016) terms "discontinuities" or interruptions (in terms of disappointment about the lack of priority given to MFL) and her negative encounters with the reality of her particular classroom context of her first school training placement.

4.1.1 Early Self-Doubt

Maria seems to have been experiencing the self-doubt that typifies many of the emotions of teachers in the early stages of their careers when they encounter negative experiences (Fantilli and McDougall 2009). She revealed some disappointment at the lack of interest or focus on language teaching and concern about the challenges of student behaviour management: "language teaching wasn't a priority. Stopping the children from hurting each other was". It was at this point that she felt a certain lack of clarity about her role and some self-doubt as she says: "I was slightly wondering what was going on because I hadn't felt that I had been massively successful". This suggests that there was a degree of challenge to Maria's identity as a language teacher and her affiliation (Werbińska 2016) or desire for recognition as a valid member of that community.

Nevertheless, Maria continued her training. As Ewing and Manuel (2005) point out, the factors that determine why and how some trainees are able to move forward from negative early experiences are not well understood. In the case of Maria, she reported having clear ideas about being a language teacher before she started her training: "My mum was an MFL teacher. I had a sense of what and who I wanted to emulate". Her ability to draw on a positive role model (Knowles 1992) in her mother and her mother's disciplinary affiliations (Pennington 2015) appears to be a factor in her desire to continue to pursue her career.

Maria's autonomy at this stage can be seen in her apparent belief in her own self-efficacy or ability to influence student behaviours or achievement (Guo et al. 2010), her motivation to teach and her "agentive-reflective powers or autonomy" (Werbińska 2016, p. 135). Werbińska (ibid.) uses the term to refer to "a teacher's capacity to act while being guided by a sense of self-dependence and responsibility for educational reflection formed by ongoing reflection" (2016, p. 137). Maria's matter of fact statement about the behavioural challenges: "language teaching wasn't a priority. Stopping the children from hurting each other was" suggests that she is not over-awed by the challenges. This is also a point she makes later in the interview: "I wasn't fazed by the behaviour stuff". She can manage despite the challenges to her belief sets. She shows autonomy in her ability to reflect on these tensions and maintains a degree of resilience (Ewing and Manuel 2005).

4.2 Phase 2: Early Days of First Appointment: Encountering New Methods and Approaches/Consolidating Practices

Maria's professional development can be seen to be fairly rapid: she was appointed Head of Department in her second year of teaching. At the beginning of her second critical phase, Maria came across new methods that presented a departure from what she had encountered during her training (Morrison 2013) and hence maybe engendered a reassessment of her thinking in the face of the unfamiliar as Werbińska (2016) suggests.

Maria's development could be seen to enter a phase where she was exposed to new ideas and responded critically to new influences which appear to have helped her to crystallise her views of herself as a teacher

(Hodkinson and Hodkinson 2004): what she valued and practices she distanced herself from. She can be seen to be engaging with a community of practice as a site of learning (Hodkinson and Hodkinson 2004) in relation to a new Target Language-based method and more broadly about being a language teacher. This approach can be described as a model of Communicative Language Teaching (CLT) which unlike the more standard form of CLT used in schools, features almost exclusive use of the target language by both teacher and students. Lessons typically include strong elements of competition as well as games and songs.

In the following section, conceptualisations of communities of practice in relation to Maria's teaching context are discussed. I follow this with an examination of the influence of the shared practices within the department as regards the use of the new teaching approach.

4.2.1 Influence of Subject Department: Communities of Practice

During her early years at School X, Maria's views of herself as a teacher seemed to be shaped by a colleague from her subject department and his embracing of a new teaching method. Maria found this method inspirational: "I was genuinely very inspired by his way of teaching […]. I think he was the biggest influence on my teaching style". Although Maria reported feeling inspired by her mentor colleague, she saw her identity as a teacher as being separate from the method. She revealed some reservations about the method: "there were elements of that I felt comfortable with and elements I didn't so I picked only those". The more playful elements of the approach, allowing students to interact in a more "teasing" way, or engaging in "verbal duelling" (Cook 2000) did not always appear to sit comfortably with Maria. Whilst appreciating some of the light-heartedness of the method, she rejected the exchanging of insults.

However, Maria appears to have seen in the playful nature (Rampton 1999) of this method a point of connection to her sense of identity (Borg 2006), stating "I tended to use humour quite a lot and that method allowed me to be who I knew I needed to be", suggesting that she saw the use of humour as a valued quality in a languages teacher (Prodromou 1991).

4.3 Phase 3: Finding a Place: Making Connections and Encountering Conflict

Ewing and Manuel (2005) maintain that it is during this phase that teachers begin to understand how important it is to make connections and to *find a place*. Furthermore, they assert that it is during this period teachers frequently realise the challenge of managing conflict with other teachers and navigating a politically complex setting.

4.3.1 Making Connections: The Challenges of Getting Colleagues on Board

Although Maria's early experiences as a teacher of MFL suggest an affiliation with the community of practitioners of the new method in her school, notably her mentor, she subsequently met with some resistance when, a year later, as Head of Department, she attempted to encourage her colleagues to engage with the method by visiting another school and to consider taking on board some ideas from them: "there was no way in which they could conceive of borrowing ideas".

4.3.2 Affinities and Fragmentation

Maria's affinities with other colleagues appeared to shift as influential staff and new staff came in. When taking over as Head of Department in her second year as a qualified teacher, she became increasingly aware of fragmentation or divisions in the department. As stated by the participant, despite her colleagues' resistance, when her mentor left the school, Maria and another colleague continued to use elements of the new approach. Affiliation with this colleague as a member of the community of practitioners was through a shared endorsement of elements of that approach and a similar teaching style whereby they created a professional connection and potential for collaboration, elements which are recognised as highly significant in the development of the identify of early career teachers (Morrison 2013). In addition to the colleague who also embraced the new approach, there were some colleagues who shared broadly similar teaching styles to her and with whom she developed closer links: "There were pockets of only two who taught German then there was one who I could share ideas with. We would have a regular slot even it was just a quick chat".

The teachers in this instance were connected by teaching styles and shared assumptions (Wenger 1998) about what worked in language lessons. In terms of working together and sharing of materials, the affinities were most clearly related to shared practices such as the use of games in the language classroom.

According to Maria, the department of six teachers was somewhat divided with significant differences in approach between teachers who were "old school where the classes were silent" and the noisier classes where teachers were "more fun". Maria aligned herself with the latter set of teachers. She also reported disagreeing with colleagues about issues such as grammar, stating in relation to one of her colleagues, "one thing we used to argue about was grammar". Whilst discussion is not always harmonious, Wenger et al. (2002) argue that a sparky disagreement can be part of the positive energy of a community of practice and can stimulate reflection and problem-solving.

4.3.3 Beliefs and Values

During the period of consolidation of her practice at her school, Maria appeared to have reinforced some of her educational beliefs (Pajares 1992; Borg 2006) and her values. Maria reported viewing language as performance and valuing the use of humour in language teaching to help create an environment where making mistakes is seen as a natural part of language learning. She embraced the new approach as a way of providing some light-heartedness in the lessons and to help students to develop a good-humoured and positive approach to making mistakes in language.

She reported allowing her students to be "put on the spot" to some extent to help them develop wider life skills of dealing with making mistakes with good humour, although like Morreall (1983), she was concerned by the idea that laughing with someone at their mistake might mean laughing collectively at someone.

4.4 Phase 5: Building a Professional Identity and Voice: Teacher as Agentive Educator

There are two key threads that run through Maria's biographical account: the constancy of a wider teacher identity and a strong sense of agency (Edwards 2015). Maria's view of herself as a teacher appears to have broadened as she progressed through her career, leading her to identify herself most strongly as an educator rather than as an MFL teacher. Seeing herself as an educator means working across different contexts and applying her generic teaching skills with a view to educating children holistically. Increasingly she is able to identify and reflect on her values and belief sets as will be illustrated in this section.

Although Maria had a break to have children, she still viewed herself as a teacher, as illustrated below. Since she left her school in 2008, she has undertaken a coaching role and maintains that: "it's bigger that just this classroom identity … I don't feel that I have left teaching". However, she felt that absence from formal teaching had embedded the permanence of her identity as a teacher, albeit an identity that is shifting and broadening over time and space (Norton 2013). Similarly, whilst working in a different context or space as a coach later on, it became clear to Maria that as a teacher she had a set of skills and knowledge that remained with her and could be transferred from one context to another: "it's teaching, you realize that those skills don't ever leave".

4.4.1 Beliefs and Values

As illustrated below, Maria viewed herself primarily as an educator. As such, her attitudes to herself were underpinned by strong beliefs about educational responsibility for the development of the whole child. What she enjoyed as an educator was communication and connection with learners and the: "responsibility of being an educator of a child' and 'making eye contact responding thoughtfully to a child". Her comments suggest a recognition of the moral underpinnings of education (Sockett 2008) together with a valuing of the relational aspects of teaching (Gatti 2016). Through her continuing role as a coach she can continue to be an educator and to connect with young people: "I'm somebody who values connection with people, finding out why people are finding certain things difficult".

What also emerged from the interviews was that Maria valued her general teaching skills, such as behavior management and clear communication very highly. For Maria it was very important to see herself as more than a modern language teacher to help her deal with challenging times in the work place: "conceptualizing yourself as an educator rather than simply and straightforwardly as a modern language teacher really helps you to see those times through".

Maria's comments suggest that as she has become more experienced, she has become less influenced by the immediate environment and contextual factors (Lave and Wenger 1991) and has become more independent in her identity as a teacher. Whilst she is not currently teaching MFL in a school, she has been able to reflect on not only her own teaching but also on her educational values. She exhibits a confidence and a sense of clarity about her teacher identity. At the same time, she exhibits the desire to challenge and question, suggesting that she would welcome the opportunity to engage with critically reflective discourse communities of experienced teachers or professional development programmes involving university tutors and school teachers (Thomas et al. 1998) or, indeed as she has done, to undertake further study.

5   Conclusion

This chapter has examined the concept of language teacher identity, looking at perceptions of identity; to what extent contextual and social factors such as communities of practice and affinities have shaped the development of the case-study participant, Maria; and how these influences have changed over time. I now return to my research questions:

In relation to RQ1, it is clear that Maria identifies most strongly as an educator rather than as an MFL subject teacher. This is an identity which, although shifting in nature, endures over time. Embedded in this view of herself as a teacher are sets of general beliefs and values sets about education as well as more specific ones that relate to language learning. Maria sees her teacher identity as extending beyond the classroom into different contexts where she can bring her valued teaching skills in relation to communication with young people and behaviour management to bear. Nevertheless, as an MFL teacher, she is clear about what she valued: seeing language as performance, using humour in language teaching and learning and creating a safe classroom space for making mistakes.

Turning now to RQ2, the contextual factors that shaped Maria's sense of identity over time and space, it is clear that identifying with and sharing approaches and practices at her school, helped her to develop confidence and an increasing clarity about who she was as a teacher in the early stages of her career. Whilst benefitting from some degree of sharing of practice and affiliations during the early and middle stages of her career, Maria appears to have had the confidence to be independent in her thinking and her practices which has sustained her in her career. The apparent lack of reliance on a large community practice after her mentor left is significant as it raises questions about the extent to which communities of practice are enduring in their influence or are sustained by other members (Hodkinson and Hodkinson 2003).

Although she appears to have briefly faltered slightly, Maria showed resilience (Ewing and Manuel 2005), and seems to have benefitted from emotional distancing through her higher-level studies, which perhaps has enhanced her sense of identity as a teacher to enable her to develop her disciplinary affiliations (Pennington 2015) and educational beliefs (Borg 2006).

Whilst individual case studies are bound to the particular case, they nonetheless provide nuanced accounts of teacher development. I would argue that this study offers interesting and potentially important insights with implications for teacher education. First, it adds to the body of literature that highlights the important relationship between teacher, subject affiliation, identity and agency, suggesting that a strong identity as an educator, a strong sense of agency and ongoing engagement with formal education and research may be key factors in sustaining a satisfying and ever-developing teaching career. Nevertheless, a greater focus on teacher identity in teacher education programmes would certainly be beneficial.

Further studies are needed with a wider range of participants into the factors that influence the development of teacher identity over time and space to ascertain whether it is familial influences or personal characteristics and beliefs or indeed a complex mix of all of these (Beauchamp and Thomas 2009) that are most significant. Also worthy of further investigation is the role played by the development of disciplinary knowledge as teachers develop as researchers through undertaking collaborative research projects, or indeed through language education studies, in consolidating and clarifying teachers' views of themselves as teachers (Pennington and Richards 2016).

It is striking that Maria identified most strongly as an educator rather than as an MFL teacher and that she has an enduring desire to develop her teacher role to become a producer of knowledge (Johnson 2006) and a theoriser in her own right, a role that would resonate with Zeichner et al.'s work (2015) advocating a more democratic epistemology in teacher education through a re-framing of whose knowledge counts and how school teacher and teacher educators interact across institutional and ideological boundaries.

References

Alshenqeeti, Hamza. 2014. Interviewing as a Data Collection Method: A Critical Review. *English Linguistics Research* 3: 39–45.
Barkhuizen, Gary, Phil Benson, and Alice Chik. 2014. *Narrative Inquiry in Language Teaching and Learning Research*. New York: Routledge.
Beauchamp, Catherine, and Lynn Thomas. 2009. Understanding Teacher Identity: An Overview of Issues in the Literature and Implications for Teacher Education. *Cambridge Journal of Education* 39 (2): 175–189.
Beijaard, Douwe, Paulien C. Meijer, and Nico Verloop. 2004. Reconsidering Research on Teachers' Professional Identity. *Teaching and Teacher Education* 20 (2): 107–128.
Bloomer, Martin, and Phil Hodkinson. 2000. Learning Careers: Continuity and Change in Young People's Dispositions to Learning. *British Educational Research Journal* 26 (5): 583–597.
Borg, Simon. 2006. The Distinctive Characteristics of Foreign Language Teachers. *Language Teaching Research* 10 (1): 3–31.

Bourdieu, Pierre. 1984. *Distinction: A Social Critique of the Judgement of Taste*. London: Routledge & Keegan Paul.
Bourdieu, Pierre, and Loïc Wacquant. 1992. *An Invitation to Reflexive Sociology*. Chicago and London: University of Chicago Press.
British Educational Research Association (BERA). 2018. *Ethical Guidelines for Educational Research*, 4th ed. London: British Educational Research Association. https://www.bera.ac.uk/researchers-resources/publications/ethicalguidelines-for-educational-research-2018. Accessed 1 August 2018.
Charmaz, Kathy. 2003. Qualitative Interviewing and Grounded Theory Analysis. In *Inside Interviewing: New lenses, New Concerns*, ed. James A. Holstein and Jaber F. Gubrium, 311–331. Thousand Oaks, CA: Sage.
Cook, Guy. 2000. *Language Play, Language Learning*. Oxford: Oxford University Press.
Cooper, Karyn, and Margaret R. Olson. 1996. The Multiple 'I's' of Teacher Identity. In *Changing Research and Practice: Teachers' Professionalism, Identities, and Knowledge*, ed. Kompf Michael, Terence Boak, Richard Bond, and Don Dworet, 78–90. London: Falmer.
Day, Christopher. 2012. New Lives of Teachers. *Teacher Education Quarterly* 39 (1): 7–26.
Day, Christopher, and Qing Gu. 2010. *The New Lives of Teachers*. London, UK: Routledge.
Day, Christopher, Pam Sammons, and Gordon Stobart. 2007. *Teachers Matter: Connecting Work, Lives and Effectiveness*. New York: McGraw-Hill Education (UK).
Dimmock, Clive, and J.C.-K. Lee. 2000. Redesigning School-Based Curriculum Leadership: A Cross-Cultural Perspective. *Journal of Curriculum and Supervision* 15 (4): 332–358.
Edwards, Anne. 2015. Recognising and Realising Teachers' Professional Agency. *Teachers and Teaching* 21 (6): 779–784.
Ewing, Robyn, and Jacqueline Manuel. 2005. Retaining Quality Early Career Teachers in the Profession: New Teacher Narratives. *Change: Transformation in Education* 8 (1): 1–16.
Fantilli, Robert D., and Douglas E. McDougall. 2009. A Study of Novice Teachers: Challenges and Supports in the First Years. *Teaching and Teacher Education* 25 (6): 814–825.
Gatti, Lauren. 2016. *Toward a Framework of Resources for Learning to Teach: Rethinking US Teacher Preparation*. New York: Springer.
Gee, James Paul. 2000. Identity as an Analytic Lens for Research in Education. *Review of Research in Education* 25 (1): 99–125.

Glaser, Barney, and Anselm Strauss. 1967. *The Discovery of Grounded Theory*. Chicago: Adeline.

Goetz, Judith Preissle, and Margaret D. LeCompte. 1981. Ethnographic Research and the Problem of Data Reduction. *Anthropology & Education Quarterly* 12 (1): 51–70.

Guo, Ying, Shayne B. Piasta, Laura M. Justice, and Joan N. Kaderavek. 2010. Relations Among Preschool Teachers' Self-Efficacy, Classroom Quality, and Children's Language and Literacy Gains. *Teaching and Teacher Education* 26 (4): 1094–1103.

Hodkinson, Phil, and Heather Hodkinson. 2003. Individuals, Communities of Practice and the Policy Context: School Teachers' Learning in Their Workplace. *Studies in Continuing Education* 25 (1): 3–21.

Hodkinson, Heather, and Phil Hodkinson. 2004. Rethinking the Concept of Community of Practice in Relation to Schoolteachers' Workplace Learning. *International Journal of Training and Development* 8 (1): 21–31.

Huberman, Michael. 1993. Step Towards a Developmental Model of the Teaching Career. In *Teacher Professional Development: A Multiple Perspective Approach*, ed. Lya Kremer-Hayon, Hans C. Vonk, and Ralph Fessler, 93–118. Amsterdam: Swets & Zeitlinger.

Huberman, Michael. 1995. Networks That Alter Teaching: Conceptualizations, Exchanges and Experiments. *Teachers and Teaching* 1 (2): 193–211.

Johnson, Karen E. 2006. The Socio-Cultural Turn and Its Challenges for Second Language Teacher Education. *TESOL Quarterly* 40 (1): 235–257.

Knowles, J. Gary. 1992. Models for Understanding Preservice and Beginning Teachers' Biographies: Illustrations from Case Studies. In *Studying Teachers Lives*, ed. Ivor Goodson, 99–153. New York: Teachers College, Columbia University.

Lanvers, Ursula, and James A. Coleman. 2017. The UK Language Learning Crisis in the Public Media: A Critical Analysis. *The Language Learning Journal* 45 (1): 3–25.

Lave, Jean, and Etienne Wenger. 1991. *Situated Learning: Legitimate Peripheral Participation*. Cambridge: Cambridge University Press.

Macaro, Ernesto. 2000. Issues in Target Language Teaching. In *Issues in Modern Foreign Language Teaching*, ed. Kit Field, 163–181. London and New York: Routledge.

Morreall, John. 1983. *Taking Laughter Seriously*. Albany: SUNY Press.

Morrison, Chad. 2013. Teacher Identity in the Early Career Phase: Trajectories That Explain and Influence Development. *Australian Journal of Teacher Education* 38 (4): 91–107.

Norton, Bonny. 2000. Language and Identity. *Sociolinguistics and Language Education* 23 (3): 349–369.

Norton, Bonny. 2013. *Identity and Language Learning: Extending the Conversation*. Bristol, Buffalo, and Toronto: Multilingual Matters.

Norton, Bonny. 2017. Learner Investment and Language Teacher Identity. In *Reflections on Language Teacher Identity Research*, ed. Gary Barkhuizen, 80–86. New York: Routledge.

Norton, Bonny, and Kelleen Toohey. 2011. Identity, Language Learning, and Social Change. *Language Teaching* 44 (4): 412–446.

Pajares, Frank M. 1992. Teachers' Beliefs and Educational Research: Cleaning Up a Messy Construct. *Review of Educational Research* 62 (3): 307–332.

Pennington, Martha C. 2015. Teacher Identity in TESOL: A Frames Perspective. In *Advances and Current Trends in Language Teacher Identity Research*, ed. Cheung Yin Ling, Ben Said Selim, and Park Kwanghyun, 16–30. London: Routledge.

Pennington, Martha C., and Jack Richards. 2016. Teacher Identity in Language Teaching: Integrating Personal, Contextual, and Professional Factors. *RELC Journal* 47 (1): 5–23.

Pollard, Andrew, Kristine Black-Hawkins, Gabrielle Cliff-Hodges, Pete Dudley, Steve Higgins, Mary James, Holly Linklater, Sue Swaffield, Mandy Swann, Mark Winterbottom, and Mary Anne Wolpert. 2019. *Reflective Teaching in Schools*. London and New York: Bloomsbury Publishing.

Prodromou, Luke. 1991. The Good Language Teacher. *English Teaching Forum* 29 (2): 2–7.

Public Accounts Committee. 2018. Retaining and Developing the Teaching Workforce. 31 March, HC 460, 2017–2018. https://publications.parliament.uk/pa/cm201719/cmselect/cmpubacc/460/460.pdf. Accessed 1 March 2019.

Pyhältö, Kirsi, Janne Pietarinen, and Tiina Soini. 2015. Teachers' Professional Agency and Learning—From Adaption to Active Modification in the Teacher Community. *Teachers and Teaching* 21 (7): 811–830.

Rampton, Ben. 1999. Deutsch in Inner London and the Animation of an Instructed Foreign Language. *Journal of Sociolinguistics* 3 (4): 480–504.

Richards, Keith. 2006. Being the Teacher: Identity and Classroom Conversation. *Applied Linguistics* 27 (1): 51–77.

Richards, Jack C. 2010. Competence and Performance in Language Teaching. *RELC Journal* 41 (2): 101–122.

Richardson, Christina. 2011. *Supporting the Dyslexic Pupil in the Curriculum: Exploring Inclusive Practice in Mainstream Schools with Special Reference to*

Dyslexic Learners in the Modern Foreign Language Classroom (Unpublished PhD thesis). King's College London.

Sharkey, Judy. 2004. TESOL Teachers' Knowledge of Context as Critical Mediator in Curriculum Development. *TESOL Quarterly* 38 (2): 279–299.

Sockett, Hugh. 2008. The Moral and Epistemic Purposes of Teacher Education. In *Handbook of Research on Teacher Education: Enduring Questions in Changing Contexts*, ed. Marilyn Cochrane-Smith, Sharon Feiman-Nemser, D. John McIntyre, and Kelly E. Demers, 45–65. New York and Oxford: Routledge.

Speck, David. 2019. Revival Hopes for Language GCSEs with New Centre of Excellence. *Times Educational Supplement.* 10 January. https://www.tes.com/news/revival-hopes-language-gcses-new-centre-excellence. Accessed 20 March 2019.

Steadman, Sarah. 2018. Defining Practice: Exploring the Meaning of Practice in the Process of Learning to Teach. *Teacher Education Advancement Network Journal* 10 (1): 3–9.

Swarbrick, Ann. 2002. *Teaching Modern Languages.* Oxford: Routledge.

Thomas, Guy, Sam Weinberg, Pam Grossman, Oddmund Myhre, and Stephen Woolworth. 1998. In the Company of Colleagues: An Interim Report on the Development of a Community of Teacher Learners. *Teaching and Teacher Education* 14: 21–32.

Tinsley, Teresa, and Nina Dolezal. 2018. *Language Trends 2018.* London: British Council.

Toom, Auli, Kirsi Pyhältö, and Frances O'Connell Rust. 2015. Teachers' Professional Agency in Contradictory Times. *Teachers and Teaching* 21 (6): 615–623.

Tsui, Amy. 2007. What Shapes Teachers' Professional Development? In *International Handbook of English Language Teaching*, ed. Cummins Jim and Davison Chris, 1053–1066. Norwell, MA: Springer.

Varghese, Manka, Brian Morgan, Bill Johnston, and Kimberly A. Johnson. 2005. Theorizing Language Teacher Identity: Three Perspectives and Beyond. *Journal of Language, Identity, and Education* 4 (1): 21–44.

Visscher, Adrie, and Bob Witziers. 2004. Subject Departments as Professional Communities. *British Educational Research Journal* 30 (6): 785–800.

Wenger, Etienne. 1998. *Communities of Practice: Learning, Meaning, and Identity.* Cambridge, UK: Cambridge University Press.

Wenger, Etienne. 2010. Communities of Practice and Social Learning Systems: The Career of a Concept. In *Social Learning Systems and Communities of Practice*, ed. Blackmore Chris, 179–198. London: Springer.

Wenger, Etienne, Richard Arnold McDermott, and William Snyder. 2002. *Cultivating Communities of Practice: A Guide to Managing Knowledge*. Boston, MA: Harvard Business Press.

Werbińska, Dorota. 2016. Language-Teacher Professional Identity: Focus on Discontinuities from the Perspective of Teacher Affiliation, Attachment and Autonomy. In *New Directions in Language Learning Psychology*, ed. Christina Gkonou, Tatzl Dietmar, and Sarah Mercer, 135–157. Basel, Switzerland: Springer.

Zeichner, Ken, Katherina A. Payne, and Kate Brayko. 2015. Democratizing Teacher Education. *Journal of Teacher Education* 66 (2): 22–135.

Znaniecki, Florian. 1934. *The Method of Sociology*. New York: Farrar & Rinehart.

8

Constructing Hybrid Identities in the Language Classroom

Lorenza Boscaini and Debora Quattrocchi

1 Introduction

This chapter presents the personal accounts of two teachers of Italian, in the UK. In both narratives the authors look at the impact of pluricultural settings on identity construction and projection in the context of MFL teaching and learning.

Lorenza's narrative shows how the love of reading can be a motivating factor for language learning and, by extension, for developing the complex identities that interact in the language classroom. By doing that, she also explores the feelings of anxiety she experienced as a bilingual learner and later on as a language teacher in the classroom; it also highlights the importance of flexibility and acceptance of linguistic differences in the process of developing language teacher's agency.

L. Boscaini (✉) · D. Quattrocchi
The Open University, Milton Keynes, UK
e-mail: l.boscaini@open.ac.uk

D. Quattrocchi
e-mail: d.quattrocchi@open.ac.uk

© The Author(s) 2019
M. Gallardo (ed.), *Negotiating Identity in Modern Foreign Language Teaching*, https://doi.org/10.1007/978-3-030-27709-3_8

Debora's narrative shows how the conventionally attributed identity of the MFL teacher as monolingual/monocultural *ambassador* has become too confining in the context of the diverse and multicultural realities present in our world. In her narrative she suggests that the role of *mediator* (Kohler 2015; Liddicoat 2014) can better address the idea of difference embedded in the dynamics of the language classroom, especially at a time of demographic and social changes as a result of migration. In her narrative she reflects on the tensions that as a transnational language teacher in the UK she experiences in the context of the MFL classroom and the difficulties in reconciling cultural and linguistic differences in her teacher/mediator role.

2 Lorenza's Narrative

2.1 Growing Up in Two Languages

I have many fond memories of the rural community where I grew up on the outskirts of a provincial town in the northeast of Italy boasting Palladian buildings of unparalleled beauty, rivers, open views towards the mountains and fields running alongside a cycle lane leading to town. In this community a variant of the Venetian dialect was (but is no longer) the language spoken by its 5000 inhabitants. This co-existed in a state of *diglossia* with the official language. Italian was used in education and formal situations because it was regarded as culturally and linguistically more prestigious, also owing to a larger body of literature written in Italian.

My childhood in *diglossic* Vicenza meant that I became bilingual (Grosjean 2008), using the local dialect in (both formal and informal) conversation at home or socially, particularly with school friends, and Italian for reading and writing at home or in school. I recollect reading avidly from an early age any printed text, even newspapers. This love of reading was instrumental to developing my Italian language skills and general knowledge, as it was later on in my life to developing my desire and motivation to learn other languages (a factor considered by Gardner and Lambert 1972) and to have strong affiliations with the wider Italian

8 Constructing Hybrid Identities in the Language Classroom 169

language community, as well as with other speech communities of the languages I have learned.

At an early age I discovered that Italian or Venetian were not simple means of communication and that instead they were loaded with, what Norton calls "their social meaning" (Norton 2000, p. 5). This tension between language and dialect had never affected me until I started primary school, where the freedom to speak my dialect was denied because in the Italian education system at the time the use of the Venetian dialect was deemed unacceptable, while Italian was considered a language better placed to describe the dominant culture and therefore, the key to future success. This idea of different languages co-existing within one community was new to me. I imagine that many children around the world must experience similar feelings when transplanted to a new linguistic environment in school, especially after migrating to a new country. The two languages co-existed and interacted within myself, but expressing thoughts and feelings in Italian was at times awkward, embarrassing, unlike the richness of scope when using the Venetian dialect. Concurrently, there were situations when it was not easy to communicate in Italian.

I recollect one shaming critical incident in the classroom when my teacher tried to find out which was my natural writing hand and I replied in my dialect that I was ambidextrous. She surprised me by demanding that I should speak Italian. I remember asking myself: "why?", while trying subconsciously to justify the teacher. That experience led me to acknowledge a nexus between language, culture and identity, but also to learn to disguise my accent and switch from Venetian to Italian in order to fit better in society. This spurred me to adopt a more flexible approach as a "speaker-hearer" (Grosjean 2008, p. 9) later in life and even gave me the willingness to use foreign languages unconventionally (including code-mixing or *romance-esque*) (Block 2010), when communicating with other interlocutors.

Being an avid reader led me consciously to develop confidence in my language skills and to accept that I had two speech communities: Venetian for family or neighbours, Italian for my formal educational environment in which I developed an imaginary and creative world. (I would spend hours absorbed in reading children's tales in Italian to reimagine my own version of the events, identifying myself in characters such as *Thumbelina*, or *Pinocchio's Blue Fairy*). Retrospectively, it could be said that, at an early age, I acquired a sense of self by negotiating multiple identities (Venetian child and daughter, Catholic choir girl, volleyball team player, actress in the local theatre, Italian student, etc.), while trying to reconcile myself subconsciously with the community dialect, the social power of the national language and the new horizons it opened for me. Inevitably, the acceptance of my new Italian speech community would lead to feelings of detachment from the connections that I used to share in my childhood.

I did not study another language as the Italian primary curriculum then had no MFL provision. Nevertheless, I spent time fantasising about what it would sound like speaking Russian, French or English. Later on, in middle school, I enthusiastically began learning English, mainly through grammar and mechanical non-communicative drills. I embraced new forms of thinking and identified with those attached to rather stereotypical ideas of the UK, which, of course, were epitomised by my love of British pop music. In addition to English, in high school I learned Latin and French, and at university I read modern languages. Subsequently, my identity as a language learner opened new horizons and challenges through prolonged absences studying and living abroad in Finland, Hungary, Moscow and London, places where I learned and used other languages and felt a sense of affiliation to transnational and transcultural communities, which extended beyond local relationships and concepts of nationhood. Undeniably, those experiences have formed the plurilingual citizen of the world that I have become today. They also effectively represent a partial loss of my original identity which, although compensated by multiple newly acquired identities, has resulted in me being perceived often as an outsider.

On the term *plurilingual* I draw here from Álvarez and Pérez-Cavana (2015) who make a difference between *multilingualism* and *plurilingualism*. Although often used interchangeably, such terms differ from one another as the former refers to separate co-existing languages in society, while the latter refers to the languages an individual can use (including one's own mother tongue) as being "in a sophisticated interrelationship" (2015, p. 62), and constructed in social interrelation. As we will now see I consider an essential aspect of my role as a teacher of Italian that of supporting the expansion of the language learner's own multilingual, pluricultural and transnational identity.

2.2   On Being a Teacher of Italian

As a plurilingual individual with strong affiliations to different European cultures (Italian, British, French and Russian) and sub-cultures (Italians in London, MFL teachers' community, etc.), my professional identity as a language teacher is deeply embedded within my beliefs, my passion for teaching and my personal multiple and contradictory identities, which are at times fragmented (because they pull in different directions: local versus global, traditional versus new roles). I live and teach Italian in Britain, spend periods of time in Italy and other European countries to visit family and friends or travel to other parts of the world. At the intersection of different cultures, life can be complex, particularly when negotiating transnationalism with nationalism. With the former being a fluid and the latter a fixed concept, uneasiness in individuals and society can be exacerbated as exemplified by reactions to immigration. My professional identity is also very much influenced by my past experiences as a learner of English and Russian, my bilingualism and the sense of achievement in mastering Italian at the expense of the partial loss of my dialectal competence.

As a young graduate I worked as a freelance translator. This activity was solitary. So, longing for a diverse workplace and interaction, in the UK I fulfilled my aspirations becoming a teacher of Italian to adults, and moving on to teach in secondary institutions and Further Education. In my career as a language teacher, I have renegotiated my teacher's identity according to new professional and academic goals, different institutions' pedagogical and social norms, cultures and structures and personal academic interests, particularly process drama, in which I have developed professional expertise and knowledge. I have been an active agent in transforming my teaching practice, for example by encompassing drama and performing in language learning because as Eteläpelto states: "Although human actions have a social genesis, they also emerge from subjects' personal histories" (2014, p. 650).

My identity as a teacher is co-constructed through personal agency, but also through interaction with my UK learners (a mixture of domestic and international students). Within the language classroom the societal microcosm of learners' identities correlates to the ambitions and motivations of its members: that is why it is important to adopt flexibility and demonstrate acceptance of differences. As in my case, their learning is affected by perceptions, beliefs, history and their own awareness and understanding of cultural identity. In the language classroom students engage in what Norton (2000) calls "constantly organising and reorganising who they are and how they relate to the social world" (2000, p. 11), although this process sometimes can create conflict, as illustrated by the following example.

Early in my teaching career, one of my degree students burst into tears in the classroom saying that she felt so hopeless and inadequate, that she could never bring herself to speak Italian. When she was three her Italian father had severed his ties with her whole family. Consequently, she experienced painful emotions and struggled to renegotiate her identity through the new language. As with my own experience in primary school this episode illustrates the strong emotional and cognitive dimension implicit in language learning. When the afore-mentioned student told me her story, I felt uncomfortable and, to this day, I feel guilty because Italian had triggered for her memories of a difficult past. Professionally, this early critical incident focused my attention on the interrelations between language and memories and taught me never to underestimate their potential emotional impact on language learning.

In my teaching career I have learned to evaluate situations in the classroom, consider options and long-term implications and make decisions on how to move forward. For instance, when a learner is reluctant to enact a role-play, I always think that s/he may have reasons for this. As a strategy, I reinforce the message that simulations of fictional personalities or role-plays, singing in Italian or dancing are great opportunities to learn a language. One of my ab-initio students who refused to engage in a conversation activity scheduled at the pause of a *Tarantella* being played (a performing activity aimed at creating a jovial atmosphere in the group) justified himself saying: "Sorry, I am British", invoking cultural stereotypes and implying that his cultural background prevented him from expressing emotions. This scenario made me realise that my professional choice of activities and freedom to set tasks based on my pluricultural experiences may not always make all the classroom participants feel equally at ease because of culturally rooted and socially constructed attitudes. At the same time, I feel it is important that students see me not only in my professional role but as a human being who, if necessary, is willing to use more flexible approaches, such as multiple linguistic codes and bold language constructions. For instance, I use my passive knowledge of Spanish to un-code meaning when a Spaniard mistakenly says in Italian *moglie* instead of *donna* because of its Spanish cognate *mujer*. It means that I can help them to avoid misunderstandings by suggesting the correct word in Italian.

The perception of what is a teacher's role can certainly vary from student to student and over time from institution to institution. Instructor, neutral chair, commentator, devil's advocate, consultant, actor, expert and facilitator of learning, mediator in discussions, assessor, IT expert. These are just some of the intrinsic roles of a MFL teacher. Moreover, today we cannot ignore the role of social media and the new technologies in education as these have become essential learning tools. Students' attitudes, motivation, interaction, openness or resistance to learning, even their perception of my persona affect my own sense of identity and beliefs about my teaching practice. I would like to believe that my choices and actions in the classroom, although influenced by my own personal and professional experience, go through a process of recognition, evaluation, negotiation and response to learners' demands. This is no small task and accomplishing it can be isolating, so I value supportive colleagues' collaboration and their willingness to share professional experiences. Despite having different professional affiliations, the community with which I identify most is that of international Italian language educators.

2.3 My Personal Reflections

My narrative recounts how some critical incidents that occurred to me as a language learner were pivotal experiences both in my personal and professional identity construction, as a learner and as a teacher. My bilingual language learner's experience highlights how my desire to integrate socially into the wider Italian community became a motivating factor in developing language proficiency. It also led to a passion for literature and spurred me to reflect on the nature of language, language usage and meanings. Particularly, the personal and social implications of choosing to speak one language rather than another increased my interest in the correlations between language, culture and identity.

Becoming a teacher in the UK, where I had not been educated, and teaching in different institutions was a significant milestone for me. This required continuous professional learning and the renegotiating of my professional identity. It posed many challenges (some linked to the sociocultural and material characteristics of the different institutions in which I worked) and a need to reshape my teaching practice in an agentive manner. Furthermore, as a teacher who is aware that her identity is moulded by experiences, interactions and beliefs, I became particularly concerned with the process of identity formation and the way encounters with different learners and languages affect such a process in the language classroom.

Similarly, for the learner the act of redefining one's own identity through contextualised learning can be confusing, especially when one experiences feelings of belonging to different groups with whom language, thoughts and beliefs are shared. The examples I have given in my narrative show how language learning is emotionally charged (Krashen 1981; Dewaele 2010). They also illustrate how language learners sometimes may feel pushed outside their comfort zone, just as I did when communicating in Venetian dialect in my Italian school. As a bilingual learner and as a teacher I have never really liked code-switching or code-mixing in communication and have always tried to avoid them. However, in a mixed ability group of learners with different mother tongues and backgrounds code-switching or code-mixing could avoid breakdown in communication and contribute to reduce their affective filter, hence create a light-hearted atmosphere, conducive to learning. This can give participants a new sense of freedom and empower them to use their pluricultural and linguistic competences.

As a teacher, I see my sense of agency as a combination of professional commitment, motivation, creativity, choices, life-long learning and well-being (Eteläpelto et al. 2013). I view flexibility and inclusiveness as elements that can be successfully encompassed in the teaching practice to facilitate language learning. Hopefully institutions will put more emphasis on flexible language learning approaches to increase acceptance of learning differences, tolerance of different cultures, social cohesion and intercultural awareness. As my present life, work, homes and relationships stretch beyond the boundaries of one single country, I perform at the intersections of different cultures and languages, as a multilingual, plurilingual, pluricultural, transnational individual, an experience that truly enriches my teaching.

3 Debora's Narrative

3.1 A Language Teacher's Journey

I close my eyes and see myself as a younger woman, sitting in front of a teaching recruitment panel. The Chair asks me a crucial question: "Why do you want to teach Italian in the UK?" I smile to myself, I am prepared for this, I have rehearsed it many times, I know exactly what to say: "I love working with students and teaching and promoting my culture and language; I find sharing ideas and knowledge with students and colleagues rewarding and enriching; I enjoy designing stimulating pedagogical activities. But mostly it is about my passion for promoting *my* culture and *my* language to students in a multicultural capital like London".

At that time, I had not yet developed a truly wide perspective on language teaching. As a young teacher my competence was based more on theory than experience and promoting *my* culture and *my* language seemed a very good answer. And perhaps it was so, some twenty years ago, when I was still quite new to the job and the world had only just started to proclaim itself interested in diversity and inclusivity. A world not yet transformed by the internet revolution and the impact of social media, where mass migrations had not yet happened, not at least on the wide scale and with the public resonance recently experienced. A world in which being multicultural merely meant promoting examples of banal nationalism, naively placing a few exotic flags next to the British one in the classroom. Twenty years on, this is a very different world, one where in light of a new necessary intercultural orientation, promoting *one's* culture and language suddenly feels extraordinarily "small", almost dangerously narrow-minded.

In time and with experience I could not help questioning my identity/ies as someone living in *another* country, someone who had swapped the well-known coordinates of her original language and culture with new ones, as a teacher of Italian operating in a multicultural British capital; and almost inevitably as a cultural ambassador, an *ascribed* identity (Block 2014), which I have always found far too confining, attributed to me by the educational system, the institutions I worked for, the curricular expectations, the regulatory bodies for standards in education and unwittingly perpetuated by students, colleagues and to an extent even by myself. Kramsch (2014) draws our attention on how "globalisation has changed the conditions under which FLs (Foreign Languages) are taught, learned, used. It has destabilized the codes, norms and conventions that FL educators relied upon" (2014, p. 302).

As an MFL educator living through global changes, I now view cultural and linguistic practices across the world as more and more interlinked and it seems almost unnatural to look at them as separate entities. As a result of growing mobility and interconnectedness the role of monocultural/monolingual *ambassador* seems dated and inadequate. At some point in my professional experience it felt natural to me to veer towards a mediatory approach instead, which allowed for a recognition of difference in the classroom, where so many voices are heard, not just the teacher's, but also and above all the students' voices, with their own accents, cultural traits, behaviours, memories, traumas, differences. Significantly Kramsch (2014) encourages MFL educators "not to lose sight of the whole", by which she means:

> Catching the essence of a word, an utterance, a gesture, a silence, as they occur inside and outside the classroom, and seeing them as a manifestation of the speaker's or writer's voice, informed by an awareness of the global communicative situation, rather than just by the constructing of sentences, paragraphs and texts. (2014, p. 309)

Indeed, in the language classroom students learn to develop not only their own voice but also "an ear for the voices of others" (ibid.). The teacher/mediator can help students move through and embrace difference without prejudices, with empathy and an open mind.

Moving towards a mediatory role was a conscious decision for me. We are faced by many challenges throughout our careers as educators and need to respond to social change, legislations and sector policies, yet never losing track of students' individual needs. Teachers' agency is the result of many tensions, which inevitably inform identity construction. Edwards (2015) refers to it as a combination of "commitment, responsibility, strong judgements, self-evaluation, connection to the common good and attention to what people do" (2015, p. 779). I would also add intercultural mediation to this list. As Liddicoat (2014) puts it, "intercultural mediation is a form of bringing languages and cultures into contact for individuals and groups through a sharing of understanding and cultural practices, values, norms" (2014, p. 260). This process of sharing grants us, MFL teachers and students, a unique insider/outsider position from which it becomes easier to accept/embrace multiple interpretations of cultural and linguistic practices.

3.2 Italy Is Changing

I am teaching a class, it is December 2017, and inevitably we are going to talk about the holidays. How do Italians spend the festivities? Do they gather around the family table? Do they go to church? What do they eat? Not only are there the inevitable differences between Northern and Southern Italy, different traditions, different specialities, from *tortellini* and *cappone* in the North to local *scacciate* in Sicily alongside many other significant nuances, but with the recent waves of migrations experienced by the country, the Italian population has necessarily made room for new linguistic and cultural practices, some of which might even impact the way we celebrate holidays together. So where do I start? How do I convey these changes to my students? How do I gradually undo that stereotyped image of Italian identity still promoted by text books, and tell them that Italians are changing, from the way they talk, to the way they pray, to the way they eat? I am reminded that learning a language—and the culture associated with it—is a process, an ongoing journey, for both teacher and students, and as such it never truly ends: in the classroom many voices mix and not necessarily combine together and teaching a language is about communicating, transmitting meaning, sharing knowledge but also different views and emotions. A language might be made of grammar rules, words and syntax but all of these are emotionally charged when spoken in context, when spoken to and heard/received by others. Thus the way people celebrate *le feste* in Italy is different now, because times have changed and keep changing at an increasingly fast pace; being "migrants through time",[1] today we all experience language and culture in quick transformation, having to make room for new behaviours, linguistic influences, practices, narratives of migration, trauma and integration at a growingly faster pace than in the past. How can a language teacher perform as an ambassador of one single target language and culture in today's widely interconnected and fast-changing world? And how can s/he mediate through cultures when the cultures overlap and leak into each other?

Due to its economy and geography, Italy, a country of emigration until the 1970s, has turned in the past fifty years into a country of immigration, recently experiencing an extreme level of mass migration (Crespi 2014). We have all become painfully familiar with images of refugees stranded at sea struggling to reach the coast for safety, driven by the remote promise of a better life. According to Crespi, in 2011 Rumanian citizens living in Italy reached about 1 million and "formed the largest foreign community in Italy (21.2% of the total number of foreigners), followed by Albanians (10.6%), Moroccans (9.9%) and Chinese (4.6%)" (2014, p. 250). Together with immigrants from Africa (Libya, Tunisia, Nigeria), they are gradually changing the cultural texture of the country. Significantly Crespi's data points at the number of foreign under-age children resident and/or born in Italy, growing from 412,432 in January 2004 to 932,000 in January 2010 (ibid.). This suggests that a considerable portion of young people living in Italy today have been born or brought up by at least one foreign parent, thus growing up juggling the heritage culture and language alongside the cultural and linguistic practices of the host country. Italy's demographic and cultural composition is changing and this makes teaching a class about a specific country's culture and language a lot more problematic than it might have been two or three decades ago. It also reminds us that curricula should always be fluid and ready to accommodate new topics to reflect social changes in real time.

3.3 On Being a Language Teacher in a Changing World

My narrative attempts to capture (and reflect upon) the tension that language teachers like me might experience in the context of the foreign language classroom, where we have been traditionally perceived as ambassadors of a given language and culture but where in fact today, we find ourselves to act more and more as intercultural mediators.

Delanty (2003) warns us that in our times we can no longer rely on traditional coordinates such as class, gender, ethnicity and as a result "the reference points for the self have become unstuck" (2003, p. 135). Our fluid sense of identity as transnational individuals relies on our ability to acknowledge and accept difference, to focus "on the recognition of difference rather than sameness" (ibid.). Like many MFL teachers, I have spent a considerable portion of my life in another country and have developed as a result a hybrid identity, encompassing multiple cultures (and languages). I have learnt to embrace difference, to accept otherness and make it my own. Evans (2014) proposes the notion of "valorization of difference" (2014, p. 204) and reminds us that "a foreign language and its culture reside in the concept of 'otherness'" (ibid.). Hybrid identities and transnational experiences shape classroom practices and equip us with the relevant intercultural competence needed to navigate across cultures/languages.

But, what does it mean to navigate across cultures and languages? What does it mean to act as mediator in the context of the language classroom? As a language teacher I mediate between all the cultures and languages represented in the classroom, while simultaneously negotiating my own sense of identity, often fragile, as a transnational living across languages in a fast-changing world. Through mediation I encourage reflection, analysis, multiple interpretations and, to borrow Kramsch's words once more, the capacity to develop "an ear for the voice of others" (Kramsch 2014, p. 309).

Traditionally an *intermediary*, in the language classroom a mediator is someone able to convey meaning across different parties who do not share the same language. With globalisation and increasing mobility, the recent spread of technology and its impact on communication, mediation has become the stuff of everyday life for many of us, thus contributing to promote a natural shift towards an intercultural approach in all areas, not just language teaching and learning. We all work, study, do business transactions with people from different backgrounds than ours on a wider scale than we used to. This has brought a deeper awareness of *difference*, of *otherness*, alongside a sense of displacement but also a sense of empathy and understanding and ultimately an ability to recognise, filter through and welcome multiple perspectives.

In the context of the language classroom it might be helpful to think of mediation as a journey from one linguistic and cultural system to another (and back and across) which in the process conveys not only meaning but also its affective component, thus promoting tolerance, empathy and a capacity or at least a willingness to engage with otherness. While Kohler (2015) reminds us of its common association with "notions of conflict and resolution of difference" (2015, p. 3), Liddicoat (2014) points at how "mediation is no longer seen in terms of the resolution of communication problems but rather is an interpretation of language in use" (2014, p. 261). The idea of *difference*, filtered through mediation, seems to permeate everything we do in the language classroom, as I will try to illustrate below.

As an Italian who has spent half of her life in the UK I have learnt to negotiate simultaneously *different* cultures and languages (not to mention the *different* identities attached to these), on a daily basis, both on a professional and a personal level, feeling somehow "hybrid", not entirely one or the other, but a mixture of the "Italian" and the "British" mind-sets. Inevitably I continuously have to make cultural adjustments to respond to societal behavioural requirements and reconcile the two. In my classroom, students often have a multilingual/multicultural background too, thus also finding themselves having to negotiate *different* languages and *different* identities.

As a teacher of Italian, when I teach language inevitably I also incorporate loose elements of the culture of the country in my lessons (these might range from current affairs to fashion, to specific societal rituals, e.g. the tradition of the Italian *aperitivo* or certain events in childhood, such as communion or confirmation, which reflect the strong Catholic orientation of the country and used to mark crucial stages of childhood). However, as outlined earlier, the changing social texture in Italy makes the current country's cultural framework more complex to understand. This means that the perceived idea of "Italian" culture is no longer solid and "same" but somehow diverse and shaped by *difference*. Engaging with difference through the mediation of the MFL teacher, students go through various processes of recognising, analysing, comparing (to their own experience) and rationalising "other" practices (initially alien to them) and finally accepting them and making them their own (Liddicoat 2014).

One example of this in my experience as an Italian language teacher in the UK, revolves around how loud Italians are perceived to be. Often in the classroom I am told by students of British upbringing in particular, that Italians are too loud and that they gesticulate too much. They have noticed these traits in a variety of situations, in their journey to work, at work, in the cafes, pubs and streets of London, etc. Their immediate response to this is assuming rudeness or argumentativeness, especially if compared with their own way of speaking, generally soft and less forceful (the urge of making comparisons between a system we know well and one we don't know so well is hard to resist). It is only after engaging at a deeper level with the cultural norms intertwined with the language, that students come to the realisation that despite a louder and more animated tone of voice, the conversations they thought to be arguments were in fact perfectly amicable. This is when difference is understood and internalised. In my experience of the multicultural class, when *loudness* is discussed I have noticed class participants from non-British backgrounds allying with each other and aligning themselves with the so-called *loud* Italians. This might seem a trivial example and yet it highlights the considerable role that stereotypes still play in our society as well as the tension (stemming from difference) often present in the language classroom. The tension is dissipated when students shift their perspective from a close and internal one, to an external one (putting themselves into someone else's shoes), and accept that amicable conversations can take place also in louder tones.

My role as teacher and educator is to defuse tensions but not to ignore them, even when it is difficult to reconcile them. My aim is to foster in students a willingness to recognise and embrace difference with empathy and curiosity, exercising an open-minded approach towards others/otherness. At a time of fast-pace changes, significant migrations, globalisation and greater awareness of multicultural issues, it seems crucial to re-think the role of the language teacher in the MFL classroom from ambassador for the target language to professional intercultural mediator, able to process and convey (but not necessarily reconcile) difference and change; able to help students understand and embrace otherness, develop intercultural awareness and metalinguistic competence, while they also engage with their own mediation processes.

4 Concluding Remarks

Writing these accounts, although initially challenging, has been liberating. It has given us a platform to discuss aspects of our teaching and professional learning that we had not shared before. It has also provided a focus on pedagogy and agency, with a precious opportunity to reflect on the process of renegotiation and transformation taking place within our professional and personal identity. Ultimately, it has showed us how bold we have become through our journey, in making difficult choices, questioning some of the stifling conventions imposed to us by formal teacher training or sector policies, founding instead our practices on experience and class interaction.

Our personal narratives explore the complex, fluid relationship between language and identity in the MFL context. Although coming from different perspectives (the first account focusing on identity renegotiation and agency, transformation of the language learner into a language teacher; the second one looking at the language teacher's journey from language ambassador to intercultural mediator), both narratives propose a similar approach towards language teaching and learning. Being both mindful of the impact of the affective component on language learning and the complexity of teacher–student dynamics, in these narratives we have drawn attention to issues of anxiety, trauma, difference, so often experienced by MFL teachers and learners.

Digital communication entails a wider access to languages, interdisciplinary research, foreign literature, translated ideas and information than ever before. Language, identity and culture necessarily encompass elements of transnationalism, hybridity and in-betweenness and today identity is informed more by difference and diversity than unity and coherence. It is therefore crucial to reassert the relevance of language learning and linguistic diversity in the broader educational context and continue to devise new approaches to language teaching as a means to increase social cohesion, tolerance and intercultural mediation.

Note

1. Hamid (2017, p. 209). I have borrowed this phrase from Hamid's *Exit West* because it perceptively summarises the sense of displacement experienced by many today as a consequence of the extreme acceleration of pace of life.

References

Álvarez, Imna, and M. Luisa Pérez-Cavana. 2015. Multilingual and Multicultural Task-Based Learning Scenarios: A Pilot Study from the MAGGIC Project. *Language Learning in Higher Education: Journal of the European Confederation of Language Centres in Higher Education (CercleS)*: 59–82. http://oro.open.ac.uk/44650/1/. Accessed 08 January 2019.

Block, David. 2010. Speaking Romance-Esque. In *Language and Culture Reflective Narratives and the Emergence of Identity*, ed. David Nunan and Julie Choi, 40–46. New York and London: Routledge.

Block, David. 2014. *Second Language Identities*. London: Bloomsbury.

Crespi, Isabella. 2014. Foreign Families in the Italian Context: Migration Processes and Strategies. *Journal of Comparative Family Studies* 45 (2): 249–260. https://www.jstor.org/stable/24339609. Accessed 24 February 2019.

Delanty, Gerard. 2003. *Community*. London: Routledge.

Dewaele, Jean-Marc. 2010. *Emotions in Multiple Languages*. London: Palgrave Macmillan.

Edwards, Anne. 2015. Recognising and Realising Teachers' Professional Agency. *Teachers and Teaching: Theory and Practice* 21 (6): 779–784. https://www.researchgate.net/publication/278741031. Accessed 06 December 2018.

Eteläpelto, Anneli et al. 2013. What Is Agency? Conceptualising Professional Agency at Work. *Educational Research Review* 10: 45–65. https://www.researchgate.net/publication/254863609. Accessed 21 January 2019.

Eteläpelto, Anneli et al. 2014. Identity and Agency in Professional Learning. In *International Handbook of Research in Professional and Practice-Based Learning*, ed. Stephen Billett et al., 645–672. New York: Springer. https://doi.org/10.1007/978-94-017-8902-8_24. Accessed 21 January 2019.

Evans, David. 2014. *Language and Identity*. London: Bloomsbury.

Gardner, Robert, and Wallace Lambert. 1972. *Attitudes and Motivation in Second Language Learning*. Rowley, MA: Newbury House.

Grosjean, François. 2008. *Studying Bilinguals*. Oxford: Oxford University Press.

Hamid, Mohsin. 2017. *Exit West*. London: Penguin Random House.

Kohler, Michelle. 2015. *Teachers as Mediators in the Foreign Language Classroom*. Bristol: Multilingual Matters.

Kramsch, Claire. 2014. Teaching Foreign Languages in an Era of Globalisation. *The Modern Language Journal* 98 (1): 296–311. https://www.jstor.org/stable/43651759. Accessed 06 December 2018.

Krashen, Stephen. 1981. *Bilingual Education and Second Language Acquisition Theory*. Los Angeles: California State University.

Liddicoat, Anthony, J. 2014. Pragmatics and Intercultural Mediation in Intercultural Language Learning. *Intercultural Pragmatics* 11 (2): 259–277.

Norton, Bonny. 2000. *Identity and Language Learning: Gender, Ethnicity, and Educational Change*. Harlow: Longman/Pearson.

9

The Journey to Becoming a Language Teacher: Motivation and Engagement with the Process of Professional Development and Lifelong Learning

Laura Puente Martín and Susanne Winchester

1 Introduction

Involved in a myriad of daily activities, planning lessons, attending meetings, marking students' work, it is easy to lose sight of oneself as a teacher. We live in the now, constantly adapting to change and moving on to the next step. It is hardly a surprise that we do not often stop to think about how far we have travelled since the start of our teaching careers.

We have been lucky to be offered the opportunity to undertake this journey as authors of this narrative. We were invited to delve into a crucial aspect of our personal lives that we can now identify as a motivating factor in becoming a language teacher, and in steering the direction of our professional development. We were both moved by each other's accounts:

L. Puente Martín (✉) · S. Winchester
The Open University, Milton Keynes, UK
e-mail: l.puente-martin@open.ac.uk

S. Winchester
e-mail: s.winchester@open.ac.uk

© The Author(s) 2019
M. Gallardo (ed.), *Negotiating Identity in Modern Foreign Language Teaching*, https://doi.org/10.1007/978-3-030-27709-3_9

on the one hand, the early discovery of a love for words, and how this passion is closely interconnected with family memories; on the other hand, a more bittersweet journey, now triggering the opportunity to raise awareness of the personal difficulties that some teachers may experience simply because of the way they look—a case which will probably resonate with many colleagues.

Nevertheless, our stories of how we became language teachers converge in a vivid passion for both learning and helping others to learn, assisted by our own engagement with specialised professional development.

2 Laura's Narrative

2.1 "Miss, Where Are You Looking At?"

I was in front of a group of teenage pupils, in a small classroom in a comprehensive school somewhere in England. I had arrived there just a few weeks before, to work as a Spanish Language Assistant in three local state schools: two grammar (selective) schools and one comprehensive (non-selective) school. I had been appointed for one of the few hundred jobs available, thanks to my academic results in my final year studying for an English Philology degree in Spain, and I had been feeling rather too pleased with myself. For a long time I had dreamt of living and working abroad, and now I was finally here, in England. This was going to be my big adventure, and, as it turned out, the start of my teaching career.

The comprehensive school where I was teaching had been a bigger culture shock than the carpet in the bathroom of the house I shared with other foreign language assistants. I was very impressed by the facilities the school had, such as the Year 11 common room, but very disappointed about the lack of interest the pupils had in their learning. I knew behaviour was generally poor, and these pupils were very vocal about the fact that they saw no point in learning foreign languages. "Why do I have to study Spanish?", they would ask, "I am never going to go to Spain".

However, the negative attitude of the pupils towards learning was not the biggest stumbling block for me as a teacher. The biggest stumbling block was something I actually thought very little about: my strabismus.

I had suffered from it from birth; an operation at the age of five was very successful with one eye, but there was overcompensation with the other. I had never suffered from bullying at school in Spain; it was something that people simply made no comment about, at least in front of me. These positive experiences did not prepare me well for teaching teenagers at a secondary school. Whenever I asked a student to do something in class, they would ask me to confirm if I meant them. Often, they would turn around to look behind them, as if I were looking at something just beyond, over their shoulder. For a start, the students were probably genuinely confused: it could be that they had never had a teacher with strabismus before. However, they soon repeated this process constantly and deliberately in the class, with a smirk, challenging me explicitly with the question "where are you looking at, miss?".

Undoubtedly, the pupils' reactions and behaviour had a negative effect on my self-esteem and professional enjoyment of the teaching experience at this comprehensive school. However, pupils at the grammar schools where I was also contracted to work behaved quite differently and seemed to enjoy my lessons, particularly the oldest ones who were studying at GCE level. As a consequence of this overall experience, by the time the academic year ended, I had resolved in the first instance to continue my studies with a Ph.D., in order to work in higher education in the long term. I had already looked into this possibility before leaving for England, so it was relatively straight forward to start working towards a doctorate in English literature. Although this approach may sound rather pragmatic, in practice at the time I was mostly looking forward to some uninterrupted time devoted to research and scholarship in a field, literature, I am still passionate about. Thankfully, I was privileged to have a very supportive and encouraging supervisor, as well as the financial help of a research grant that enabled me to take this path.

On the other hand, encouraged by the more positive experience of teaching in the grammar schools, where students had never made any comments about my strabismus, and I had been happy teaching, I decided also not to give up on teaching altogether. Nowadays, I am an Associate Lecturer at The Open University, where I have worked for over fifteen years.

2.2 Perceptions of Difference

So far, during the rest of my teaching career, I have never encountered antagonism or negativity due to my strabismus: my experience at the comprehensive school remains an isolated, if important, critical incident. However, the negative impact that strabismus can have is well-documented. As stated by Astle et al.:

> People with strabismus often report problems making eye contact when speaking with others (Nelson et al. 2008; Satterfield et al. 1993). Abnormal gaze cues associated with strabismus may explain why they have more difficulty in social situations and why others develop negative impressions of them. (2016, p. 122)

For teachers, difficulties with making eye contact with students can have a negative effect when managing a class or a specific activity. The realisation that a problem can occur indeed may prompt teachers into developing coping mechanisms and seeking advice or specialised help, if available. They may choose to be upfront with their pupils about their strabismus, thus creating a wider learning opportunity, too. For instance, a teacher suffering from a rare form of dwarfism, diastrophic dysplasia, provides an example of how this may work in real practice:

> In my work, I've also learned that children are not afraid to ask upfront questions like "Why do you look different?" When my students ask why I perform simple tasks in a particular way, we often try to imitate differences in movement to make comparisons. For example, I show them how I lift myself onto a student chair and use a ruler to tap the light switch on or off. This becomes a way to explore how people may do things differently, even though we all have similar thoughts, dreams, and feelings. (Venter 2017, n.p.)

This example reveals how self-reflection can help to resolve a problem and develop agency, where the teacher takes control of a situation by making a proactive intervention: in this case, talking openly and graphically about dwarfism.

I remain full of admiration for what this teacher did. Even now, reflecting on my experience and writing this story, I feel as if I were exorcising a demon. So, what did *I* do? I want to believe that, in a very sketchy manner, I was beginning to be what Schön (1987) and others refer to as a self-reflective practitioner.

As described by Boud and Walker (1990), self-reflective practitioners take time to think about their lessons *after* they have finished. They rehearse in their memories parts that went well and parts that went not so well. Pinpointing what made these sections successful and unsuccessful helps teachers to develop further those valuable techniques, and to readjust or abandon altogether the resources or strategies that simply did not work. In this process self-reflective practitioners proactively seek the support of relevant, up-to-date, innovative literature and training; banks of resources; line managers and networks of teachers.

So, I was aware that my classroom management skills could be improved, and I started seeking a wider range of teaching resources. For instance, I exchanged activity ideas and resources with other language assistants in the schools I was working at. I also enquired after supplementary classroom resources, and some of the teachers guided and encouraged me. For example, I remember using supplementary worksheets that were available as part of the textbook packages the schools used, but the teachers had no time for during normal lessons. Some of the resources provided by the Consejería de Educación (part of the services of the Spanish Ministry of Education in the UK) were also very helpful. One particular example comes to mind: a magazine that gathered activities created by Spanish language assistants across the country, which I received at one of the schools. Nowadays this resource still exists, albeit with a different name, *Acti/España*.

There is then some evidence that I was on the journey to becoming a self-reflective practitioner, but it is also true that there are things that I did *not* do. Even if I did not allow the experience to bring me down—my adventure year in England was, otherwise, going pretty well-, I *did not* confide in my line manager about the pupils' comments about my strabismus: it would have been just too humiliating. To a degree, I was suffering from professional isolation, as I did not trust anybody enough to be open about something that I felt was very personal. A strong culture of hierarchy in Spanish universities in my undergraduate years also made it difficult for me to take the step to approach a manager with a professional situation that could be potentially read as a weakness, a failing, or a liability. The working culture in higher education in the UK can be described as more collaborative, diverse and inclusive, and I think this culture has made me more willing to reach out to my managers and colleagues later in my career. For instance, conversations in professional forums, workshops and conferences have helped me to adapt to institutional and industry changes, such as new policies and tuition systems. At a more personal level, contact with colleagues strengthens my personality and agency as a teacher, as well as contributing to a feeling of belonging within an academic community.

Part of being an effective teacher and self-reflective practitioner is a desire to become acquainted with your pupils´ specific needs in order to adjust your teaching to them. Although I could sense a fundamental difference between some of the pupils in the comprehensive and grammar schools where I was teaching, I did not have enough knowledge at the time to pinpoint exactly how these differences came about in the first place. On the other hand, nowadays I have a better understanding of British society and I am able to ascertain the reason why many of these pupils at the comprehensive school were not interested in learning foreign languages. It was partly because they had very low expectations about their future, due to their socioeconomic background: that's why they thought that they were never going to travel to Spain. Besides, they had an internalised perception that education was not for them, and, if they acted defensively, it was because they felt excluded. I, however, was brought up in an inclusive society that, although not without its own endemic problems, arguably valued education for everyone, regardless. I have always been passionate about the benefits of lifelong learning, and I have a wide range of interests, including literature, history and foreign languages. At a more material level, education can increment your chances in life drastically; it can also enrich your inner life and train you to think critically. I am sure that teachers at the comprehensive school where I worked made every effort to motivate their pupils to take advantage of the opportunities that education afforded them to improve their socioeconomic situation, empowering them for instance by developing their reading and writing skills.

I wish I had been more willing and able to integrate myself successfully within this collective endeavour, but thankfully at a later stage in my professional career I have been able to attempt to remedy this. Nowadays, I work for an institution with a strong ethos promoting lifelong learning and equal opportunities, and I want to encourage my students to achieve their goals in life. I find a high degree of communion with my managers, colleagues and students in the value we all place on education, while advocating that all school children, such as some of those I encountered in the early stages of my career, should be encouraged to feel confident about their individual potential, and to have high expectations for their future. As Toom et al. (2015) emphasizes, in order to stimulate agency in teacher education there needs to be the necessary social support and culture, as well as equality and acknowledgement. My personal experiences have made me sensitive to the needs of my learners, particularly those with specific learning differences and any medical conditions that potentially can have a detrimental impact on their studies. For example, as part of my continuous professional development I have specialised in Specific Learning Differences (SpLDs), in particular, dyslexia. At my institution I have supported numerous students who had disclosed SpLDs, showing them techniques to structure, develop and proofread their writing for their Spanish and Applied Linguistics modules. I have helped dyslexic students understand the syllabic structure of the Spanish language in order to enable them to bridge the gap between the written and the spoken word. In tutorials, I have learned that simple things, such as taking care to keep your worksheets and slides clear and uncluttered, can help not just students with SpLDs, but all students in general.

Both specialised training and shared experience have been instrumental in the process of refining the skills required to best support students with SpLDs. Nevertheless, the unspoken connection I feel with learners dealing with these kinds of obstacles remains a key motivating factor. Empathy, and the willingness to listen and intervene, sometimes proactively, are important elements for me as a teacher, and there is evidence that students find this helpful, because they mention it in their feedback. This is very rewarding for me. Back in that comprehensive school, I may not have felt quite like a teacher yet, probably, quite rightly. However, I would have been relieved to learn that "teachers' professional agency is not a fixed disposition of an individual teacher, rather, it is constructed situationally in relation to the current context and past personal experiences (Emirbayer and Mische

1998; Greeno 2006; Lipponen and Kumpulainen 2011)" (Toom et al. 2015, p. 616). In other words, you are not born a teacher, you make yourself one.

3 Susanne's Narrative

3.1 My Little Book of Words

From an early age, I have been fascinated by words and languages. I grew up surrounded by pocket dictionaries which my father used in the 60s and 70s when English was not the Lingua Franca that it is now. My father worked as an engineer in many countries, in remote places, where knowing some of the native languages was important for survival. My father enjoyed language learning and was to a large degree an autodidact—he would buy dictionaries (we had Greek, Spanish, many French and English and Italian phrasebooks and dictionaries) and teach himself, using the language knowledge of Latin, French and English which he had learned at school. Of all the countries he worked in, Italy was the one he travelled to most often and loved. In fact, my mother and father lived in Italy before I was born. I remember my mother recounting how pronunciation and mispronunciation could distort the meaning of a word in Italian—and any other language!—so much that one would not be understood. She demonstrated this with the Italian word for egg, *uovo*. As a young child, I found it great fun, trying to pronounce the two initial vowels in a way other than I had known from my mother-tongue, German. I was amazed to find that there were so many other languages that expressed the same thoughts and ideas but just in other words. I found the idea fascinating!

I knew that these little phrasebooks and dictionaries were special; for a five-year-old girl, they held some magic within. Sometimes, my father would make phone calls to Italy and often, before a conversation, would look up specific terms. Then, I would listen to him in wonderment, speaking in Italian, saying ordinary things in this beautifully elegant sounding language. I would always ask him what he had been talking about and his answers always left me feeling astounded that there was more than one way, more than one language, to talk about the world.

One day, during my kindergarten years, I got up very early one morning, before anyone else had woken up; I went to our bookshelf and chose the smallest and—to me—most appealing dictionary and painstakingly copied out one small page. It was my father's tiny Italian dictionary. I hadn't yet learned to write, so I have no idea how it must have looked. The page was supposed to be a present for my friend. Proudly, I handed it over to him in the morning, and in the afternoon, my mother was asked to see the nursery teacher. They thought it was an unusual present. Why would a child, who could not write, copy out a page in a dictionary, in a foreign language, as a present for a friend? There was curiosity as to what had motivated me to do this; I don't know how the conversation with my mother went as I had to wait outside the office, but I felt disappointed. In a way, I felt that the magic of the little present had escaped them. How could they possibly fail to see how special these words were? I was sharing the most precious treasures with my friend!

3.2 Learner and Teacher Agency

It must have seemed odd at the time, but the fascination did not pass and became a lifelong passion. Apart from my compulsion to collect words, another quest shaped my childhood life: I wanted to find out who had "invented German" and I would frequently ask adults this question on first encounter. I was fascinated by the idea of language itself and that ideas could be expressed in many different ways.

I don't ask so much about the invention of German anymore—I have learned!—but I still like words and share them with others! This resulted in my decision to join the Doctorate in Education programme at my institution. The focus of my research was on vocabulary learning and involved producing vocabulary sets on digital flashcards for beginner students of German. This enabled me to research a topic I am passionate about and to share it with a wider audience.

The fact that early childhood experiences can have a significant influence on later professional development was acknowledged by Knowles (1992) and in my case, the early fascination with words steered my entire life and career. As all German pupils in the 80s, I started learning English when I was ten and, a year later, French. Many lists of vocabulary were written—some of them were learned, many forgotten. As a pupil and student, I experienced a lot of frustration during my language studies, always feeling that there was a lack of words in my foreign language knowledge. As a pupil and student in Germany, in my language classes, I was encouraged to read long texts in French and English and to produce my own vocabulary lists with translations. These were often incorrect because I had misunderstood the text and context. When we were given vocabulary lists by our teachers, I always managed to know the first few items on the list, but my recall diminished the further I got down in the list. And I felt further frustrated by the fact that I could understand every word my teachers were saying but could never achieve the same standard when I spoke. Unfortunately, when I learned languages in the 80s, I received no training in how to learn effectively. With more guidance on learning strategies and a warning that language learning needs determination, resilience and acceptance of failure, my learning may have been more efficient and less emotionally challenging. Later in my life, I studied other languages, out of curiosity, enabling me to see the world through different lenses and giving me an opportunity to explore different options for learning words. Just as one of the characters in Khaled Hosseini's novel *And the Mountains Echoed*, I felt that "if culture is a house, then language was the key to the front door; to all the rooms inside…" (2013, p. 362). It is often said that dictionaries represent not only the language used but also the beliefs, ideologies and values of any given speech community. So, words and what they represent in different language communities create a direct route to understanding a different culture, too. The words and languages I collect help me to understand the world that goes beyond my own language community.

In terms of learning words, I often had the image of myself as that of a Victorian butterfly collector, hunting and trying to capture particularly beautiful specimens, realising that these beautiful creations are elusive and fragile and can easily disappear again which is why I examined the role of memory, of how to commit vocabulary to memory to prevent the hard-earned foreign vocabulary from escaping.

In my school and university days, very little attention was paid to learning skills, so when I came across Sebastian Leitner's (1974) work on learning how to learn, I felt a sense of empowerment because it validated my beliefs of teaching and learning: that knowing how to learn is vital, that learners need to be instructed in learning strategy use, that vocabulary learning should be approached systematically and that it is best to adhere to a particular learning schedule to ensure that nothing is forgotten. I stumbled upon his work at a time when I worked as a private tutor, teaching French and English and recognising that what my students needed was not only help with learning the language but also knowing how best to learn. Leitner's effective way of self-testing and making judgements on what parts of the learning material needed more attention than others was a simple system. It revolutionised the way I tackled vocabulary learning and started my interest in learning strategies in language learning.

This interest continued throughout my professional and personal life as teacher and language learner. I was asked many times by students how best to learn vocabulary because they, just as I, felt that simply writing vocabulary lists did not do the job sufficiently. When I worked as Modern Foreign Languages Curriculum Coordinator for a consortium of Adult Education centres, I was also in charge of professional development of MFL tutors and was fortunate enough to receive training as an e-guide—a champion for implementing technology in teaching and learning. It was during that time that I realised the huge potential of technology in language learning and teaching. It was during one of the training sessions that I came across upon flashcard programmes and realised what a powerful tool they could be for my students. I started collecting vocabulary from my students' textbook, translating it and uploading it to Quizlet, a flashcard programme which not only helps students to memorise vocabulary but also provides a range of different activities to practise retrieval of vocabulary. These sets can then be shared with students via a link—and here I was again: collecting words and sharing them with others!

Students welcomed this learning strategy; in data I gathered (questionnaires and focus groups) for my research on vocabulary learning, one student stated that learning vocabulary with my translated and uploaded sets was for them "the best thing ever"; another student reported that they had considered leaving the course but the availability of the flashcards had changed their mind. The response by students had confirmed my hunch as a language learner myself: students felt a need for more support for vocabulary learning and that they felt more secure in their learning with the availability of translated vocabulary sets.

As a teacher I felt empowered to see myself as an action researcher and take agency of my own professional identity. My discussion with students and my research findings demonstrated that my beliefs were shared by others and that my own attitude to learning had influenced my teaching and professional identity. Extending my beliefs beyond that of language learner and applying it in my professional practice had struck a chord with my students. I felt that my views had validity—I had found my professional voice as a researcher. Coldron and Smith (1999) suggested: "People find a kind of agency in positioning themselves [...] in response to needs that arise from an assessment of the circumstances in which they find themselves." (1999, p. 714) Furthermore, Edwards (2015), drawing on the work of Taylor (1989, 1991) and Eteläpelto et al. (2013) explains that agency is based on our capability of making judgements about the goals for our actions and involves teachers forging their own professional practice and identity. Once I had recognised that my experience as a language learner was shared by many others, my professional knowledge enabled me to seek a solution and thus shape my own professional identity and autonomy in the process. I have also realised that my identity as a language teacher is intertwined with my experiences and identity as a language learner.

I am fortunate in that the higher education institution I work for allows for professional development in the form of taking modules alongside other students. The experience of being a student and a teacher in parallel is of enormous value; having the opportunity of being a student empowers me in my identity as teacher. My students value my expertise as a teacher and my experience as a student. The availability of professional development does not only help to become a better practitioner but also to see oneself as a researcher. The availability of professional development opportunities as practitioner-researcher allowed me to follow the Doctorate in Education (EdD) programme and to research a field I was passionate about. For me, the choice of opting for an EdD rather than a Ph.D. was rooted in my drive to improve learning for others, for which an action-research approach was ideal.

My research, sparked by my curiosity as a child and my intuition as a language learner and teacher, has been shared with students and colleagues. My practice and beliefs are thus deeply settled in my historical self. My journey has come full-circle but I intend to travel the path again, with new knowledge and understanding.... and more sharing of words!

To refer to Cooper and Olson's terminology (1996), I most certainly see myself as a composite of multiple "I"s'; foremost I am a teacher and leaner in equal measures: I teach my native language, German, in the UK, with English being my language of habitual use. I have now reached a point in time where I have lived in the UK longer than in my native country, yet I still see myself as a learner of English—a truly lifelong learning process. To me, learning has made me who I am—not only in terms of knowledge but also in terms of my identity. This is reflected in Lave's assertion that "learning is... more basically a process of coming to be—of forging identities in activities in the world" (1992, p. 3).

My experiences as a learner and teacher feed into a perpetual cycle of personal and professional development. My sense of shifting, multiple identities is echoed in Cooper and Olson (1996) who view professional identity as multifaceted and conclude that a number of factors influence teacher identity. Referring to Mishler (1999), Beijaard et al. (2004) conclude that

> It is better to recognize in the definition of identity that a plurality of sub-identities exists. To give expression to this, Mishler used the metaphor of "our selves as a chorus of voices, not just as the tenor or soprano soloist [...]. Identity development occurs in an intersubjective field and can be best characterized as an ongoing process, a process of interpreting oneself as a certain kind of person and being recognized as such in a given context". (2004, p. 113)

In my identity as language learner with a passion for words, I will continue to gather these lexical building blocks, full of culture and ideas, while my professional, teacher identity will keep looking for ways to make learning more effective and enjoyable.

4 Conclusion

When we started work on this chapter, we sent each other our narratives first and both of us had an initial crushing feeling that we didn't have anything profound to share, nothing to say. We felt that our voices were very much like the voices of many other language teachers in similar situations. We felt that, because our voices were similar to those of others, we did not have a voice at all. However, when we reflected on and talked about our experiences, we realised that both our narratives were not quite so different in that they described a critical incident in our lives that shaped our identity as teachers. While one incident occurred very early on in life, the other happened when already firmly set on the path of being a language teacher. Nonetheless, the two incidents determined what came next and influenced our understanding of who we are as people, as language learners and language teachers. Of course, while one perspective and understanding stems from a retrospective examination of events that shaped the person, the other choice of action and construction of voice and agency occurred much later in life than childhood. What both of these incidents show is that they served as turning points. For one, in their young life, there was an intuitive feeling that language holds something special and that those cherished words served to unlock some kind of hidden world. For the other, it was the experience in the classroom that determined her future career path.

In the foreword to Nunan and Choi's *Language and Culture: Reflective Narratives and the Emergence of Identity* (2010), Bonny Norton recognises that "the validation of past history and experience" (p. xi) can be difficult for students and teachers who are, academically, not accustomed to using their own voice to support their research. In defining voice, we utilise Nunan and Choi's definition as "the centrality of the human story to qualitative research in terms of what the story is and how the story is told" (2010, p. 1). These authors' assertion that the act of writing can become the act of enquiry itself was enlightening. They explain that the procedure of writing is complementary to the final product, i.e. our exploration of the path to our identity as teachers is equally as important as our identity itself. Our account, our giving voice to the *Werdungsprozess*, the coming into being of who we are as people and as professionals is just as essential as examining the status quo of our identities. Personal narratives, thus, can be encouraged as a valuable research tool that can also open a window onto our colleagues' practice and identity, a world otherwise relatively private, but immensely varied internationally, enriching our own teaching potential and contributing to a feeling of community beyond our own specialisation and educational institutions.

References

Astle, Andrew T., Thomas Foulsham, and Paul V. McGraw. 2016. The Consequences of Strabismus and the Benefits of Adult Strabismus Surgery. *Optometry in Practice* 17 (3): 121–130. https://www.researchgate.net/publication/306019013/download.

Beijaard, Douwe P., et al. 2004. Reconsidering Research on Teachers' Identity. *Teaching and Teacher Education* 20 (2): 107–128. https://doi.org/10.1016/j.tate.2003.07.001.

Boud, David, and David Walker. 1990. Making the Most of Experience. *Studies in Continuing Education* 12 (2): 61–80.

Coldron, John, and Robin Smith. 1999. Active Location in Teachers' Construction of Their Professional Identities. *Journal of Curriculum Studies* 31 (6): 711–726. https://doi.org/10.1080/002202799182954.

Cooper, Karyn, and Margaret R. Olson. 1996. The Multiple 'I's' of Teacher Identity. In *Changing Research and Practice: Teachers' Professionalism, Identities and Knowledge*, ed. Michael Kompf, W. Richard Bond, Don Dworet, and R. Terrance Boak, 78–89. London: Falmer Press.

Edwards, Anne. 2015. Recognising and Realising Teachers' Professional Agency. *Teachers and Training* 21 (6): 779–784. https://doi.org/10.1080/13540602.2015.1044333.

Emirbayer, Mustafa, and Ann Mische. 1998. What Is Agency? *American Journal of Sociology* 103: 962–1023.

Eteläpelto, Anneli, Katja Vähäsantanen, Päivi Kristiina Hökkä, and Susanna Paloniemi. 2013. What Is Agency? Conceptualizing Professional Agency at Work. *Educational Research Review* 10: 45–65. https://www.researchgate.net/publication/254863609_What_is_agency_Conceptualizing_professional_agency_at_work.

Greeno, James G. 2006. Authoritative, Accountable Positioning and Connected, General Knowing: Progressive Themes in Understanding Transfer. *Journal of the Learning Sciences* 15: 537–547.
Hosseini, Khaled. 2013. *And the Mountain Echoed*. London: Bloomsbury.
Knowles, Gary J. 1992. Models for Understanding Pre-service and Beginning Teachers' Biographies: Illustrations from Case Studies. In *Studying Teachers' Lives*, ed. Ivor F. Goodson, 99–152. London: Routledge.
Lave, Jean. 1992. Learning as Participation in Communities of Practice. Paper Presented at the Annual Meeting of the American Educational Research Association, San Francisco, CA. http://www1.udel.edu/educ/whitson/897s05/files/Lave92.htm.
Leitner, Sebastian. 1974. *So Lernt Man Lernen*. Freiburg: Herder.
Lipponen, Lasse, and Kristiina Kumpulainen. 2011. Acting as Accountable Authors: Creating Interactional Spaces for Agency Work in Teacher Education. *Teaching and Teacher Education* 27: 812–819. https://doi.org/10.1016/j.tate.2011.01.001.
Mishler, Elliot G. 1999. *Storylines: Craft Artists' Narratives of Identity*. Cambridge, MA: Harvard University Press.
Nelson, Bradley A., Kammi B. Gunton, Judith N. Lasker, Leonard B. Nelson, and Lea Ann Drohan. 2008. The Psychosocial Aspects of Strabismus in Teenagers and Adults and the Impact of Surgical Correction. *Journal of AAPOS* 12: 72–76, e71. https://doi.org/10.1016/j.jaapos.2007.08.006.
Norton, Bonny. 2010. Foreword. In *Language and Culture: Reflective Narratives and the Emergence of Identity*, ed. David Nunan and Julie Choi, 2. New York and London: Routledge.
Nunan, David, and Julie Choi. 2010. *Language and Culture: Reflective Narratives and the Emergence of Identity*. New York and London: Routledge.
Satterfield Denise, John L. Keltner, and Thomas L. Morrison. 1993. Psychosocial Aspects of Strabismus Study. *Arch Ophthalmol* 111: 1100–1105. https://doi.org/10.1001/archopht.1993.01090080096024.
Schön, Donald A. 1987. *Educating the Reflective Practitioner: Towards a New Design for Teaching and Learning in the Professions*. San Francisco: Josey Bass.
Taylor, Charles. 1989. *Sources of the Self: The Making of Modern Identity*. Cambridge, MA: Harvard University Press.
Taylor, Charles. 1991. *The Ethics of Authenticity*. Cambridge, MA: Harvard University Press.

Toom, Auli, Kirsi Pyhältö, and O'Connell Rust Frances. 2015. Teachers' Professional Agency in Contradictory Times. *Teachers and Teaching* 21 (6): 615–623. https://doi.org/10.1080/13540602.2015.1044334.

Venter, Alison. 2017. What I've Learned as a Teacher with a Disability. *Educational Leadership* 74 (7): n.p. http://www.ascd.org/publications/educational-leadership/apr17/vol74/num07/What-I've-Learned-as-a-Teacher-with-a-Disability.aspx.

Conclusion

The context of modern foreign language teaching in the UK is a rich field of investigation. MFL teachers represent a community of practice whose experiences and stories are key to understanding the impact of MFL policies in the education system, as well as to how the existing fragmentation of the language teaching environment affects practitioners. Their stories as migrants and/or as pluricultural and plurilingual individuals are also important to determine the impact of socio-political and demographic phenomena on the profession and on society as a whole.

The decision to write this book about MFL teachers' identity arose from a personal reflection on my own experience as a member of the profession. The encouragement and predisposition I encountered among the group of colleagues who eventually became contributors to this book—fellow women language teachers and teacher educators with transnational lives in many cases has resulted in a fruitful and congenial collective endeavour which has made us reflect on our individual and professional trajectories. The cathartic experience of writing the individual chapters has given us an opportunity to share lived experiences, visions for the future of the profession and desires for change. It has also made us realize how important the task of giving voice to other language teachers is; to hear through their words about their role in the constantly changing educational, social and political scenarios in which they live including the current climate of the national decline of the subject and the fractured environment in which these teachers often operate. We have done so in the hope that it will help to better understand who MFL teachers are, what moves them to become teachers and what they bring to their learners.

It is often said that in order to understand language teaching and learning we need to understand teachers and to appreciate the professional, cultural, social and individual identities which they claim or which are assigned to them. Through the chapters in this book we gain an understanding of how MFL teachers themselves make sense of their experience of teaching a language in the UK and of how teachers' personal and professional journeys and their sustained immersion in diverse linguistic and cultural milieux have, undoubtedly, an impact on individuals' sense of identity and their professional practices. We have addressed those aspects in this volume as follows:

The study on transnationallanguage teachers in the UK in Chapter 2 reveals that teachers' sense of self is not fixed by a particular culture or language and that their experiences of managing conflicting attitudes and values across diverse socio-cultural and linguistic worlds conveys the constant process of rethinking their identity. This chapter also reveals that in spite of the educational changes, uncertainties and difficult conditions of service that affect many of these professionals, their sense of identity remains strongly connected to their practice and the relationship with their learners and other practitioners.

In Chapter 3 we learn about the role that dilemmatic agency plays in the process of identity construction among the Russian professional female community of teachers/translators in the UK. Through Irina's voice, a representative of that community of professional women, we learn about the dilemmatic decision-making process involving constancy and change, being the same as others and being different, resisting and at the same time conforming to gender and professional ideologies.

Chapter 4 unveils how the lifeworld of being a language teacher is contradictory in nature, although contradictions, for the participating language teachers, are experienced as harmonized and energizing. More specifically, the need to project a persona or a fictitious identity seems to be at the centre of the lifeworld of being a language teacher which also manifests in its role as intermediary, mediating between connection and distance, interpreting between languages, cultures and individuals.

Expanding on previous chapters, the study in Chapter 5 gives evidence of language professional journeys into teaching as characterized by complex personal dynamics of migration and negotiation of identities in new cultural and linguistic landscapes and by a clear sense of personal investment in the teaching profession. In addition, we can see that teaching the mother-tongue clearly represents for teachers something much more than just teaching a subject; it is an act invested with profound personal meanings, with cultural, social and moral values that are embedded in past experiences.

In Chapter 6 we learn of the importance of modern language teachers engaging with action research projects as a compelling form of identification because it involves teachers investing themselves in what research activity they do and in the relationships that they develop as part of that process. The Exploratory Practice project co-directed by the author lays out a model which can be replicated in other language centres.

Chapter 7 adds to the findings of previous chapters by emphasizing the role played by the development of disciplinary knowledge as teachers develop as researchers through undertaking collaborative research projects, or indeed through language education studies, in consolidating and clarifying teachers' views of themselves as teachers. In this study the participant, an MFL secondary school teacher, not only identified herself most strongly as an educator rather than as an MFL teacher, but she had an enduring desire to develop her teacher role to become a producer of knowledge and a theorizer in her own right.

The final two chapters in the book capture personal reflections from practicing MFL teachers who explore the complex, fluid relationship between language and identity in the context of their professional and personal lives. In these chapters, the authors acknowledge finding the exercise of writing their stories challenging and liberating at the same time. They also recognize the value of the experience from which they have emerged confident and reassured as it showed their resilience in overcoming the difficult choices and the rejection of conventional practices in their journey to become the professionals they are today.

The voices that emerge from the nine chapters in this volume illustrate the diverse and at times contradictory, fragmented and creative landscapes MFL teachers navigate. They also evidence teachers' agency in responding to and acting upon the social environment and in developing, maintaining and constructing their identities as members of academic departments and educational institutions, but also as pluricultural and plurilingual individuals. It is this sense of agency and also their resilience in their decision-making abilities, which enable them to develop their potential and enrich their professional lives. In addition, in this book we have highlighted the importance of language teachers engaging with research and demonstrated that the barriers between teaching and researching, the dichotomy of the teacher-researcher, can be softened. The chapters in this book evidence that MFL teachers develop as researchers through undertaking collaborative, exploratory and auto-ethnographic research which allows them to consolidate and clarify their views of themselves as professionals and as part of communities of practice (Pennington and Richards 2016). In all cases, practitioner inquiry and/or auto-biographical narrative have served as empowering instruments with transformative values that have helped us to bridge the gap between the practitioner and the researcher. As teacher-researchers we have engaged with the process of research as a method to generate knowledge about MFL teachers' identity that can enhance how they are perceived in social and educational establishments and raise awareness of key issues affecting the profession.

We hope this book makes a contribution to the field of language teacher identity research by offering a fresh insight into understanding a key element in the educational and socio-political debate surrounding the discipline of modern foreign languages in the UK—namely the teachers' voices and their sense of agency in shaping their professional lives.

We also hope the stories and reflexions in the chapters inspire others to pursue further research in this field.

Reference

Pennington, Martha C., and Jack Richards. 2016. Teacher Identity in Language Teaching: Integrating Personal, Contextual, and Professional Factors. *RELC Journal* 47 (1): 5–23.

Index

A
Affiliation 3, 5, 9, 19, 20, 27, 32, 36, 37, 46, 60, 144, 146, 153, 154, 156, 160, 168, 170, 171, 173
Agency 2–7, 9, 19, 25, 27, 33, 34, 39, 46–48, 50, 53–57, 59–63, 92, 93, 98, 102, 120, 124–126, 129–131, 133, 143, 144, 149, 158, 160, 167, 172, 174, 177, 182, 188, 190, 191, 193, 196, 198
Autobiography 5, 7, 21, 22, 38, 46, 92, 100, 103

B
Beliefs 1–3, 5, 6, 18–20, 23–26, 36–39, 127, 128, 147, 150, 154, 157–161, 171–174, 194–197

Bilingual 27, 28, 45, 46, 49, 51, 58, 63, 167, 168, 173, 174

C
Collaborative 3, 4, 56, 161, 190
Communities of Practice (CoP) 3, 4, 6, 9, 19, 118, 130, 144–148, 150, 155, 159, 160
Culture 2, 3, 19, 25, 27–33, 35, 37, 38, 46, 47, 55, 59, 60, 62, 95, 107, 109, 118, 169, 171, 174–182, 186, 189–191, 194, 197, 198

D
Diaspora 3, 26, 36, 48, 62
Difference 10, 29, 30, 36, 38, 52, 58, 109, 129, 157, 167, 168, 170,

© The Editor(s) (if applicable) and The Author(s) 2019
M. Gallardo (ed.), *Negotiating Identity in Modern Foreign Language Teaching*, https://doi.org/10.1007/978-3-030-27709-3

207

172, 175–177, 179–182, 188, 190, 191

E
Emotions 2, 5, 6, 25, 29, 37, 102, 120, 125, 129, 131–133, 153, 172, 178
Exploratory Practice (EP) 3, 6, 9, 117, 118, 120–130, 134–136

F
Foreign 1, 4, 6, 8, 30, 34, 37, 52, 53, 119, 134, 150, 169, 176, 178, 179, 182, 186, 190, 193–195

G
Globalisation 176, 179, 181

H
Higher Education (HE) 6, 9, 33, 91, 93, 118, 119, 130, 135, 144, 187, 190, 196

I
Identity 1–7, 9, 10, 17–21, 23, 25–39, 45–64, 91, 92, 94–97, 99, 104, 106–112, 117, 118, 120, 122, 124, 125, 127–135, 143–153, 155, 158–160, 167–174, 176, 177, 179, 182, 196–199
Integration 18, 19, 32, 36, 38, 130, 178

J
Journey 3, 6–8, 38, 62, 91–93, 95, 96, 98, 102, 104, 106, 107, 110–112, 125, 126, 175, 177, 180–182, 185, 186, 189, 197

K
Knowledge 1–5, 19, 28, 34, 35, 39, 92, 97–99, 103, 104, 111, 122, 123, 129, 130, 147, 150, 153, 158, 161, 168, 171, 173, 175, 178, 190, 192, 194, 196, 197

L
Language learning 9, 46, 94, 118, 119, 143, 157, 159, 167, 171, 172, 174, 175, 182, 183, 192, 194, 195
Language teacher 1–10, 17–23, 25, 26, 28, 30–33, 35–39, 51, 64, 91–97, 105, 108, 109, 111, 112, 117, 119–121, 123, 124, 136, 144–148, 151, 153–155, 159, 167, 168, 171, 175, 178, 179, 181, 182, 185, 186, 196, 198
Lived experiences 1, 6, 8, 36, 118, 124, 151

M
Memories 7, 29, 30, 168, 172, 176, 186, 189
Migration 3, 4, 27, 46, 108–111, 168, 175, 177, 178, 181
Modern Foreign Language (MFL) 1–10, 17, 18, 20, 22, 23, 36, 39, 143, 145, 147–150, 153,

154, 156, 158–161, 167, 168, 170, 171, 176, 177, 179, 181, 182, 195
Multicultural 19, 105, 168, 175, 176, 180, 181
Multilingual/multilingualism 28, 47, 48, 105, 170, 171, 175, 180

N

Narrative Inquiry 6, 21, 39, 49, 99
Narratives 4, 5, 7–9, 18, 19, 21–25, 27, 31, 33, 34, 36–38, 46, 47, 49–53, 56, 57, 60–63, 92, 98, 99, 102–105, 107, 108, 111, 117, 118, 124–128, 133, 151, 167, 168, 173, 174, 178, 179, 182, 185, 198, 199

P

Pluricultural 1, 4, 5, 167, 171, 173–175
Plurilingual 1, 4, 5, 170, 171, 175
Practitioner Inquiry (PI) 5
Practitioners 1, 2, 4–7, 9, 10, 20, 33, 38, 39, 63, 117, 121, 123, 124, 126, 128, 133, 134, 136, 148, 156, 189, 190, 196

Professional 1–10, 18–21, 25, 26, 30, 32, 33, 35, 37–39, 45–64, 91–100, 104–111, 117–122, 124–128, 131–136, 143, 144, 146–154, 156, 158, 159, 171–174, 176, 180, 182, 185–187, 189–191, 193, 195–197, 199

R

Reflective 1, 10, 18, 21, 24, 36, 49, 63, 100, 102, 103, 105, 121, 128, 154, 159, 189, 190, 198

S

Second Language Acquisition (SLA) 1, 6, 8, 25, 94, 95
Subjectivity 37, 97, 103, 110

T

Transcultural 4, 7, 18, 21, 23, 29, 31, 37, 38, 170
Transnational 1, 2, 4–7, 10, 17–21, 23, 26–28, 30–32, 36–39, 168, 170, 171, 175, 179

Printed by Printforce, the Netherlands